CATERING SALES AND CONVENTION SERVICES

CATERING SALES AND CONVENTION SERVICES

Ahmed Ismail

Delmar Publishers

I(T)P® an International Thomson Publishing company

Albany • Bonn • Boston • Cincinnati • Detroit • London • Madrid
Melbourne • Mexico City • New York • Pacific Grove • Paris • San Francisco
Singapore • Tokyo • Toronto • Washington

NOTICE TO THE READER

Cover Design: Elaine Scull

Delmar Staff
Publisher: Susan Simpfenderfer
Acquisitions Editor: Jeff Burnham
Developmental Editor: Jeff Burnham
Editorial Assistant: Judy Roberts

Production Manager: Wendy Troeger
Production Editor: Elaine Scull
Marketing Manager: Katherine M. Hans

COPYRIGHT © 1999
By Delmar Publishers
an International Thomson Publishing company

The ITP logo is a trademark under license.
Printed in Canada

For more information contact:

Delmar Publishers
3 Columbia Circle, Box 15015
Albany, New York 12212-5015

International Thomson Publishing Europe
Berkshire House
168–173 High Holborn
London, WC1V7AA
United Kingdom

Nelson ITP, Australia
102 Dodds Street
South Melbourne,
Victoria, 3205 Australia

International Thomson Publishing France
Tour Maine-Montparnasse
33 Avenue du Maine
73755 Paris Cedex 15, France

Nelson Canada
1120 Birchmont Road
Scarborough, Ontario
5G4 M1K Canada

International Thomson Editores
Seneca 53
Colonia Polanco
11560 Mexico D. F. Mexico

International Thomson Publishing Gmbh
Königswinterer Strasse 418
53227 Bonn
Germany

International Thomson Publishing Asia
60 Albert Street
#15-01 Albert Complex
Singapore 189969

International Thomson Publishing Japan
Hirakawa-cho Kyowa Building, 3F
2–2–1 Hirakawa-cho, Chiyoda-ku,
102 Tokyo, Japan

ITE Spain/Paraninfo
Calle Magallanes, 25
28015-Madrid, Espana

2 3 4 5 6 7 8 9 10 XXX 05 04 03 02 01 00 99

Library of Congress Cataloging-in-Publication Data
Ismail, Ahmed.
    Catering sales and convention services / Ahmed Ismail.
      p.   cm.
    Includes index.
    ISBN 0-7668-0037-7
      1. Caterers and catering—Marketing.   2. Congresses and conventions—Marketing.   I. Title.
  TX911.3.M3I84   1999
  642'.4'0688—dc21   98-33393
                          CIP

ISBN 0-7668-0037-7

Delmar Publishers is pleased to offer the following books on
HOSPITALITY, TRAVEL, AND TOURISM

- **Catering Sales & Convention Services**
  Ahmed Ismail

- **Conducting Tours, 2E**
  Marc Mancini

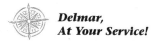

- **Destination: North America**
  Dawne M. Flammger

- **Dining Room and Banquet Management, 2E**
  Anthony Strianese

- **Domestic Ticketing and Airfare**
  Linda Hood

- **Geography of Travel & Tourism, 3E**
  Lloyd Hudman and Richard Jackson

- **Hospitality and Travel Marketing, 2E**
  Alastair Morrison

- **Hosting the Disabled: Crossing
  Communications Barriers Group Travel, 2E**
  Martha Sarbey deSouto

- **Hotel, Restaurant and Travel Law, 5E**
  Norman Cournoyer, Anthony G. Marshall
  and Karen Morris

- **Hotel Sales & Operations**
  Ahmed Ismail

- **International Air Fares Construction and
  Ticketing**
  Helle Sorensen

- **International Travel and Tourism**
  Helle Sorensen

- **Introduction to Corporate Travel**
  Annette Reiff

- **Learning Apollo: Basic and Advanced Training**
  Talula Austine Gunter

- **Marketing & Selling the Travel Product, 2E**
  James Burke and Barry Resnick

- **Math for Food Service, 3E**
  Robert Haines

- **Passport: An Introduction to Travel & Tourism, 2E**
  David Howell

- **Practical Food & Beverage Cost Control**
  Clement Ojugo

- **Practical Guide to Fares and Ticketing, 2E**
  Jeanne Semer-Purzycki

- **Sabre Reservations: Basic and Advanced Training**
  Gerald Capwell and Barry Resnick

- **Selling Destinations: Geography for the
  Travel Professional**
  Marc Mancini

- **Travel Agency Management**
  Gerald Fuller

- **Travel Perspectives: A Guide to Becoming a
  Travel Agent, 2E**
  Susan Rice and Ginger Todd

- **Welcome to Hospitality: An Introduction**
  Dr. Kye-Sung (Kaye) Chon and Dr. Ray Sparrowe

 Delmar,
At Your Service!

 Delmar Publishers

an International Thomson Publishing company I(T)P®

Contents

Preface

Catering Sales and Convention Services approaches the intricate world of hospitality in a unique way. Each aspect of catering is covered to provide the student or the inexperienced catering sales professional foundational concepts and keys to selling food and beverage and its corresponding service requirements.

The text is organized logically so that each chapter builds on the previous one. Considerable effort was made to ensure that Catering Sales and Convention Services was presented in a way that promotes learning and discussion. Each chapter ends with a summary of key concepts and a series of review questions to provoke thought.

Throughout Catering Sales and Convention Services the reader will find case studies that encourage thinking "outside of the box." An innovative component of this text, called "Industry Perspectives," was developed to give the reader real-world views of various relevant topics. Graphs and charts are displayed in easy-to-follow format.

Acknowledgments

The author's thanks go to the many people who helped make this text. The professionals who gave their support and input include Penny Woodruff; Lori Perry; Dawn Hill; Dawn Miller, CMP; Joe Murray; John Pohl; Kelly McNeely; Dr. Sotiris Avgoustis; Jil Froelich, CMP; and Kathy Ray, CMP. My thanks also go to my brother, Tarek, and my beautiful wife, Jamie.

About the Author

Ahmed Ismail is an acknowledged authority in the hospitality industry. Currently serving as a university instructor and working in the meeting industry, he received a bachelor of arts degree in international management from Gustavus Adolphus College. His professional experience spans over a decade in hotel sales, catering, and marketing with Marriott, Hyatt, and Renaissance Corporations. Throughout his career, he has received numerous awards for leadership and innovation. He is sought after by many corporations for consulting and speaking engagements. He has guided many to rewarding and successful careers in hospitality.

CHAPTER 1

The Catering World: An Introduction

INTRODUCTION

The catering industry is divided into two fundamentally different disciplines: **facility catering** and **outside catering.** A **facility** is a hotel, banquet hall, conference center, convention center, or other venue that has space an organization can use. Facility catering, therefore, is the discipline in which a facility provides food/beverage and logistical support to an organization that needs **function space** at that facility. Function space is the term used to describe the meeting rooms, ballrooms, exhibit halls, and other banquet spaces a facility makes available to organizations for various uses. In contrast to facility catering, outside catering is the discipline in which a facility provides food/beverage and the requisite logistical support and service to an organization or individuals in a venue other than the facility.

Facility catering and outside catering share some characteristics but not all. The fundamental difference between the two disciplines is that facility caterers must consider the availabilities and best uses of their function spaces, which may be limited. Outside caterers are not necessarily limited by function space. They are limited by their abilities to locate venues, and to achieve adequate kitchen capacities and staffing levels.

The two catering disciplines share the characteristics of menu and event planning, as well as certain operational issues. The objective for both disciplines is the same: to achieve maximum catering results. Figure 1–1 illustrates how the two disciplines relate.

This chapter outlines the similarities and differences between outside and facility catering, as well as examines catering career management.

FACILITY CATERING

Maximizing space is using as much function space as possible as efficiently as possible. Facility catering differs most dramatically from outside catering in this regard. Maximizing function space is important because facilities rely on their spaces to generate most of their catering revenue.

Catering facilities fall into two basic types: hotels with function space and stand-alone banquet facilities. A **hotel** is a facility that rents sleeping rooms to overnight guests. A hotel with function space has both sleeping rooms and function space. A **stand-alone facility** has function space but lacks sleeping rooms.

Hotels have, as an integral part of their overall success, tied sleeping room usage to function space usage. Stand-alone facilities lack this tie because they lack sleeping rooms, but they have other factors to consider.

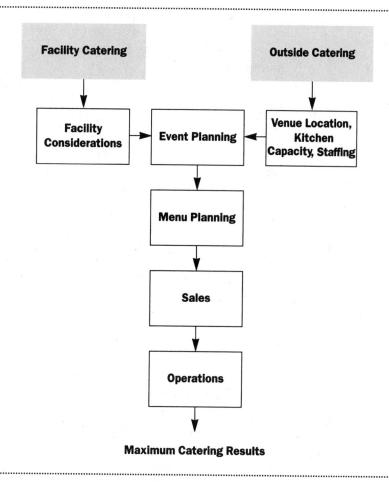

FIGURE 1–1

The world of catering

ROOM RENTAL

The aspect of function space usage stand-alone facilities share with hotels is **room rental**.

ROOM RENTAL

Room rental is the cost of using function space. Like the rates for sleeping rooms, room rental for function space generates revenue for use of the space for a specified time frame. The *renting* of this space is not considered part of the cost of a meal or a meeting. Often called a "setup fee," room rental can add significantly to the overall revenue of a function. Most facilities consider room rental pure profit.

Many catering sales staff are uncomfortable charging room rental. Many fear that charging for the use of function space will dissuade potential customers from using their facilities. Room rental is a bargaining tool for the salesperson and should therefore not be disregarded. Charging room rental is the same as charging a sleeping room rate at a hotel. A hotel should no more give away a function room than it should give away a sleeping room.

Because room rental is part of the revenue the catering department receives, it plays a role in the profitability of the facility's catering sales department. Any revenue generated from function space use is viewed as catering revenue.

Market Tolerance and Room Rental. A facility that is in the enviable situation of being the only facility in its market need not concern itself with competition. This situation is rare, however. In today's catering facility marketplace, many facilities of similar size usually compete in close proximity. These competing facilities most often seek the same client pool.

The market dictates room rental according to city. Competitors in a city quote room rental rates based on different criteria. Rates drastically above what the market dictates translate into little business (too expensive); rates drastically below translate into lost profit (too inexpensive). Room rental quotes should fit both the facility's needs and the client's expectations.

Hotels quote room rental rates using the market tolerance principle they use to calculate sleeping room rates. Hotel managers deviate from the market tolerance principle by considering the quality of their function spaces. Some managers, for example, view their facilities' function spaces as superior to those of their competition. Others discount their function spaces because those spaces are in poor condition. Managers who drastically reduce function space fees to guarantee bookings may value room rental less than other hotel revenues. A facility with function space characteristics that are unique among the facility's competitors may be able to charge, and obtain, premium room rental rates. Unique function space characteristics include:

- High ceilings
- Large, continuous ballrooms (without pillars, posts, or other obstructions)
- New carpeting, lighting, equipment, and so on
- Advanced in-house sound systems or multimedia control centers
- Theater auditoriums
- Windows with unique views
- Centrally located meeting spaces
- Soundproof walls and room dividers

Client Education and Room Rental. Like market tolerance, client education can impact the rental rates a catering facility and its competitors quote. In certain locations (e.g., downtown), potential clients may find that there is too little function space to satisfy demand. In situations where function space is at a premium, most facilities charge higher room rental rates. The market, in turn, assumes those values on function room rates. In other words, clients expect hefty charges for room rental downtown. These clients have been educated to expect high charges. The market tolerates the high charges for room rental only because the client pool expects them.

The opposite also applies. If facilities in certain locations find that they are losing business to competitors due to room rental costs, those facilities will likely discount their rental prices quickly. Hotels that historically discount or give away meeting space teach clients that they can avoid paying higher costs. Again, the clients have been educated to expect certain charges.

Types of Room Rental. Room rental rates should be broken down by specific times of day and meeting room. Each facility should have a **room rental tariff sheet** that breaks down what management has determined to be the value of each meeting room and each function space in specific time frames. These predetermined tariffs should be based both on market tolerance and client education level. These figures can be divided by length of time and time of day.

With standard time frames, management can determine a general room rental quote. Facility management should preset the value of its function space without considering other factors, such as sleeping room usage or food functions.

Room rental tariffs can be predetermined in different ways. The most common method is to determine a dollar value for each square foot of function space based on the set room rental revenue budget established by the facility (again based on market tolerance and client education). If, for example, a catering facility has 10,000 square feet of total function space and the daily room rental target is $5,000, the predetermined room rental for each square foot of function space is $0.50 (5,000 ÷ 10,000).

LENGTH OF TIME

The length of time an organization holds a function space dictates how many other organizations can use the space.

- **24-Hour Hold**   Reserving space for an entire day and night precludes the facility from reselling that space to any other group during that time.
- **Weekend Hold**   A weekend hold on function space is common for groups that require vast amounts of setup or teardown time. Conventions, for example, may have intricate displays and ancillary materials that require preparation and dismantling. The facets of a meeting room are often set up or cleaned and packaged for removal (torn down) over weekends. Social events like weddings may require partial weekend holds for decoration prior to the event itself.

TIME OF DAY

The standard breakdown of when groups meet encompasses the average length of time room rental tariffs are applied. The most common meeting times and lengths are:

- **Half-Day** Half-day meetings occur between 8:00 AM and 12 PM or 1 PM and 5:00 PM. The half-day time frames most often occur between major food functions (i.e., after breakfast, before lunch, after lunch, or before dinner).
- **Full Day** Groups meeting for full days usually request the hours of 8:00 AM to 5:00 PM.
- **Evening** Evening functions most often occur after 5:00 PM. Receptions and dinners may be precluded from booking at a facility that has an evening function booked in the corresponding meeting space.

Applying the square footage guideline for rental to the specific time frames discussed earlier indicates the predetermined room rental charge for any event function type. Again, the predetermined room rental tariff should not consider other revenue factors, such as sleeping room usage and food functions. This tariff is simply the cost of the function space.

MAXIMIZING FUNCTION SPACE IN A HOTEL

In general, hotels build function space to complement, or encourage the use of, sleeping rooms. The profit margin on the sale of a sleeping room is very high (70 to 80 percent is common). As a result, most hotels endeavor

SAMPLE ROOM RENTAL TARIFF SHEET

Function Room/ Square Footage*	Room 1 1,500	Room 2 1,500	Salon A 1,500	Salon B 2,500	Salon C 3,000	Total Rental (Dollars)
Time Frame						
Full-Day	750	750	750	1,250	1,500	5,000
Half-Day	375	375	375	625	750	2,500
Evening	375	375	375	625	750	2,500
**24-Hour Hold	1,125	1,125	1,125	1,875	2,250	7,500

*At $0.50 per square foot.

**Note: The 24-hour hold rental tariff is greater than the predetermined square foot allotment because holding a room beyond the full day involves holding the additional evening time frame. Because a 24-hour hold on a room precludes the room from availability for evening functions, the room rental loss should include both tariffs. Weekend holds, because they can vary in length, can use the same guideline. Any setup or teardown time that is needed should be included in the rental quote based on the time frames that are precluded from sale.

primarily to sell all their sleeping rooms each night. In reality, however, most hotels do not sell all their rooms every night. In fact, in many markets the number of rooms occupied, or the **occupancy level**, falls well below 100 percent. To create more demand for sleeping rooms, hotels first must analyze and understand the nature of their guests.

Understanding Hotel Guests. Years ago hotels discovered that the individual or **transient hotel guest** could not be counted on to fill their rooms each night. Individual business and leisure travel fluctuated wildly from day to day and year to year. It became difficult for hotels to **forecast** or predict occupancy with these fluctuations. In part from this need to better forecast, a new type of hotel booking was identified: the group. Organizations that seek to hold meetings, conventions, and other functions at a hotel are considered groups. A **group booking** is a group of reservations made at a hotel for one or more nights that correspond to a specific event. Most hotels categorize a booking of ten or more rooms per night as a group booking.

Understanding the Booking Cycle. Group and transient guests together compose a hotel's overall room demand. The time between the booking of a reservation and the arrival of the guest(s) is the **booking cycle**. Because group bookings require much more planning than do transient reservations, their booking cycle is much longer. A group booking cycle of 3 to 5 years is not uncommon. The transient booking cycle, in contrast, can be as short as 2 weeks. Because a hotel can have a base of group rooms on the books before it books transient rooms, the transient sales effort is awarded the flexibility to book rooms based on how many rooms remain. Transient rooms often cost more than do group rooms due to supply and demand. The fewer the rooms that are available, the higher their rate. In addition, the desire to book groups in advance is so intense that hotels often offer them lower sleeping room rates than transient guests. In effect, most hotels trade lower rates for a guaranteed **group base** of rooms.

Figure 1–2 illustrates a fictitious hotel's occupancy for 1 week. This hotel has 400 rooms available for sale each night. As the figure shows, the number of group rooms differs throughout the week as groups enter and exit. In this example, the hotel nearly but never fully sells its rooms based solely on group demand. Ultimately, the hotel's transient rooms fill the voids left by the group base each night.

Hotels may target the number of rooms they expect the group base to reach on a given night. This targeted number of group rooms is called the **group ceiling**. The number of group rooms is often fixed (hence the term *ceiling*) because of the aforementioned trade-off of lower rates for guaranteed occupancy. A hotel wishing to maximize its room rates will mix lower rated group rooms with higher rated transient rooms. Using **yield**

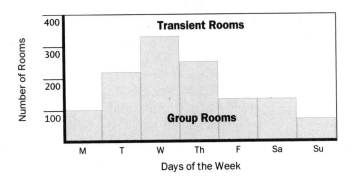

FIGURE 1–2

Transient and group
occupancy

management, a hotel tries to come as close to full occupancy each night as possible while maximizing room rate revenue.

Understanding the Impact of the Group Guest. Understanding how group guests impact a hotel's function space helps explain the fundamental differences between hotels and stand-alone banquet facilities. An organization that seeks to book a group at a hotel typically does so because it wishes to have these people attend or be part of a function or an event. Hotels, in an attempt to increase group bookings, built properties with function space so they could house group guests and host their functions. Before hotels with function space evolved, organizations had no incentive to book their groups at any one hotel. In fact, it was common for groups to spread their members among several hotels near the banquet facility in use.

The realization that group rooms are almost always tied to events that require function space dictated how hotels viewed the maximization of their space. If a hotel had only half its group ceiling filled but no function space available, it would be unable to book additional group rooms. Remember, the group ceiling is set to supplement the number of transient rooms for sale.

Calculating the Rooms-to-Space Ratio. The preceding scenario can be avoided by relating the group's sleeping rooms to the hotel's function space. Optimizing the sleeping room commitment of each new group while remembering function space availability ensures that space is maximized. The **rooms-to-space ratio** is the number of overnight rooms needed by a potential business opportunity relative to the total square feet the group needs for function space. The actual ratio differs from hotel to hotel. In general, the total number of rooms in the group ceiling on a given night dictates the number of sleeping rooms that should be occupied each night by the group. This number, when divided by the available function square footage, results in a figure that allocates a specific number of square feet to each sleeping room. The lower the number of rooms left to book within the group ceiling, the greater the amount of function square feet that can be available for sale.

Consider an example of rooms-to-space ratio as it might relate to a new group booking opportunity. Figure 1–3 shows a day in the function space availability of the XYZ Hotel. Currently, this hotel has booked the ABC Group. Assume that the group ceiling for the night in question is 250 rooms and that the ABC Group has reserved 175. The hotel has committed half its ballroom, one-third its breakout space, and all its specialized food function space for the ABC Group. **Specialized space** is simply function space that cannot be used for any other function. Specialized function rooms are permanently set up to host a specific food or event function. Permanent boardrooms or dining rooms, for example, cannot be changed to suit another function.

If a new group called the 123 Co. asked the XYZ Hotel for 25 overnight rooms and all its remaining space, should the hotel book it? Assume it does. The revised availability display would look like Figure 1–4.

The 123 Co. now takes all remaining function space at the XYZ Hotel. At first glance, it may seem the hotel made the correct booking decision. Closer examination, however, shows it did not. An additional 25 sleeping rooms for the 123 Co. would bring the total number of group rooms on that night to 200. The XYZ Hotel had set its group ceiling at 250 rooms. Booking the 123 Co. precludes the hotel from booking additional group rooms. The group ceiling will probably remain unattained, and the hotel will sit with empty rooms.

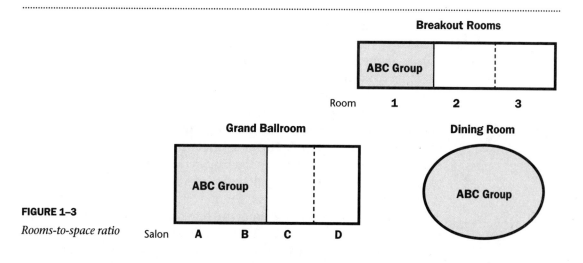

FIGURE 1–3

Rooms-to-space ratio

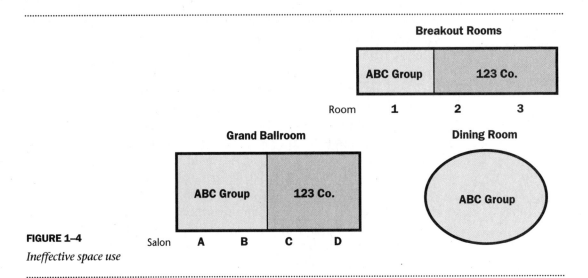

FIGURE 1–4

Ineffective space use

Introducing the Conference Center. A relatively new phenomenon in the industry, the **conference center**, has affected the number of new hotels built with extensive function space. A conference center is a meeting and/or an event facility that generally has no sleeping rooms. Some conference centers have sleeping rooms, but they are not the centers' primary revenue source, as they are in hotels. In fact, the numbers of sleeping rooms at conference centers are often low relative to the centers' function space capacities. A conference center that has a large sleeping room component is, after all, nothing more than a hotel with meeting space.

Conference centers differ from traditional stand-alone facilities in that they actively target the meeting market. This focus has put them in direct competition with hotels that seek the same market. Without the sleeping room component, conference centers have been able to impact the catering business at some hotels.

Because of the labor, equipment, and other costs needed to host group functions, some newly built hotels have chosen to cut back or eliminate their function space. These new hotels are often built near conference centers so they may house the conference centers' groups. In effect, conference centers act as the function spaces of hotels, which allows each facility to focus on its core strengths and let the other accommodate its weaknesses. A problem results from this relationship, however: Each facility may be limited by the other's capacity. For example, a hotel built next to a conference center may be limited in its group bookings by the number of groups the conference center can accommodate. A large conference center may be unable to host large groups because the nearby hotel may have too few sleeping rooms available in its group ceiling.

FUNCTION SPACE SALES RESTRICTIONS IN A HOTEL

Two basically different types of catering business exist in a hotel's catering effort. **Group catering** is catering derived from group bookings (sleeping rooms). **Local catering** is catering derived solely from the catering function (no sleeping rooms). Specifically, local catering is business in which the function or the meal is the primary focus. A dinner dance is local catering, while a convention dinner is group catering.

Group and local catering combine to best use the hotel's function space. Group catering is typically booked first, as the booking cycle dictates. Like the yield management of group and transient rooms, local catering should build on the "base" group catering creates (see Figure 1–5).

The need for hotels to maximize their function space in conjunction with sleeping room usage has given rise to certain catering sales restrictions. These restrictions aim to determine whether certain function space opportunities will hamper sleeping room booking. Local catering and its impact must be desirable for the hotel as a whole.

The analysis of desirability is not clearcut. A business opportunity can be more desirable for one hotel than another based on certain factors. The first step in determining desirability is basic: Should the hotel consider the opportunity? Again, because sleeping and function room usages are intertwined in a hotel, catering must not keep sleeping rooms from being occupied. Therefore, most hotels empower their group sales directors to

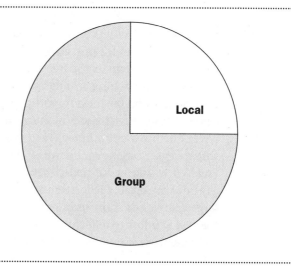

FIGURE 1–5

Group versus local catering

impose local catering sales restrictions based on the group base of sleeping rooms. In catering, the tools for ensuring the desirability of potential business opportunities are the **open sell date**, the **free sell date**, and the **space release**.

Open Sell. These tools allow local catering functions to be sold for some future date without hampering the group room sales effort. To ensure it succeeds, the group team gets the first opportunity to book the space on any given day. In most cases, the group ceiling dictates if and when catering can pursue a local business opportunity. Once the group team sells the preset number of guest rooms for a given date (i.e., reaches the ceiling), the remaining function space is made available to local catering. Throughout the year, the group team books groups for future dates. On many of these future dates one may find they have already reached their group ceiling of overnight rooms. With the approval and guidance of the group director, these dates can be listed for the future. Those dates where the team has met the ceiling will now become available to local catering. These are open sell dates. Local catering is now open to pursue all opportunities that fall on these dates without worrying about hampering the group team.

There is some debate in the industry as to exactly when space should acquire open sell status. If, for example, the group team reached its ceiling on Wednesday but on the Tuesday before had sold no rooms, should the space become available to catering on Wednesday? Most salespeople will argue that a potential group for Wednesday will check into the hotel the night before, on Tuesday. Therefore, would it make sense to sell the function space to catering groups on Wednesday and thereby preclude groups from checking in the night before? In many cases, a director of sales will determine open sell dates based on the night before, the night of, and the night after to ensure no opportunity is lost.

Free Sell. Whether a hotel has an open sell policy or not, other avenues are open for pursuing local catering business. One derivation of the open sell theory is the free sell time window, which allows space that is rapidly approaching and has not yet been sold by the group team to be sold. Short-term business opportunities are the focus of free sell windows. In most cases, the chances of the group sales team filling its group ceiling a week before are minimal. The theory that someone should book something to get some revenue into the hotel is the driving force of free sell. Free sell windows are tied closely to a hotel's booking cycle. The longer the booking cycle, the longer the free sell time frame. A hotel that books a large number of short-term group business opportunities will shorten its free sell window to reflect the short booking cycle. The most common free sell time frames are 45 to 90 days out (see Figure 1–6).

Free Sell Window

Function Space
Available to Local
Catering

Days from Arrival

FIGURE 1–6

Free sell window

Space Release. At times, business opportunities fit into neither the free sell nor the open sell window. In these cases, individual local catering opportunities may be able to gain a space release. A space release is a method instituted by some hotels to waive booking restrictions on local catering business when warranted. Usually, the business completes a form highlighting the date, potential revenue, and so on and submits it to the hotel director of sales for approval. A space release is granted when the group sales effort traditionally underproduces. Space releases are most commonly granted for **national holiday time frames** and winter **holiday parties**.

National Holiday Time Frames. Holiday time frames are unique when it comes to analyzing the space intensity of a potential function. National holidays in America, such as Memorial Day, Labor Day, Fourth of July, and Thanksgiving, are often quite slow for group business. Religious holidays can have a similar impact depending, in large part, on where the hotel is located in the country. In Canada, Boxing Day and the Canadian Thanksgiving are similar in effect. These dates (hotels may have others based on local events that impact them similarly) should be left open to local catering booking without consideration of their impact on sleeping rooms. Anything that can be booked during these days would likely displace no potential group revenue.

National holidays impact Canada and America differently. Because no American group wants to book a function on the Fourth of July does not mean no group will book. Canadians, for example, do not celebrate the Fourth of July. Thanksgiving in America is on a different day than that in Canada. The international market can provide many opportunities to fill holiday time frames with local catering.

Holiday Parties. Often called Christmas parties, these holiday local catering functions occur during the late fall and early winter. Many organizations host parties during this time of year to thank their employees and members for their hard work. These functions are not listed among holiday time frames, even though they are obviously part of the holiday season, because they are a unique type of catering function and have different characteristics. These functions are very high food and beverage revenue producers. Also, they are held by groups and organizations to celebrate the holiday season but are seldom held during the week of Christmas. Most holiday parties are held on the Fridays and Saturdays in the first 2 or 3 weeks of December, and possibly in the last week of November. They are even sometimes held in January to accommodate holiday schedules.

MAXIMIZING FUNCTION SPACE IN A STAND-ALONE FACILITY

While stand-alone banquet facilities generally lack a sleeping room component, there are other considerations when maximizing their function space. The previous example of the relationship between conference centers and hotels touched on one facet of stand-alone facilities and their unique needs. Banquet facilities have primarily one feature for sale: their function space. Therefore, with no sleeping room component, stand-alone facilities' catering business is entirely local. This means that stand-alone facilities must ensure that their space is used in the best way. To understand how well space is being used, one must understand the concept of **space intensity**.

Space Intensity. Space intensity is a measure of the function space being used for an event or a function versus what is considered typical for the facility. A facility with limited function space cannot allow a group to use all its space. A large convention center with hundreds of thousands of square feet of meeting space may be able to be more generous in its space allocation. Space-intensive functions are not considered "best use" in a typical day.

"Common" or "typical best use" differs from facility to facility. For example, if a group of thirty people wants to book but insists that their meeting be placed in the entire ballroom instead of a smaller ballroom section that could also accommodate their needs, the meeting could be considered space intensive. A small lunch for ten might fit into a hotel's breakout rooms instead of the rooftop dining hall. The stand-alone facility must be able to direct clients into function space that can best accommodate their functions while optimizing its overall space usage.

The facility in Figure 1–7 has two options for placing the meeting of the XYZ Company. Option A uses a permanent conference room that can

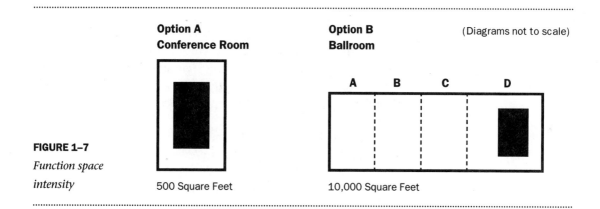

FIGURE 1–7

Function space intensity

accommodate up to fifteen people. Option B uses one section of the 10,000 square foot ballroom. Which option is the least space intensive?

The conference room in Option A is set up to host the meeting exclusively. No opportunity would be displaced or lost if the XYZ meeting were booked in this room. No bigger groups could better use the space.

Using Section D of the ballroom, as shown in Option B, would preclude the facility from using the entire ballroom for a much larger meeting or meal function. With this option, the facility would incur an **opportunity cost**. This cost would be incurred because the facility would have lost the opportunity to book better business.

Space intensity can be complicated by the lengths of time functions are held in specific rooms. Functions that are booked on a 24-hour-hold basis do not necessarily operate 24 hours a day. A 24-hour-hold simply guarantees that a function room will not be sold to another group after scheduled hours. An organization may ask that its function room be held on a 24-hour basis even though its meeting is only scheduled from 8:00 AM to 5:00 PM. (Groups that have brought extensive materials into rooms and do not want them moved or that have security concerns often make this request.) The 24-hour-hold does not allow for the room in question to be sold outside of the 8:00 to 5:00 time frame. A dinner starting at 7:00 PM could have been booked in the same room.

Space intensity can also be complicated by groups requesting extensive setup and teardown times. A group requesting entry into a room 6 hours before a scheduled function for setup has likely prevented the facility from selling that room for a meal function.

Space Efficiency. Another consideration in maximizing function space at a stand-alone facility is **space efficiency**. Space is used efficiently by minimizing the labor and opportunity cost incurred by changing function rooms from one event to another. Function space that can be prepared rapidly for a function when another ends allows the space's potential to be maximized. The time it takes for a facility to change a room from one event to another is called **turn time**. Most facilities need an hour of turn time between functions. Facilities can reduce turn time by booking functions that use similar seating styles (see Chapter 4). A **stay set** is a function that is booked after another using the same setup. Hotels with function space share the desire for space efficiency with stand-alone facilities.

Meeting Package Pricing. Conference centers and stand-alone banquet facilities that actively seek the meeting/event market (i.e., functions with no sleeping room components) have become popular with some event planners. One benefit of booking at these facilities is their unique pricing structure. Conference centers commonly use a pricing concept called **bundling**. Bundling is a process by which two or more elements of a meeting's costs are combined and quoted as one. Bundled prices are perceived by some planners as easier to use because they are quoted on a per person basis. The **day meeting package (DMP)** bundles the cost of the meeting space, food and beverage (often continental breakfast, coffee breaks, and lunch), and a limited amount of audiovisual (AV) equipment. The **complete meeting package (CMP)**, also called the comprehensive meeting package, is used by hotels and conference centers with sleeping rooms. The CMP bundles the cost of a sleeping room with the DMP.

FACILITY CATERING DEPLOYMENT

The structure used to ensure that all functions held at a facility are completed correctly vary from facility to facility, particularly in hotels. Stand-alone facilities have more limited options. This section looks at the catering structures of both.

Hotel Catering Deployment. As was mentioned previously, the catering effort at a hotel is categorized as group or local. In most facilities, the individuals responsible for each type operate in separate but related departments. The catering department focuses on local catering business, while the convention services department focuses on group catering. The biggest difference between the two is that convention services' main role is, as its name implies, **servicing**. The extent to which a hotel separates the two departments may vary greatly on the hotel's size and philosophy.

Group servicing is the on-property coordination of the specifics of a group. Depending on the size of hotel, these specifics can be food and beverage related or sleeping-room related. Again, depending on the size of the hotel, this servicing can be done by the catering or the convention services department. In some cases, three departments are involved in booking and servicing a group: The room salesperson books the group, the catering salesperson coordinates all menus, and the convention serviceperson manages the servicing once the group is on property. Despite the number of departments involved, the sales department books the group and another department takes over as the group's arrival date nears (except in the case of "meetings managers," which is addressed later).

Some hotels have no convention services departments. In these hotels, the catering department assumes all servicing duties. The three most common ways of deploying the sales and service sides of a hotel are **three-tiered deployment**, **two-tiered deployment**, and **two-tiered modified deployment**. Figures 1–8 through 1–10 illustrate these deployments.

Three-Tiered Deployment. Three-tiered deployment (see Figure 1–8) requires that the three branches of the hotel sales team work together. Each branch has a specific role in bringing a group from booking to arrival.

Two-Tiered Deployment. Two-tiered deployment (see Figure 1–9) exists in hotels with no convention services departments. The catering department assumes the servicing and menu planning roles of all group business, as well as the booking of all local catering.

Two-Tiered Modified Deployment. The two-tiered modified deployment scenario (see Figure 1–10) employs both the catering and convention services departments. However, the catering department does not play a role in servicing groups. The convention services department does all menu planning and group servicing, while the catering department works strictly on local catering.

The management of group servicing at any hotel begins when the room salespeople and the catering and/or convention services department(s) communicate about group details. **Turnover** is the process by

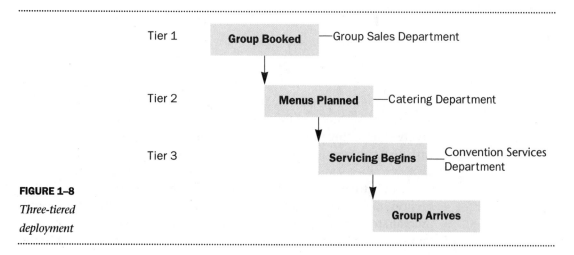

FIGURE 1–8

Three-tiered deployment

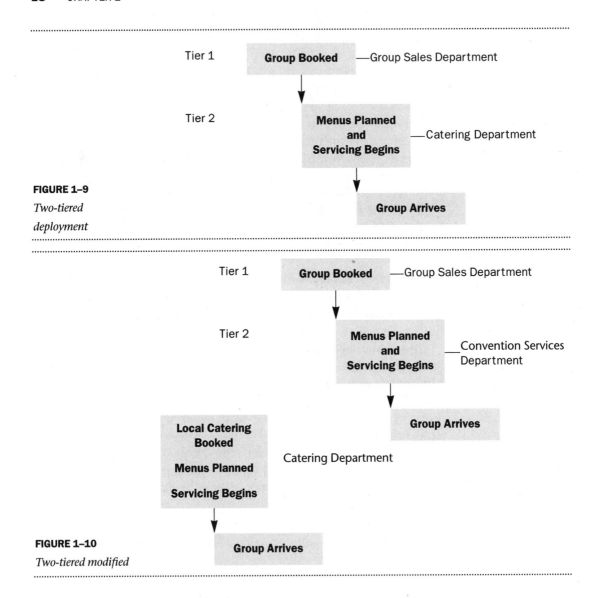

FIGURE 1–9

Two-tiered deployment

FIGURE 1–10

Two-tiered modified

which a group salesperson makes the catering and/or convention services department(s) aware of the details of a group. Because the salesperson involved in selling rooms is most often the first to actually communicate with the group (and thus knows more than anyone at the hotel), the turnover process must be as complete and as detailed as possible.

Group turnover is the method by which a catering or convention services manager becomes aware of a group and the details of the group's program to that point. Done properly, the turnover gives an "at a glance" look at a group, as well as valuable information about the client and the contact(s).

The turnover process should be completed on a schedule that gives the catering/convention services manager ample time to prepare. A large convention should be turned over no later than 1 year out. This time is needed to coordinate the hotel's efforts on behalf of a group as well as to manage the catering/convention services manager's slate of upcoming groups.

STAND-ALONE FACILITY DEPLOYMENT

As has been reviewed, the stand-alone facility, which lacks a sleeping room component, has no need for a convention services department. The servicing would be completed strictly by the catering personnel, and there would be no turnover process. The tiered structure for a stand-alone facility is, in essence, **one-tiered deployment** (see Figure 1–11).

FACILITY CATERING ORGANIZATION

The relationships of personnel at a catering facility are vital to the facility's success. Figure 1–12 illustrates a common catering reporting structure.

Each person in facility catering has a distinct role. The biggest difference between a hotel's organizational chart and that of the stand-alone facility is the convention services department. A facility with no sleeping rooms has no group catering component, so separate departments are unneeded. The following sections briefly describe each job.

Director of Food and Beverage. The director of food/beverage runs each department that sells, buys, or makes food and beverage products for a facility. The catering, restaurant/outlet, and kitchen staff report to him or her. The directors of catering and convention services (in some facilities those positions are combined) report to this person. The operational staff who coordinate all function space requirements report directly to this director but report indirectly to the directors of catering and convention services, respectively.

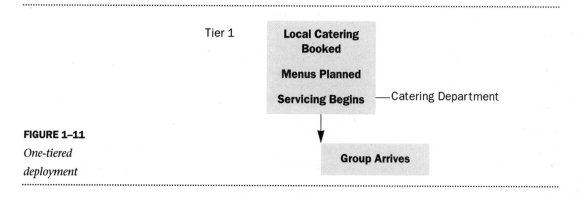

FIGURE 1–11
One-tiered deployment

Director of Catering. The director of catering is responsible for the catering side of the sales effort. He or she must be able to direct all local and, sometimes, group catering efforts on property. Typically, the catering sales staff as well as the operational catering staff reporting indirectly to the director of catering. In very large hotels, the catering sales staff may report to the director of catering, while the operational staff may report to a director of food and beverage. The director of catering works closely with the executive chef to develop menus and with the director of convention services to service groups (in three-tiered deployment). The director of catering reports directly to the director of food and beverage.

Director of Convention Services. The director of convention services (often abbreviated as CS) is responsible for servicing all group catering. This director works closely with the director of catering in three-tiered

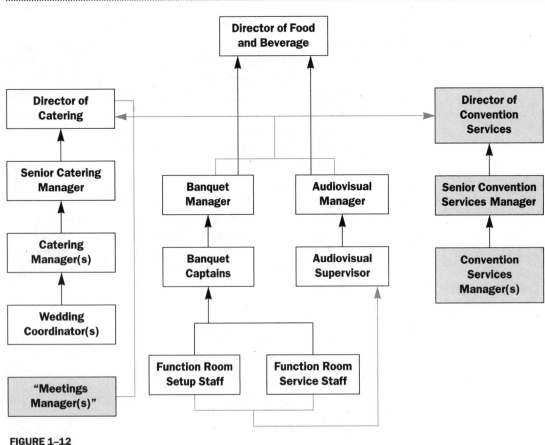

FIGURE 1–12

Facility organizational chart

Gray lines represent indirect reporting structure.
Shaded boxes indicate positions applicable only to hotels.

deployment and individually in two-tiered deployment. Operational staff may report directly or indirectly to the director of convention services as Figure 1–12 shows. The director of CS reports to the director of food and beverage.

Senior Catering/Convention Services Manager. Reporting to their respective directors, the "seniors" often deal with day-to-day operational issues. They often lead their teams of managers by example.

Catering/Convention Services Manager(s). Often called the "work-horses" of a facility, catering/convention services managers deal with most of the local and group catering business. Reporting to the senior or director of their department, these managers must be able to work well together to ensure every function in a facility is executed correctly.

Banquet Manager. The banquet manager's role in servicing is very important. He or she coordinates the staff in charge of setting up function rooms, serving meals, and cleaning up. The banquet manager works with the catering and/or convention services department(s) to ensure that all service sides of a program are completed correctly. The banquet manager is often the manager closest to the clients during a program, so his or her customer service skills should be well developed. Sometimes called a banquet maitre'd, the banquet manager often reports indirectly to the directors of catering and convention services and directly to the food and beverage director. The banquet manager reports indirectly to operational hotel personnel because local and group catering must receive equal amounts of attention by those servicing. A direct report to the director of one or the other might reflect a conscious effort by the facility to focus on group versus local or vice versa.

Audiovisual Manager. The audiovisual (AV) manager is responsible for setting up and servicing all AV needs of a function. Whether an organization needs a simple slide projector and screen or a large multimedia satellite setup, the AV department ensures the equipment is set up correctly. Technology in today's meeting and convention industry mandates that the AV department know the latest trends in equipment and technology.

Banquet Captain(s). Reporting directly to the banquet manager, each banquet captain is responsible for a specific function. Because it is unrealistic to expect the banquet manager to supervise each event in a facility, the captains serve as his or her representative in ensuring that levels of quality and service are met.

Function Room Service Staff. The service staff coordinate all food and beverage services at a function. They report to their assigned banquet captain. They work hand in hand with the setup staff to ensure a function room performs its duty.

Function Room Setup Staff. The setup staff in a hotel is in charge of physically arranging meeting rooms. The tables, chairs, displays, and related items must be tailored to each function. The setup staff ensures that the rooms are ready for the service staff to begin work. The setup and service staff report indirectly to the AV manager because it is sometimes necessary to coordinate the setup and service of a function around extensive AV arrangements.

Wedding Coordinator. Some hotels become very proficient at coordinating and executing weddings and wedding-related events. If a hotel establishes a reputation as a quality reception or rehearsal site, a wedding specialist may be employed by the catering department to develop this market. Developing the skills and knowledge required to effectively communicate and coordinate this market can take a great deal of time. This position frees the rest of the catering staff to concentrate on other local catering and group business.

Junior Sales Manager/"Meetings Manager." Many hotels employ one or more "meetings managers" to coordinate small to medium meetings and conferences. The idea is to empower salespeople to singlehandedly coordinate all the room and catering aspects of a group. In essence, they can be considered both sales and catering managers. This combination gives clients the ease of working with only one salesperson. The small meetings market is growing rapidly in many areas of the country. This position is viewed as useful training ground in which entry-level hotel professionals can learn all aspects of hospitality sales and catering.

OUTSIDE CATERING

An outside catering operation must be flexible and adaptable. Because outside caterers have not set function rooms to use, they must be willing and able to execute every aspect of what they need on the road. Logistics are an important part of the outside caterer's responsibilities. Within logistics, the outside caterer must focus on two primary components: preparation and transportation.

PREPARATION

The client who chooses an outside caterer rather than a catering facility to provide food and beverage for a function does so primarily because he or she wants a different venue. An outside caterer can provide food and beverage virtually anywhere. While the outside caterer is adaptable and flexible, adaptability means nothing without preparation. In outside catering, preparation is determining if and how an event will be run.

Can It Be Done? The outside caterer must first determine if the venue the customer has chosen is viable given his or her capabilities and limitations. No outside caterer should accept a large function if he or she lacks the staff or experience to handle it. It is best for the outside caterer to be honest when he or she is not certain he or she can accomplish something. A small group that needs a formal dinner in a remote location may be easier for one outside caterer than another.

In **specialized outside catering**, organizations focus their catering abilities in single directions. Street-corner vendors are considered specialized caterers because they are mobile, specialize in food items (e.g., hot dogs, pretzels), and target single, specific markets. Specialized caterers are becoming more and more popular. Specialized caterers provide food and beverage service at:

- Motion picture filming locations
- Weddings
- Construction sites
- Carnivals, fairs, festivals, special events

Kitchen Capacity. To determine if he or she can handle a job, the outside caterer considers two main points: **kitchen capacity** and **staffing**. Kitchen capacity is the amount of food that is produced within safety guidelines in a set time frame. The capacity of an outside caterer's kitchen goes beyond the sizes of the ovens, fryers, and burners. Large ovens help produce large amounts of food only when their operators know how to use them. The experience and deployment of an industrial kitchen staff is crucial to determining kitchen capacity.

Kitchen Deployment. The person who leads food preparation is called a **chef**. Often, a chef must study for years and continue learning in various working apprenticeships. The most skilled chefs are highly sought after by restaurants, hotels, and stand-alone banquet facilities, as well as outside catering companies. In commercial food operations, the title **executive chef** is given to the leader who has a staff of chefs working with him or her. The executive chef must coordinate the kitchen team in food preparation and operational menu implementation. This team can be composed of the chef alone (in a small operation) or hundreds of staff. Figure 1–13 shows a possible deployment scenario for a medium-sized catering kitchen. The organization of each kitchen differs. In a hotel, the executive chef may report to a director of food and beverage or directly to the general manager. In a stand-alone facility or a catering operation, the executive chef may also be the general manager.

The levels a chef must climb to reach the position of executive chef reflect the apprentice-like training he or she needs. This apprentice structure is more formal in Europe than it is in North America, but the titles of each level are similar:

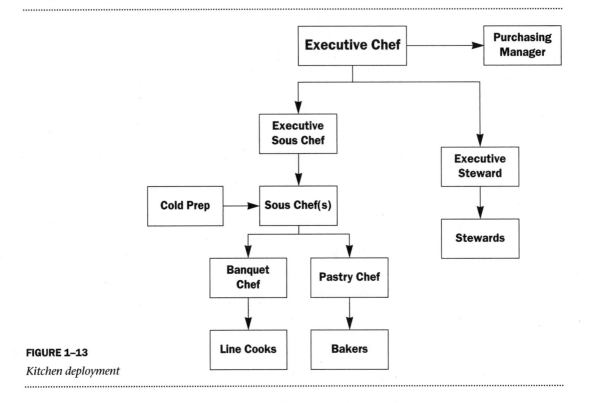

FIGURE 1–13

Kitchen deployment

- **Executive sous chef**—This chef is typically the leader of food production. The executive chef in a large kitchen may develop into more of a manager than a "hands-on" chef. The executive sous (pronounced *sue*) chef implements the directives and ensures that the team runs well.
- **Sous chef**—The sous chef leads a department within the kitchen. One sous chef may prepare sauces while another may focus on soups. These chefs often rotate responsibilities to master each part of the culinary process.
- **Banquet chef**—A banquet chef's sole responsibility is to ensure that all catered (i.e., nonrestaurant) meal functions are completed. Not all kitchens have a banquet chef. This chef is more common in a facility kitchen. Some kitchens employ the executive sous chef in this role.
- **Pastry chef**—The pastry chef is a master of desserts. This chef creates all cakes, pies, cookies, tarts, breads, and so on. Often the first person in the kitchen each morning, the pastry chef works with a staff of bakers to create the baked goods needed for breakfast, as well as the desserts needed for other meals.

- **Executive steward**—An executive steward is responsible for inventorying and cleaning servingware and eating utensils. The steward must ensure that the caterer has enough plates, forks, knives, and spoons. More than simply a dishwasher, the steward plans for a large, catered function to supply enough clean cups, glasses, and so on. Not all kitchens have stewarding departments.
- **Purchasing/beverage manager**—The purchasing/beverage manager ensures that the right quantity of food and beverage is ordered and in stock when needed. He or she keeps the kitchen supplied as well as plans for specific catered meals.
- **Cold preparation**—The individuals working in "cold prep" work strictly with foods that need no cooking (e.g., salads, fruits). These staff report to a sous chef because the foods they prepare are often parts of other food items.

Determining kitchen capacity starts and ends with the executive chef. He or she alone is qualified to judge the size and scope of an outside caterer's capacity. He or she serves the same role in facility catering. A kitchen staff of three cannot execute a dinner for 2,000 optimally despite how hard it tries. Whatever the scope of the catering operation, the outside catering professional, as well as the facility catering personnel, would benefit greatly from spending time with the chef and the rest of the kitchen staff. Understanding the scope and ability of a kitchen helps the catering professional make educated decisions.

Staffing Levels. Once kitchen capacity has been determined, the outside caterer must calculate the number of servers and other operational staff needed to execute a function. The number and guidelines vary drastically according to food function type and desired service level. (See Chapters 4 and 5 for more on these topics.) As a general benchmark, outside catering functions require:

- One food server for every forty attendees
- One food **runner** for every 100 attendees
- One seating setup/teardown person for every 200 seats
- One bartender for every 100 people
- One bar runner for every five bars

These staffing levels are not absolute. For example, a formal dinner with several food courses might require one server for every twenty or thirty attendees. More bars are needed when the client desires a "no-line" service level. Additional kitchen personnel are also needed with this service level to ensure the food is served within quality and safety guidelines.

TRANSPORTATION

Transporting food from where it is prepared to where it is to be served is vital to the outside catering operation. This is not as vital when the caterer has access to a venue's kitchen, but venue kitchens rarely have the facilities caterers need. A venue kitchen is best used as a backup for preparing last-minute items or replenishing foods.

The transportation used in outside catering comes in two forms: the **mobile kitchen** and the **general-purpose vehicle**. The mobile kitchen is essentially a kitchen on wheels. It is used most often by small caterers who need not create large amounts of food in short times. Mobile kitchens are limited by their cooking and storage capacities. The general-purpose vehicle is used to transport and store fully cooked food. These vehicles are most commonly used for large events. They are valuable to the caterer because they can be used to transport anything: food, equipment, staff, and so on.

Refrigeration trucks, mobile grills, and beverage vehicles are part of the catering transportation component. Events that occur over long periods must have places in which to store food until it is needed. Mobile grills can be thought of as extensions of the mobile kitchen in that they prepare food on location, but only by grilling. Mobile grills are therefore limited in the types of foods they can prepare. The beverage vehicle is commonly thought of as a beer truck. A van or another type of vehicle that has taps on the outside and coolers on the inside are useful because large quantities of beverage can be served without a bar.

Outside caterers who wish to expand their businesses must actively seek **preferred vendor** status. A preferred vendor is a supplier of goods or services another business has certified or approved in some way. Certification can entail rigorous quality testing, or it can involve simple product sampling. A preferred vendor in outside catering usually has been selected by a venue as the sole caterer, or one of the few caterers, who may serve the facility. An outside caterer should try to earn certification in as many venues as possible. Unique venues like museums, historical homes, government buildings, and recreation/team building venues can be lucrative for a caterer. Clients who want catering service in these venues will have to choose from the preferred catering vendors.

Outside catering is an exciting and rewarding industry. One person can cater small, intimate dinners, while a large operation can cater almost limitless events. With the emerging importance of convention centers, many outside caterers are finding opportunities to cater very large events. These convention centers often lack the internal kitchen capacities to manage all the events' food and beverage requirements, however. A large convention may require catering service for 5,000 meals or more.

Facility catering operations have begun to venture into the outside catering arena. In so-called **off-premise catering**, facilities use their large internal kitchens to provide food and beverage services to other venues. The Regency Caterers Division of Hyatt Corporation is perhaps the best known off-premise caterer.

CATERING CAREER MANAGEMENT

Hospitality careers can be very rewarding. A catering career must be fostered, like the skills in this text. This section analyzes two components of catering career management: beginning a catering career and fostering one.

BEGINNING A CATERING CAREER

Education is a critical first step toward entering the catering industry. Hospitality students often wonder which paths to catering positions are best. Without experience on a resume, how can one best enter hospitality?

Hospitality careers are not limited to catering. Hotel opportunities abound in group sales, accounting, food and beverage, human resources, engineering, retail, and customer service. The hotel industry is unique in that differing disciplines converge under one heading. Without hotel experience, however, a person who wants to begin a catering career in a hotel or another facility must do some work.

The current state of expansion in the industry makes working at a facility very possible. Facilities of every size, location, product type, and service level are always looking for new employees. Some large chains employ several employees whose sole purpose is to canvass higher learning campuses seeking talent. Small chains and independents use other means to recruit employees. There are several ways to enter this field, but each requires perseverance and initiative. To enter the sales and catering department, a prospective candidate can take advantage of any of several methods.

Management Training Programs. Most large hotel chains offer extensive management training programs for recent college graduates. Hyatt, Marriott, Sheraton, Hilton, and Westin each has a prearranged training program that lasts from 6 months to 1 year or more. Each new trainee works in most or all hotel departments during the program to gain experience in all facets of operation. Some management training programs end in the department the trainee chooses. Upon completing one of these programs, the new recruit is often assigned a junior management or supervisory role at a hotel. A permanent position in the sales and catering office of the hotel may not be available, but the trainee will eventually be placed in that office if that is his or her goal. The most prevalent entry-level position in hotel sales is meetings manager.

Internships. If a management training program is unavailable, interested candidates may seek paid or unpaid internships. While not as formal as management training programs, internships often focus on providing broad exposure to hotel departments. Internships repeated while candidates seek degrees (e.g., during summers) allow interns to focus on specific hotel disciplines. Sales offices have many marketing and promotional projects that require no more than 3 months work, which makes them ideal for summer interns. Outside catering operations that face increased demand during the summer may also use interns.

Volunteering. If formal training opportunities at a facility are not available, volunteer meeting planning may be the road to catering sales. Nonprofit organizations and charities of all kinds are always looking for help planning fundraisers and other events. Experience working with a facility from the other side (planning) may capture the attention of a director of catering and lead to paid employment. If the volunteer work goes beyond planning one function, these experiences also provide opportunities to judge several different catering operations.

Cross-Training. Recent graduates may find themselves frustrated with a lack of sales and catering opportunities at their operations or facilities of choice. When other departments offer training or internship programs, job seekers should investigate them. It is common knowledge that most facilities prefer to promote from within. Housekeeping supervisors or assistant front desk managers will therefore find that their chances of entering sales and catering are much greater than those outside the hotel. If permitted, personnel should spend 1 day a week (perhaps a day off) training in other departments to gain introductory experience, because doing so can be beneficial. **Cross-training**, the ability to learn the skills of more than one discipline, makes an individual much more valuable to an organization.

Operational experience is another benefit of cross-training. The assistant front desk manager, for example, brings to the catering office customer skills gained from guest interaction, as well as in-depth knowledge of the front office.

FOSTERING A CATERING CAREER

Whether catering managers work for major chains or independent facilities, they must always think about how to enhance their careers. Assuming they enjoy what they do, what are the keys to long-term success? The best approach to fostering a career is to predetermine the career path as much as possible.

A good starting point is to map long-term career goals. Catering managers should make lists or charts that detail where they hope to see their careers in 1, 5, and 10 years. Do they see themselves as general managers? Do they want to rise through the catering ranks and lead teams as directors of catering or food and beverage? Perhaps catering managers are content with their positions. Whatever the goals, the yearly plans should reflect where the catering managers want to be and how they will get there.

One-Year Plan. The 1-year or yearly plan should reflect the manager's most recent job evaluation or review. The yearly plan should focus on the areas the supervisor has targeted for improvement. Such a plan is most useful when set up as an immediate "action plan." An action plan should specify the areas that must be worked on and the best ways of doing so. A supervisor's input is vital, because he or she controls the manager's short-term career destiny. The supervisor's input on the action plan helps the manager understand management's specific expectations and their ideas on how best to achieve those expectations.

Five-Year Plan. The 5-year plan should be a blueprint of the individual's next desired position. Those who are content with their careers must still prove to themselves and to management how they will stay productive for many coming years. Do they want to become senior catering managers or move into the kitchen soon? The 5-year plan should be documented. To advance professionally, the individual must map the career path. The individual can start this task immediately by asking his or her superiors how they achieved their positions and in what time. Positioning oneself as a leader and a team player in day-to-day activities is a very good step toward career success. Always supporting management staff and teammates establishes the caterer as a team player. Exceeding catering sales goals consistently is a must. Whenever possible, the caterer should assume extra projects and responsibilities. Being the first to address a difficult situation establishes a good reputation. Caterers will find that maintaining consistency over 5 years will put them in positions to choose their next positions.

As part of ongoing career management, catering managers and students interested in the hospitality field should keep abreast of trade journals. Publications like *Hotel & Motel Management, Meetings and Conventions,* and *Events and Hotels* offer a wide range of timely and relevant topics. Association newsletters from groups like the American Society of Association Executives (ASAE) and the Religious Convention Management Association (RCMA) can give the planner's point of view on the industry. Individuals interested in the food and beverage side of hotels should seek *Restaurant Business, Cuisine,* and *Hotel Restaurant* magazines for similar insight. Other magazines and newsletters can be resources for research, career opportunities, and networking. Some, like the following, can be very specialized:

Catering/Food and Beverage

Events

Event Solutions

Food Arts

Hotel/Restaurant

Cuisine

Restaurant Business

Wine Spectator

Event World

Special Events

General Meeting Planning

Corporate & Incentive Travel

Corporate Meetings and Incentives

Meeting News

Association Meetings

Religious Conference Management

Insurance Meetings & Incentives

Meetings in the West

Midwest Meetings

Successful Meetings

Trade Show Week

Insurance Meeting Management

Medical Meetings

Transient/Travel

Business Travel News

Tour & Travel News

Travel Age

Travel Agent

Hotel & Travel Index

The Internet has a wide array of informative Web sites for the catering and hospitality professional. The following lists a few of the organizations currently using the Web:

General Meeting/Event Planning

Business Meetings.com

Event Planner

Event Source

Event Seeker

Exhibitor Network

Guide to Unique Meeting Facilities

Incentives & Meetings Europe

Meeting Exchange

Meeting Guide

Meetingpath

Meeting Planner

Meetings & Travel Online

Meetweb

Tourism Worldwide Directory

Trade Show Central

Trade Show News Network

Transient/Travel

BizTravel.com

City.net

Citysearch.com

Conde Nast Online

Fodor's Travel Online

TravelerNet

TravelWeb

Hotels (A sampling of hotel Web sites)

www.omnihotels.com/index2.htm

www.hilton.com/

www.marriott.com/

www.hyatt.com/

www.westin.com/

www.embassy-suites.com/

www.homewoodsuites.com/

www.ramada.com/

www.sofitel.com/

www.fourseasons.com/

www.renaissancehotels.com/   www.doubletreehotels.com/
www.ritzcarlton.com/   www.harrahs.com/
www.radisson.com/mainframe.html   www.adamsmark.com/
www.wyndham.com/   www.loewshotels.com/
www.nikkohotels.com/   www.swissotel.com/

Ten-Year Plan. The 10-year plan is essentially a rough outline. Facility catering personnel will have greater or fewer options depending on the types and sizes of their companies. If a caterer works for a chain and wants to be promoted quickly, for example, he or she should be open to relocation. Human resource managers at large chains will have some type of career profile on all management staff that other facilities may look at when they have openings. Often, these other facilities will look at the employee profile before the employee knows of another opportunity.

These profiles outline salary, performance history, experience in the company, education, management suggestions or career path, and relocatability. All professionals should review their profiles periodically to ensure accuracy and make changes. Marriage, new families, and other changes in personal status may necessitate changes in employee profiles.

If a catering team member lives where his or her company has more than one operation, he or she may have career opportunities without relocating. Called **cluster cities**, these areas allow for movement from operation to operation in the surrounding region with easy commuting. Large cities like New York, Chicago, and Los Angeles are often considered cluster cities because hotel chains regularly build more than one hotel in them.

Often, a long-term career goal of facility catering personnel is to open their own outside catering operations. Anyone interested in starting an outside catering operation must use cross-training opportunities at his or her current workplace. Experience in the kitchen, sales, and operational aspects are crucial to a successful catering operation.

Whatever career goals caterers have, they must always remember to enjoy what they do and to have fun.

Industry Perspective
"What Exactly Is a Meeting Planner?"

Dawn M. Miller, CMP
Meeting Planner

What is a meeting planner? The scope of meeting planning varies. Many planners handle everything related to bookings, while others handle only small portions. A seasoned meeting planner evolves into a meeting manager and can delegate many duties. The meeting manager takes ownership of the program and therefore oversees every aspect of the program he or she is planning. Whether the planner works for an association, a corporation, or a nonprofit organization, the scope of duties are very similar. It is the budget that varies with each group.

The meeting planner does not usually drive the "content" of the program. Content is the information that is shared, both written and verbal. Therefore, it is very important for the planner to understand the objectives of the meeting. Who is attending? Why have they been asked to attend? What will the attendees learn or do during the program? What should they take away from the meeting? Where are the attendees coming from? When is the best time to schedule the meeting for all involved? Understanding the objectives helps the planner know what destination and type of property will contribute to the success of the meeting.

The meeting planner must choose the destination carefully. Are the cities accessible by air, or do you have to drive 2 hours to the airport? Does accessibility matter to the attendees? You may want to shy away from the Northeast coast in the winter and Arizona in August, unless you are looking for a great deal! Would a small hotel with a golf course a little outside of town provide better accommodations than a large full-service hotel in the heart of town? Many planners rely on experience to choose destinations. However, most of us have not been everywhere. Local convention and visitor bureaus (CVBs) can provide information on their cities and let you know what is going on in their areas during your proposed dates. These CVBs can also recommend destination management companies (DMCs). Meeting planners put a lot of faith in DMCs. They, by nature, know their areas inside and out. They provide a wealth of information and personal knowledge about the accessibility and quality of hotels in their areas. They also help with on-site logistics, such as transportation, very important person (VIP) transfers, and special events.

Once you have chosen your destination and have considered a few different facilities for your meeting, it is time to negotiate the contracts. Hotel and facility contracts can be very complicated. A new planner may wish to have an experienced planner or a legal representative review a contract before signing it. Areas of the contract to pay special attention to are room block, meeting space block, rates, taxes, commission, attrition, and cancellation. Contracts are discussed in depth later in this text.

Now that you have confirmed "when" and "where," it is time to get down to details. Proper communication with attendees is crucial. The first list of prospective attendees should come directly from the client. The meeting planner may then be responsible for informing the attendees of the upcoming meeting. The following communication forms may be used depending on the size and scope of the program: "mark your calendars" card, invitations, confirmations, preliminary study materials, welcome packets, on-site study materials, meeting results, and service evaluations. Most of these materials can be created and contracted to another vendor. Vendors can also provide mailing service.

Getting attendees to and from the meeting can be a challenge. You may or may not make the airplane reservations, or provide the "meet and greet" at the airport, but you will have to know details about transportation. Even if you are using a DMC, you should make yourself aware of the following: distance from the airport to the meeting site, parking charges, transfers to event sites, sites within walking distance of the venue, the nearest golf course, and so on.

Throughout the planning process you have communicated many details with your contact at the meeting site, usually a catering or convention service manager. Once on site, you should have a preconvention meeting with key personnel at the site. It is important because, as the meeting planner, you are responsible for everything. You must oversee arrival of meeting materials and amenities, arrival of attendees, setup of meeting rooms, audiovisual setup, guarantees for food and beverage functions, setup of entertainment and decor, and all recreational activities.

One very important aspect of meeting planning is often overlooked: security. Security details merit a chapter on their own. It should be a given that the location will emphasize security, but that is not always the case. Do you have VIPs coming to your meeting that require extra security? What about the information being presented, both written and oral? Is there confidential information in the welcome packets? If you have a large number of attendees, you may want to provide emergency medical services as well as security.

You have survived the program and everything ran smoothly, but it is not yet over. The financial details are not fun but they are important. Planners tend to focus on the creative (the show) as opposed to the numbers. It is a good thing meeting planners must be detail oriented as well as creative. During the planning process, planners are responsible for discussing budgets with clients. The client depends on your expertise to ensure the budget is accurate. During the planning process, you may be responsible for paying deposits on goods and services on your client's behalf. When the meeting concludes, you will want to sit with the financial representative of the meeting site to review the bill. Whether you pay the invoices directly or not, you are responsible for ensuring that your client is charged properly for the services and products received and that the vendors are paid in a timely manner, which may mean 30 to 60 days. After that, it is time to start planning next year's meeting.

CHAPTER REVIEW

KEY CONCEPTS

Facility catering	Group catering	Two-tiered deployment
Outside catering	Local catering	Two-tiered modified
Maximizing space	Open sell	deployment
Stand-alone facility	Free sell	Turnover
Room rental	Space release	One-tiered deployment
Booking cycle	Space intensity	Kitchen capacity
Group ceiling	Turn time	Off-premise catering
Rooms-to-space ratio	Stay set	Outside vendor
Specialized space	Three-tiered	Preferred vendor
Conference center	deployment	Cross-training

REVIEW QUESTIONS

1. Explain the relationship between group and transient sleeping rooms in a hotel.
2. How can yield management be applied to local and group catering?
3. How do open sell, free sell, and space release catering restrictions differ?
4. Define *kitchen capacity* and its role in outside catering.

CHAPTER 2

The Marketplace

MARKET SEGMENTATION

Before caterers can make sales using the skills learned in this text, they must be able to classify the types of business they are considering using **market segments**. A market segment is simply a portion or segment of the actual or potential business pool. Categorizing business into segments that share characteristics is called **market segmentation**. Market segments can be grouped in many different ways. In various combinations, all business can be classified as one or more market segment(s).

Market segments can provide general information about the characteristics and nature of a group, but market segments may differ from one facility to another. Market segments, with their traditional traits, prompt the caterer to analyze each group specifically. The following analysis looks strictly at the most common market segments: corporate, association, and other.

CORPORATE MARKET SEGMENT

The corporate market segment consists of companies that are in business to make profits. Corporate businesses may have more money to spend than those in other segments, like nonprofit or other types of businesses. Often, corporate business is more concerned with content than with cost. This market segment frequently pays more than others to ensure quality programs.

ASSOCIATION MARKET SEGMENT

Associations are groups of individuals or companies that share purposes or goals. In a way, associations are a market segment within a market segment. Associations can be made of companies in a particular industry that band together for research, educational, political, or public relations reasons. Individuals join in associations to share ideas, hobbies, beliefs, or other things. This market segment may be more conscious of cost than the corporate segment because its members often pay for their businesses' services. Associations can be very large and require large facilities.

OTHER MARKET SEGMENT

Most companies group the market segments that do not fall easily into the corporate or association category into the "other" category. Also called the primary market, the other segment consists of groups that have characteristics that set them apart from those in the corporate or association category. This is not meant to diminish the quality or impact of this segment, but rather to afford it the attention it deserves. The other market segment has five primary components: social, military, educational, religious, and fraternal (**SMERF**).

MAKEUP OF THE OTHER MARKET SEGMENT	
Primary component	**Includes:**
Social	Weddings, Proms, Fundraisers, Bar Mitzvahs
Military	Reunions, Awards Ceremonies
Educational	Continuing Education and Certification
Religious	Revivals, Enlightenment
Fraternal	Fraternities, Sororities

The groups in the SMERF market segments, which tend to look for costs more than the corporate or association, can be large or small. These groups meet for reunions, bonding, continuing education, or any number of reasons. The lack of experienced meeting planners can make working in this segment challenging, but it can be rewarding as well.

Markets can be analyzed to separate the potential business pool into even more defined and/or diverse **subsegments**.

MARKET SUBSEGMENTS		
Corporate	**Associate**	**Other**
Manufacturing	Local	SMERF
Construction	State	Tour/Travel
Distribution	Regional	Cultural
Retail	National	Sports
Printing	International	Government
Health		Seminars
Insurance		
Media		

CATERING SALES TOOLS

When preparing for sales, catering professionals must arm themselves with basic tools. The most fundamental tool in any sales discipline is knowledge of the product. Knowledge of one's facility and what it offers, two other basic tools, are crucial before selling can begin. Another basic sales tool is familiarity with the competition. Catering salespeople must know what they are selling against. The final basic tools a salesperson must master to prepare for a sale are customer communication forms and hospitality sales tools.

KNOWLEDGE OF THE FACILITY

Have you ever walked into a car showroom and asked the salesperson a question about a car and he or she did not know the answer? It can be very frustrating to deal with salespeople who do not know their products, whatever the products (cars, clothes, or facilities). Clients will ask a range of questions that salespeople often do not expect. Some questions are impossible to prepare for because they are uncommon, but others are common and therefore easy to prepare for and to answer. The most important questions to answer in catering sales are those regarding products and services.

A facility salesperson's product is the facility. The hotel is the most intricate catering facility. It is vital that hotel caterers and convention service personnel know these intricacies so they understand what might be asked of them. Salespeople should know their products thoroughly before they try to sell them. Outside catering salespeople should know their products as well. Their menus, limitations, capabilities, and so on are all parts of the knowledge base of the outside caterer.

Information gathering is the way to build this knowledge base. The salesperson should start gathering information by approaching the manager of each restaurant, lounge, and room service department and asking him or her every conceivable question. Every possible question cannot be reviewed, but the salesperson should ask about the hotel's outlet hours of operation, meeting capacity, location, special services, and amenities. The salesperson should compile a fact sheet or personal binder to keep all the information he or she collects accessible.

Stand-alone facility caterers will find much of this information applicable. While outside caterers may find little of this information relevant, the information-gathering process should reinforce for all salespeople the principle of "know your product."

QUESTIONS TO ASK THE FOOD AND BEVERAGE OUTLETS

- Has the local food critic raved about your specialty restaurant?
- Do you offer buffets at set times or as demand warrants?
- What are your hours of operation? Do these hours change during the week?
- What is your maximum capacity? Dress code? Average per person cost?
- What days of the week, if any, do you close?
- Do you offer "Early Bird" or "Happy Hour" price reductions?
- What are your signature food items? What are your most popular food items?
- What do you consider the characteristics that set your outlet apart from others?
- Does the chef prepare daily specials? If so, what are some examples?
- Do holiday hours differ from normal hours of operation?

With knowledge of their products, catering salespeople can impress clients with information about their hotels' outlets and their hotel teams' strengths. They can also steer clients away from their hotels' weak areas before those clients settle on agendas that would require the hotels to perform in their weak areas.

Every facility has things it does well and things it does less well. Every facility also has some unique capabilities, which can include any number of amenities or services. These unique capabilities should be included in the fact sheet. A facility can aid the caterer early in the sales process by using its unique capabilities to distinguish itself from the others.

Every facility that has function space should have a detailed diagram of all its function areas and any other space in the hotel available to sell to clients. This room capacity chart should outline all the possible setups and the capacity of each area in different configurations. This diagram is a fundamental document; it should be memorized. The catering salesperson should be most familiar with this document. The facility salesperson should be most familiar with space and its flexibility.

In addition to information about outlets, function space, and special facility services, catering salespeople should have good understandings of a facility's basic administration and operation as well as the facility's location and surroundings. A facility's location can be a selling point. When located right off an interstate or a major thoroughfare, a facility can use accessibility as a selling point. Accessibility is important to groups with many members who drive to attend. Salespeople who are familiar with a facility's location show clients that they are aware of their surroundings and help create trust in their clients.

QUESTIONS TO ASK ABOUT THE FUNCTION SPACE

- How many classroom tables fit in the ballroom?
- How does seating capacity differ when using rounds of eight versus rounds of ten?
- How does rear-screen projection affect maximum theater-style seating?
- What are the capacities of all function rooms using common room sets and variations?
- What type of turnaround time is needed to change room sets?
- Can you flambé dessert in the ballroom or is doing so against the fire code?
- What is the maximum number of schoolroom tables that can fit in the exhibit hall?
- What is the reception capacity of the prefunction area?
- How many tabletop exhibits fit in the ballroom?
- Are the airwalls in the ballroom soundproof?
- Where are the light and temperature controls in each room?
- When was the meeting space last renovated?
- Are all function areas accessible or Americans with Disabilities Act (ADA) compliant?

MORE INFORMATION TO KNOW AND QUESTIONS TO ASK

- Does the hotel have automatic turndown service for all guests?
- Does the hotel have an automatic checkout billing system?
- Does the hotel have special meeting services or a business center?
- Is the hotel's tennis court or golf course highly regarded?
- Does the hotel offer complimentary coffee service or free newspaper delivery?
- Does the hotel sponsor children's activities?
- Does the hotel have frequent-stay programs and tie-ins to airlines and car rental companies?
- Are the guest rooms newly renovated?
- Are there special in-room amenities (minibars, voice mail, work areas, movies, toiletries, unique views, 24-hour room service, video games)?
- Is there express check-in service?
- Is there an airport shuttle?
- Is there concierge service?
- Is there a business center and other services?

FAMILIARITY WITH THE COMPETITION

Product knowledge is the first basic sales tool in the hospitality industry. The next important sales tool is familiarity with the competition.

Catering sales would be much easier with no competition. Clients who have no option but to book at a facility offer minimal challenge. Without the challenge of competition, however, salespeople can become

ADDITIONAL ASPECTS OF THE PERSONAL FACT SHEET OR FACILITY INFORMATION SHEET

- Correct spelling of the general manager's name
- Total number of function and sleeping rooms and group ceilings as they relate to booking restrictions
- Breakdown of kings, doubles, suites, corner rooms, view rooms, rooms on business or concierge level, and so on
- Rollaway, crib, and extra person costs
- Banquet price averages for breakfast/lunch/reception/dinner, and coffee breaks
- Secretaries club, frequent-stay program, meeting incentives
- Activities and prices (e.g., golf, tennis, pool)
- Nearby attractions and their hours and costs
- Nearby restaurants, nightspots, and so on
- Competing facilities and their phone numbers, numbers of function and guest rooms, and locations
- Major airlines that service the local airport
- Major local thoroughfares and exits
- Facility ownership, corporation, management, and corporate history (if applicable)
- Route to facility from the airport; taxi or bus costs
- Directions from downtown with exit numbers, if any
- Length of the drive to the ocean or next major city
- Distance from the convention center

complacent. Competition forces salespeople to improve their selling skills. In catering sales, the strongest salesperson survives and makes the sale.

Some caterers may be in the rare position in which they have no real competition in their areas. In those cases, selling is easy. More likely, however, market factors will drive developers to seize opportunities in all areas, and caterers will face competition. Most salespeople will face the challenge of competition.

This area of competition really allows catering salespeople to better themselves and their skills. To overcome the competition, catering salespeople must accomplish two basic tasks:

1. Know the strengths and weaknesses of all competitors thoroughly.
2. An underused and often ignored tool in overcoming competition is to gain the competitors' respect.

Knowing the Competitors' Strengths and Weaknesses. A common saying is, "Knowing is half the battle." When it comes to knowing the competition, however, knowing is three-quarters of the battle. If caterers do not know what they are facing, they cannot compete against, let alone beat, the competition.

In the day-to-day sales activities of a catering professional, a client often uses phrases like "The XYZ Facility is offering this," or "The ABC Hotel is just what we need." What do caterers do when this happens? Do they allow clients to work with other facilities? Catering salespeople who know the strengths and weaknesses of the competition are in positions of power.

To best know the competition, salespeople should insert in their personal fact sheets sections that outline information on the competition. This information should include the competition's:

- Strengths
- Weaknesses
- Room rental and sleeping room rates
- Number of function and sleeping rooms
- Typical group ceiling
- Function room square footage
- Quality of meeting space
- Outlet/ancillary options
- Banquet prices
- Location relative to the surroundings and other hotels

These aspects and more are very important for the salesperson to know. The questions the salesperson asks about the competition should resemble those asked about the caterer's own catering operation. Each time salespeople move to other cities or facilities, they must orient themselves to the strengths and weaknesses of all competitors in their new areas.

Senior management at any catering operation should have a competitive survey completed for the annual marketing plan. If information for the competitive survey is outdated, it is easy to update. A good way to do this is to personally inspect all the facilities the caterer considers competitors. In a highly competitive market, team members should share inspection duties. Spending the night at a hotel reveals what the hotel truly offers. A stand-alone facility can reveal a great deal on any given day. An outside caterer should observe competitors as they set up and execute functions at various venues. Each catering manager should tour the venue and ask the following questions:

- Is the competitor's first impression a good one?
- What level of service does the competitor provide?
- What is the quality of the plate presentation?
- Are the competitor's function rooms of comparatively good or bad quality?
- How does the competitor's service staff differ from ours?
- What is the quality and condition of the competitor's function room equipment?

Each team member should examine the sets in the ballroom and other meeting rooms. Team members should experience the health club and play rounds of golf on the golf course, if one is available. Team members should absorb all that they can and document everything they have witnessed so they may share their information and observations with the rest of the team.

The team should follow its inspection with a formal meeting with counterparts in the competitor's catering department. During such meetings, catering salespeople can obtain information on published rates, menu prices, standard amenities, and the like. With good rapport with the competitor, salespeople can obtain even more information.

This information, paired with the personal inspection, can give the sales team members a good idea of what competitors in their area can and cannot do well. To supplement this information, the sales team should solicit feedback from the local convention and visitor bureau and any clients who have good rapport with the competitor. The solicitation efforts used to collate readerboard information (discussed later in this text) are also valuable to understanding the competition, because they reveal the types of clients who frequent the competitor. At the end of this process, catering salespeople should be able to insert into their personal fact sheet binders page summaries of every competitive operation.

What should the salesperson do with the information in the binder? What the salesperson should *never* do is speak disparagingly of a competitor to a client. Doing so is very unprofessional and may lose the respect of both the client and the competitor. Being magnanimous when discussing the competition is an unwritten rule in the hospitality industry. When pressed, the salesperson should tell the client what the competition does well. In fact, catering salespeople should not hesitate to recommend competitors when the salespeople cannot or do not want to accommodate particular groups. Salespeople should stress the positives in competitors even if the client demeans them.

Knowing the competition and the ways to address the competition with clients can be helpful when clients erect roadblocks to sales. For example, if a client claims a competitor is offering a lower room rental rate or menu price than the caterer quoted and if the competitors are of the same caliber, the caterer can reply, "Wow! That is a great price. It is wonderful that the XYZ Hotel can give you that high level of quality and service at that price. We would be bankrupt trying to keep our level of service at that price." With this response, the caterer places doubt in the client's mind without seeming bitter or spiteful toward the competitor. Of course, competitors have their own business cycles, so lower price quotes are inevitable. Knowing how to deal with these issues in busy times prevents catering salespeople from inadvertently lowering menu or function room quotes to secure business. Salespeople who know their competition and know how to address any problems the competition may present can overcome the competition.

Gaining the Competitors' Respect. Skilled caterers do more than simply conquer the competition. They make the competition work for them by positioning themselves as allies, not enemies, of the competition. Skilled caterers become allies most easily by getting to know their counterparts in other sales offices.

Caterers get to know their counterparts by networking and competing. Most catering salespeople face the same salespeople at competitive facilities. They also meet competitors face to face, at industry meetings and trade shows. Once they have their competitors' names and have established rapport, catering salespeople can do two things.

First, catering salespeople can refer business that cannot be booked to specific people. Clients appreciate being given the names of specific people. The caterers providing the names look both magnanimous and knowledgeable. Clients are more likely to call the caterers again, before they call other caterers, if the caterers are honest about the clients' options and provide the names of those options. The trust between caterer and client increases in these instances, even though the business was not booked.

The caterer's competition now views the caterer as someone who has the client's best interests as the ultimate concern. The competition will reward the caterer with referrals when he or she cannot or will not accommodate a group. If the competition does not want a piece of business, it does not mean the business is undesirable. The trust of the competition, in essence, creates another source of sales leads. Such leads will be prequalified and sent in enough time for the caterer to pursue them.

Therefore, the second thing catering salespeople should do is continue building rapport with their competitors. When possible, salespeople should invite competitors for lunch and tours of their facilities on days the facilities are at their best. A conference center hosting an extensive convention can look impressive if all its parts are active, for example. These tours are opportunities for salespeople to make favorable impressions. They also make it more difficult for competitors to sell against the facilities because the facilities look their best.

Caterers should not be afraid of admitting their facilities' limitations, however. For example, caterers should admit if their hotels cannot do remote check-in. The reason for this is that referral business that doesn't apply won't be of value. In the end, catering salespeople who know what their competition can and cannot do and who have their competitors' trust are at a distinct advantage.

TIME MANAGEMENT

Most busy professionals today claim there are too few hours in a day to accomplish everything they set out to do. For catering salespeople, time management is crucial to effectively completing the duties of selling and its related operational demands. The two most important time-management issues in sales are prime selling time and prioritizing.

Prime Selling Time. In certain hours of each work day catering salespeople should focus on selling and in others they should address operational issues as needed. **Prime selling time** dictates when catering salespeople should focus on sales. Prime selling time is the period during the day in which salespeople have the best chance of reaching current and prospective clients. Selling can be done at any time of day, but lead generation and customer-rapport building have the best chance of success during these times.

As a general rule, prime selling time runs from 9 A.M. to 11 A.M. and from 1 P.M. to 4 P.M. each day (see Figure 2–1) because these are the times when most people are in their offices. The prime selling times of catering operations may differ slightly based on the operations' time zone locations. A catering salesperson calling from any of the four continental time zones (Eastern, Central, Mountain, and Pacific) will have a slightly altered prime selling time. For example, salespeople who work on the West Coast may start their day earlier because their contacts on the East Coast are already well into their day. Similarly, salespeople who work until 7 P.M. on the East Coast can still reach most of their contacts on the West Coast.

Outside prime selling time, catering salespeople can concentrate on paperwork and service issues. Salespeople should complete operational issues and related paperwork around prime selling time whenever possible.

Prioritizing. Being able to judge what task must be done first and what task can wait is important if caterers are to best use their work days and take full advantage of prime selling time. The ability to prioritize helps salespeople regulate their workflow and stress levels, which in turn increases productivity.

Efficient work day prioritizing begins with a good "day planner" or computer datebook planner. Caterers should review and update these tools consistently, because these tools are of no use if they are not used consistently.

Everything must be written in these planners, including appointments, site inspections, due dates, trace dates, and special follow-up dates. These planners should be used to follow up on proposals and contracts, and all important upcoming functions should be noted. Catering staff who are assigned special projects by their managers should plot in their planners when and how they will complete those projects. Salespeople should use planners to track mileage to sales calls, expenses on sales trips, and any other items of benefit.

Prime Selling Hours

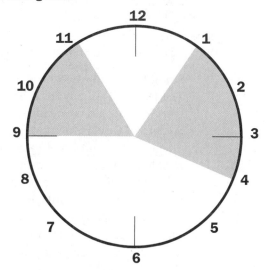

FIGURE 2–1

Prime selling time

On a day-by-day basis, these planners should serve as caterers' "prior-
itizers." Placing a day's schedule at a glance ensures that all appointments
are spaced evenly and with ample time between for preparation and follow-up. If the planner has a "to do" list area for the day, the caterer should
prioritize list items with numbers. For example, using a scale of 1 to 5, a *1*
may need to be done immediately while a *5* can be done later. The caterer
should review this list carefully at the start and the finish of each day. At
the start of each day, the caterer should review the agenda for that day, as
well as that for the next. Doing so ensures the caterer is aware of all due
dates and prepared for all appointments. If the end of the day arrives and
a *1* remains on the priority list, the caterer should stay and complete the
task. A combination of *4*s or *5*s on the list may not require immediate
attention, but the caterer must make sure to transfer those tasks to the "to
do" list of the next work day and to increase their priority levels by at least
1. Using this system, a *5* becomes a *4* the next day. This system is important because without it caterers may allow themselves to avoid indefi-
nitely tasks they do not want to do.

NETWORKING

Because the catering sales profession is people oriented, it is logical to
assume that the more people a catering salesperson contacts, the more
sales opportunities that arise. Lead generation and rapport building require
human interaction. The catering industry makes available a network of
related organizations and industry gatherings that enables caterers to meet
other salespeople and potential clients. **Networking**, or meeting and talking with these different people, can only further a sales effort.

Many different types of organizations and events provide sales and
catering teammates networking opportunities. Different locations may
have more organizations, or fewer. The following list highlights some of
these groups and what they intend to achieve:

- **Hotel Sales and Marketing Association (HSMA)**
  The HSMA is usually local hotel/facility managers and executives who meet to share ideas and network.
- **Society of Government Meeting Professionals (SGMP)**
  The SGMP is a group of local hotel and meeting facility salespeople and various government meeting planners. It is a good
  group to work with if the government is a big local player or the
  catering operation wants to focus on this market segment.
- **American Society of Association Executives (ASAE)**
  The ASAE is a national umbrella organization with state chapters. Each state chapter alters the national name somewhat

(e.g., KSAE is KY Soc. Assn. Execs). Like SGMP, ASAE combines association decision makers, hotel/facility representatives, and other vendors. In some states, the ASAE is a powerful governmental lobbying body with major impact on the catering community.

- **Meeting Professionals International (MPI)**
  Perhaps the most recognized and well-run organization of its type in the country and the world, MPI is unique in its basic structure. For catering salespeople to join MPI, they must bring meeting planners. This balance of planners and suppliers (caterers are suppliers) allows for equal influences and direction. Most local MPI chapters will help catering salespeople find planners if they want to join. Members organize national meetings, and regional seminars and even have an informative newsletter. Look for them now on the Internet.

- **Religious Conference Management Association (RCMA)**
  The RCMA is another nationally recognized organization that is focused on planning meetings and conventions for religious groups of all kinds. Its national meeting is a must for tapping into this large meeting potential.

- **Convention and Visitor Bureau (CVB)**
  Each city or region and/or state will have a CVB, which is a locally funded (usually from the hospitality community's occupancy tax or dues) organization that is set up to bring in convention group business as well as promote tourism. This is a very important entity for a caterer to become involved in. CVBs often sponsor events, familiarization trips, and trade shows in which all interested parties should participate.

- **National Association of Catering Executives (NACE)**
  The NACE is an organization of catering and convention service personnel who meet to share ideas and to network.

Networking in these and other groups helps the caterer in many ways. The more people caterers speak with, the more people who will remember the caterers. When provided opportunities to attend lunches, dinners, or receptions for any of these organizations, caterers should aim to meet at least five new people. Caterers should bring plenty of business cards and distribute them when appropriate. Some people are not comfortable at these events, but catering salespeople must think of these events as sales opportunities. After several events, salespeople will have the names of many people who may be helpful. Those people, who now feel they have viable catering contacts, may pass the salespeoples' names to other potential clients.

OTHER NATIONAL ORGANIZATIONS

- American Society of Travel Agents
- Association of Corporate Travel Executives
- Association of Destination Management Executives
- International Association of Conference Centers
- International Association of Convention and Visitor Bureaus
- International Special Events Society
- International Society of Gay and Lesbian Meeting Professionals
- National Society for Minorities in Hospitality
- National Business Travelers Association
- National Speakers Association
- Pacific Asia Travel Association
- Society of Incentive and Travel Executives

LOCAL ORGANIZATIONS

- Chamber of Commerce
- Better Business Bureau
- Kiwanis/Elks
- Rotary Club
- Downtown or Waterfront Development Commissions
- City Hall/State Capitol
- Sports Commissions
- Nonprofit Organizations like the Red Cross and the YMCA
- "Business Builder"/"Business After Hours" Networking Receptions

TECHNOLOGY

Currently, only a few of the largest hotel chains with significant financial resources have been able to computerize both their sleeping room and function space availability displays internally for sales and catering use. Creating standard, chain-wide programs for those two important functions can be cost prohibitive for many.

Sales and catering software packages are available. The most well known is Delphi. Another similar program on the market is called Miracle. Whatever systems caterers may use, they should endeavor to learn all the systems' features and applications so they can make the most of those systems.

The most important technological tool for the sales and catering office is the database. While not a new phenomenon, the database is an extremely useful information resource. Extracting historical data from a database is sometimes called **data mining**. Mining data in such a way as to extract information within set parameters allows a sales office to effectively use its resources. Data extracted from databases can identify trends or supply specific information about new sales initiatives. The most common database searches in catering sales result in information yielding history, lost business, and customer demographics.

History Reports. A database search of an organization's history at a facility can yield a salesperson valuable information. The history search can be used as a lead-generation source or a trend identifier. A pattern that is identified in history reports may indicate that changes are needed in pricing strategy or deployment. The leads generated from history are like those generated from the efficient usage of a caterer's trace files.

The biggest benefit of the history database search is the ability to tailor to specific needs. Tailored reports can be used to learn who has used a caterer's services in specific time frames, which is useful when soliciting business for need periods. Searches can be conducted to reveal information on past specific market segments. For example, if a facility wants to do a promotion for the insurance industry, the database can search all the groups within that segment. A search like this adds to the impact of a promotion, because the people being sent information already know of the facility. These searches yield information on receptive targets, which will be more likely to consider the information because they have purchased the caterer's services in the past.

Broad-based history reports (those with few parameters) can help senior management determine budgets. The creation and implementation of an annual marketing plan are more realistic when expectations are based on past performance.

Lost Business Reports. Lost business reports (LBRs) list business opportunities that did not book at a catering facility. These opportunities may have been lost to a competitor or turned down by the catering team because they did not fit the facility's strategy at the time. The LBRs should be entered into the database routinely and accessed like history reports.

The LBRs can be used to augment solicitation efforts and to solicit for need periods, as are history reports. Because the business environment changes constantly, something that was lost or turned down once may look more appealing at another time.

The LBRs can also be used to identify trends. If a catering office is routinely losing or turning down business due to rate catering prices or room rentals, a combination of LBRs can reveal the common reasons. These reports may justify reevaluating the sales strategy. Also, the loss of business due to the condition of the facility (e.g., worn-looking sleeping rooms or function space) may be reflected in the LBRs. Senior management and owners may expedite the release of renovation funds if business is being lost as a result.

The director of catering can use LBRs as coaching tools to monitor a salesperson's ability to close a sale. Those who have not yet mastered the catering success triangle may find that they are consistently losing business at the same point in the sales process. The LBRs serve as a sort of "report card" on a salesperson's technique.

Customer Demographics. Demographics help determine target markets. The ability to identify consumers based on their buying criteria is important to many industries. For example, in television an audience's demography determines which groups are watching which television shows. With that information, advertisers can place commercials that reach their targeted demographic groups.

In hospitality, demographics in a database report allow salespeople to identify group types and market segments and their respective buying habits. Certain groups share similar traits, such as space intensity and budget consciousness. A demographic report allows salespeople to search for one or more of these traits. Parameters can be set to search for specific tentative, definite, and actual status groups on the books. The LBRs can be included if the database is set up for it.

For example, if a conference center wants to increase its average menu price during a certain time frame, it can set the parameters of the demographic report to search for all groups that have paid as much as, or more than, the targeted price. The catering sales team then has another set of receptive customers who can be solicited. The same applies to searches for groups with specific beverage budgets. The more sophisticated systems allow searches by geographic region, zip code, area code, feeder city, and other characteristics.

The adage "Garbage in, garbage out" applies when working with all of the preceding reports, which means that database reports are only as good as the information put in them. Salespeople should always strive to supply complete information.

OTHER TECHNOLOGICAL TOOLS FOR HOSPITALITY SALES

- Computerized trace file programs
- Database searches from lead suppliers (e.g., Professional Convention Management Association, MPI)
- Group profitability programs
- Internet searches of the competition
- Readerboard database analysis
- Third-party reports for competitive market share
- Computerized account management programs

Industry Perspective
"Technology and the Meeting Industry"

Joseph Murray
Information Manager

The advent of computers has helped all industries accomplish many tasks. Inventory, cash balancing, word processing, and accounting have all benefited from computers in many ways. In the hospitality industry, computers and new software programs now aid meeting planners. Specific software packages, like CORE Discovery from McGettigan Partners, helps planners with almost all aspects of meeting planning.

For instance, the newest version of CORE allows users to employ the Internet to notify and register participants. With this software, a personal meeting Web site can be arranged for every meeting, thereby eliminating costly and environmentally unfriendly old methods of mass mailings and broadcast faxing. With Web site access, registration and confirmation are minutes, rather than days or weeks, away.

In addition to strictly planning software, consolidation packages are available. Consolidation is a process by which a company has a centrally located group that tracks meeting information and gives feedback on how much is being booked and spent. Because consolidation allows for detailed tracking of use and locations, it provides the organization with leverage when negotiating with facilities and venues. The total expenditure, per site, is valuable in measuring the volume of business. Because a company often books many programs at one location, clients may, depending on their salesperson, be quoted different prices for the same program. A consolidation package enables the buyer to track all quotes and to ensure the same best price each time.

The Internet is fast becoming a viable resource for meeting planners and their vendor partners. Most hotels have Internet sites that allow for fast, searchable database analysis. In fact, with the proliferation of meeting-related sites and E-mail, it is now possible for meeting planners to virtually conduct all their business on the "Net."

Anyone interested in this rapidly changing field would benefit greatly from continually seeking and learning new technological applications. The future of meeting planning is here. It is up to us to seize it.

CHAPTER REVIEW

KEY CONCEPTS

Time management

Networking

Data mining

Sales and catering
  systems

Prime selling time

Prioritizing

Networking

History reports

Lost business reports
  (LBRs)

Customer
  demographics

Market segmentation

Corporate market
  segment

Association market
  segment

Other market segment

REVIEW QUESTIONS

1. Why is time management so important? What might prime selling time be in your area?
2. Define *networking* and its importance to catering sales.
3. Name market subsegments other than those discussed in this chapter.
4. How can technology be applied to other aspects of catering? What are some as yet undeveloped possibilities?

CHAPTER 3

Finance: Managing Pricing and Profit

COST ANALYSIS

As businesses, both hotels and outside caterers want to make profits. A hotel can make money in different ways. Each area in a hotel where a product or service is sold to make money is called a **profit center**. Profit centers in a hotel are typically sleeping rooms, restaurants, function space, and catered food functions. To a lesser extent, other profit centers in a hotel are telephone, minibars, gift shops, garage, and valet. The outside catering operation only makes profit in catering sales. In either catering operation, the real-world constraints of profitability and costs determine if the operation makes money.

Catering cost analysis begins with two important assumptions. First, catering professionals know that most of their menu sales come from items on preprinted banquet menus. For the most part the price of each item is already determined (notable exceptions are the prices of fresh seafood items, which are determined by the current day's market price). Understanding how prices are determined helps all catering professionals price menus for special meals and other circumstances for which preprinted banquet menus do not suffice. Caterers who understand pricing strategy can in the early stages of planning steer clients to items they know better suit the clients' budgetary needs.

The second assumption of catering cost analysis is, no matter how much caterers understand about food cost and pricing theory, they should strive to quote special menu prices to clients only after checking with their kitchens. Kitchens know the many intangibles of pricing that catering personnel may not. In catering, chefs are often constrained in what their catering operations can sell by what is available on the market. Some metropolitan areas can obtain any food items with little notice. By virtue of their locations, smaller, remote, or isolated areas may be unable to obtain certain food items, which makes those items not cost effective. A remote resort in Oklahoma, for example, may be unable to get fresh salmon at a reasonable price. In this situation, the chef and the catering team will only offer clients the menu items that are most available and consistent in Oklahoma. The reality of availability often prohibits **off-menu pricing** as a rule. Off-menu pricing simply is creating then pricing menu items not currently on the preprinted banquet menu.

FOOD COST

Food cost is the cost of a food item relative to its selling price. Food cost is often measured as a percentage. Food cost percentage is the percentage of the profit taken by the actual cost of the food item. To calculate food cost percentage, divide the purchase price of the item by the menu price (Food Cost = Purchase Price/Menu Price).

SAMPLE FOOD COST PERCENTAGES*

Item	Purchase Price (Dollars for Each)	Menu Price (In Dollars)	Food Cost (In Percent)
Steak	5.95	22.00	27.0
Chicken	3.95	17.95	22.0
Caesar Salad	1.99	9.95	20.0

*The prices and costs shown here are strictly for demonstration. They include the total cost (starch, vegetable, and beverage, if applicable).

Catering food and beverage operations are often measured in how well they control food costs relative to profits. High food costs could result when a facility charges too little for its menu items. Very low food costs could mean the outside caterer is overcharging for menu items. Food costs are deemed too low or too high in large part by the management philosophy of the operation and the market in which the operation is competing. Food cost percentages between 30 and 50 percent are common.

If the catering operation's target food cost percentage is known, the caterer can use the food cost percentage equation to determine the price at which a food item should sell. This equation can be worked in different ways to determine specific information. If two of the three figures are known, for example, the third can be calculated. Assume the purchase price of a steak is $4.95 and the target food cost is 30 percent. The resulting equation would look like this:

$$0.30 = \frac{\$4.95}{X} \qquad X = \text{Menu Price}$$

$$X(0.30) = \frac{(\$4.95)X}{X} \qquad \text{Multiply each side by } X.$$

$$X(0.30) = \$4.95 \qquad \text{The } X\text{s cancel out on the right side.}$$

$$\frac{X(0.30)}{0.30} = \frac{\$4.95}{0.30} \qquad \text{Divide each side by 0.30.}$$

$$X = \frac{\$4.95}{0.30} \qquad \text{The (0.30)s cancel out on the left side.}$$

$$X = \$16.50 \qquad \text{Divide 4.95 by 0.30 to calculate the menu price.}$$

BEVERAGE COST

Beverage cost is calculated like food cost. The price of a drink at a reception bar, for example, is determined by the beverage cost target. Dividing the purchase price of a drink by its selling price yields the drink's cost. Traditionally, the beverage cost percentage is lower than the food cost percentage because there is more of an opportunity to make a profit in beverage sales. A beverage cost percentage of 15 to 25 percent is common.

The low beverage cost percentage allows the caterer to discount beverage prices more than food. Again, the caterer should review any pricing decisions with the appropriate department. In certain ongoing beverage promotions, suppliers sell products at less than wholesale to move stock or to establish brand loyalty. Large hotel chains may secure national agreements to use certain beverage suppliers in exchange for significant cost savings. Wine distributors may offer incentives to catering facilities to promote their brands in the facilities' lounges, banquet function spaces, and restaurants. Special beverage requests (such as unique imported wines) should be deferred until it is certain that local distributors can locate the requested items and at defined charges.

LABOR COST

The labor cost component of pricing differs slightly from food or beverage cost. The main difference is the human element. In short, labor cost is the amount of human energy or labor intensity that goes into making a meal or setting a function room. A labor-intensive meal might require hours more preparation or service than would a basic meal. A labor-intensive room set would use more hours in setup and teardown.

Labor cost, like food cost and beverage cost, is measured as a percentage. Each catering operation has targeted labor cost, just as it does a food cost and a beverage cost. At first glance, labor cost may appear to be determined based on wages paid. Like the fixed prices of food and beverages, one might assume that labor is fixed. Labor cost analysis involves many more factors than just wages, however. Because it includes a human element, labor cost can be based on wages, benefits, overtime, sick leave, vacations, **no-shows** (employees who fail to show for scheduled shifts), turnover, salaried management contributions, and level of intensity.

As was mentioned earlier, certain meals can be labor intensive. Such meals require specialized preparation. Those that necessitate several cooks are more labor intensive and thereby drive up the labor cost.

CASE STUDY

Labor Cost Case Study

A catering manager recently attended a small industry function at a competitive facility. Attendees were served a lunch that consisted of a standard chicken entree and a unique potato dish, called mushroom potatoes. These potatoes were cut into small mushroom shapes and served with a mushroom sherry sauce. The catering manager was very impressed with the potatoes and decided to use them for a dinner function he was planning. The dinner was to be served to over 400 people. The catering manager charged the standard banquet menu price and proceeded with his duties as normal.

The catering manager erred when he failed to follow up with the chef about the impact of his special menu request. It turned out that mushroom potatoes require a great deal of preparation. Each mushroom must be hand carved from a potato. The labor intensity of this meal turned out to be much higher than the catering manager had anticipated. Because the chef had to use her entire kitchen staff for more hours than she had planned, her labor cost skyrocketed. This catering manager did not foresee the problem because he saw the potatoes served at a competitive hotel of equal quality. He assumed that his hotel would have no problem with the dish. In reality, the labor intensity of the dish was the same as that for the other hotel, but the other hotel did the potatoes for a small number. In addition, the management of the other hotel wanted to impress the attending hotel employees. Obviously, they succeeded.

The labor cost considerations of events are not limited to meal preparation. The **service level** of an event also can contribute to labor intensity. The service level is the amount of attention catering staff give an event. A standard reception, for example, will have a minimal service level because the hors d'oeuvres are typically served on a self-serve buffet table. If the facility serves those hors d'oeuvres **butler style**, sometimes called **French service** or **white-glove service**, which means each item is served by roaming waiters, the labor cost would rise because additional servers would be needed. Special meal presentations, like flambé desserts or food prepared **tableside**, raise labor costs. (Tableside preparation, which requires an attendant at each dining table to prepare the food, can include food items like Caesar salad or chateaubriand, which is beef tenderloin.) A meal that has several courses or that requires an undue amount of a server's attention can be labor intensive.

This is not to say that caterers must avoid labor-intensive circumstances. On the contrary, special meal presentations can have very positive visual impacts on attendees. For example, a cherry jubilee flambé dessert looks wonderful when prepared by a skilled maitre d'. When an event is going to impact labor cost, the caterer should try to recover that cost by charging the client a service fee. Caterers can also offset labor costs by charging slightly more than listed menu prices.

OUTSIDE VENDORS AND CATERING ACCOUTREMENTS

Crucial to pricing and profit management, the catering staff of any facility and outside operation must realize their abilities as well as their limitations. In some situations, staff cannot realistically accomplish what is asked of them. Any catering operation only has the resources to perform well within a set range of expectations. What would caterers do if their clients asked them to hand-make Christmas tree centerpieces? What if clients requested bluegrass bands to play at their opening reception? Could the catering staff play the instruments?

Question
How many catering people does it take to make a handmade Christmas tree?

Answer
Five. One to call the outside vendor and four to argue about the design.

The preceding anecdote serves as a lighthearted example of what a caterer should do when asked for an unusual item. There are numerous examples of the services and products customers need in catering outside of food and beverage. Any catering operations attempting to become all encompassing and to perform some of those outside tasks would be detracting from their core strengths. When any business entity engages in tasks outside its core strengths, it inevitably incurs the additional costs that often result in higher prices to the clients. In these instances and many more, to avoid unnecessary costs a caterer should look to an **outside vendor** for assistance.

As its name implies, an outside vendor is simply a resource for catering professionals to use when they cannot realistically accomplish a needed task. Outside vendors can include:

- Musicians
- Performers
- Gift basket makers
- Florists
- Disc jockeys

- Decorators
- Props
- Rerental equipment companies
- Pyrotechnic suppliers
- Balloon providers
- Providers of special linens, dishes, silverware, chairs, and so on

All catering professionals, facility and outside alike, should have databases or Rolodexes of reputable outside vendors whom they can contact when in need of the special services and/or products known as **catering accoutrements**. Caterers should remember that outside vendors are direct reflections of their catering operations. Outside vendors who are not professional in appearance or demeanor reflect poorly on the caterers, not the vendors. Caterers can show they appreciate outside vendors who represent them well by rehiring those vendors when need arises.

Whenever possible, caterers should only use outside vendors who have earned preferred status. Such a vendor is a **preferred vendor**. With some catering operations, this status is nonnegotiable. Some clients may want friends to have parts in a function. This may be acceptable in a few cases, but there have been too many instances in which nonqualified individuals have been put in charge of the DJ booth, wedding cake, or other aspect, and disaster resulted. The client who placed these individuals in these roles may have known the individuals' true backgrounds and skill levels. More often than not, however, function attendees assume that these individuals have some connection with the caterer and view the caterer poorly.

When booking a musical act or some other kind of talent (e.g., hypnotist, juggler, comedian), the caterer should be wary of "talent brokers" and agents, because their main purpose is to secure work for their staff (which enhances their commissions), which does not always result in the best fit for the client or the catering operation. Not all talent brokers and agents are disreputable, but it is best to contact other caterers for references.

Once a client has decided to hire an outside vendor for some service, the caterer should try to compensate in some way. After all, a facility will most likely have to expend certain resources (e.g., labor) to accommodate the outside vendor. Before giving a client a quote, which the caterer should always do personally, the caterer should add a small amount to the total. Industry standard is 10 to 20 percent. This policy is justified easily. Most outside vendors expect payment for their services on the day or night of the function. Very few wait until the group pays its total bill, which can take 30 days or more. Caterers in this situation should explain to clients that the catering operation is in the hospitality business, not the banking business, and that they must compensate for financing outside vendors. Many meeting planners understand that they may not always get the cheapest vendors but that they will get the best vendors who will reflect well on both parties.

Caterers should use this pricing surcharge as a benchmark for the cost of performing the required task or service themselves. For example, if a catering kitchen can prepare a fruit-and-cheese basket for less than an outside vendor can (plus the 10 to 20 percent markup), then the caterer should provide the basket. A fruit basket does not engage the kitchen in any activity outside its core strengths, and the client should always be given the most reasonable price for a product or service.

CATERING FORECASTING

Every business operation must manage its pricing structure if it is to maximize its profit. One key to pricing management is knowledge of forthcoming revenue. The ability to predict revenue is called **forecasting**. Forecasting plays a very important role in catering.

Many decisions in a catering operation are based on knowledge of upcoming events. The purchase of food and beverages, staffing, and miscellaneous operational issues are gauged to upcoming event needs. Perhaps the most important factor in forecasting is the determination of incoming revenue. Owners, senior managers, and other catering personnel often are measured by this future revenue stream. The overall health of the operation can be predicted with forecasting.

An accurate catering forecast hinges on two important items:

1. A valid and conservative estimate of potential revenue that is based on each confirmed event
2. A valid and conservative estimate of potential revenue that is based on each unconfirmed event

Estimating revenue from confirmed events is relatively easy, because the clients of confirmed events have already dictated their menus and confirmed their attendance numbers. Multiplying attendance numbers by menu prices yields a fairly good estimate of upcoming revenue. Conservative catering forecasts reduce this estimate slightly to compensate for unknowns (e.g., cancellations, attendance reductions, acts of nature).

Estimating unconfirmed upcoming catering revenue can be more complicated. More often than not, the farther caterers look into the future, the less likely they are to have established many event details. This is especially true in hotels in which turnover has yet to occur. To compensate, the caterer attempting to forecast unconfirmed events should assign and estimate revenue for each event. Because even unconfirmed events must have reasonably accurate attendance numbers for function space to be assigned properly, the forecaster can simply multiply these numbers by average menu prices. For breakfast, lunch, dinner, and so on, caterers should determine conservative averages of what their operations offer for each meal. Caterers can also estimate room rental and other service charges based on average figures. By tallying these figures and then reducing them for the sake of conservatism, caterers can determine valid totals. Caterers should reduce forecast figures for unconfirmed events even more than those for confirmed events, because unconfirmed events have greater uncertainty.

By combining forecasts of confirmed and unconfirmed future events, senior management and other interested parties can judge, with a reasonable amount of certainty, future performance. The results of these forecasts are most often presented chronologically. A 30-, 60-, or 90-day forecast is commonly done monthly. A 6- or 12-month forecast is often done quarterly. These forecasts are then compared with past historical performance over the same period as measures of accuracy performance. Forecasts that are repeatedly too high relative to actual revenue can be revised with even more conservative figures. Even if forecasts are accurate, if they show significant drops in revenue as compared to past performance, corrective action may be taken before it is too late.

CHAPTER REVIEW

KEY CONCEPTS

Profit center	Beverage cost	Outside vendors
Off-menu pricing	No-shows	Catering accoutrements
Food cost	Service level	Forecasting
Labor cost		

REVIEW QUESTIONS

1. Discuss the importance of forecasting to a catering operation.
2. What should a caterer look for in an outside vendor?
3. List some catering accoutrements not listed in this text.
4. Determine the food costs for the following items:

Item	Purchase Price (In Dollars)	Sale Price (In Dollars)
Fresh Salmon	9.00 (per pound)	20.00 (per pound)
Filet Mignon	7.50	17.25
Free Range Chicken	4.00	13.00

5. Why would a catering operation allow different food and beverage costs among menu items? How do consumers affect pricing?

CHAPTER 4

Planning the Event

INTRODUCTION

A hotel with banquet function space or a stand-alone catering facility requires its staff to know the procedures and analyses involved in utilizing space. An outside caterer who operates a meeting or conference for a client must also know these procedures and analyses, which fall under the heading of **event function planning**. Event function planning includes the nonfood- and beverage-related aspects of securing function space. A broad definition of event planning encompasses additional logistical issues. **Event planning logistics** include securing transportation (ground and air), managing programs (organizing attendee invitation responses, scheduling food and beverage), overseeing content (speakers, function agendas, program materials), and organizing activities (spouse programs, off-site locations, recreation). Event logistics fall under the purview of event **planners**.

The space considerations of event function planning are vital for every facility. Securing function space optimally is one portion of the following catering success equation:

$$\text{Optimal Event Planning} + \text{Creative Menu Planning} \times$$
$$\text{Effective Selling} = \text{Maximum Catering Results}$$

For event function planning to be optimal, the potential of the catering facility's function space must be maximized. To maximize function space, one must understand how the space is used.

FUNCTION SPACE CONSIDERATIONS

Stand-alone banquet facilities and hotels with meeting space must make the best use of their function spaces to maximize their catering revenue potentials. Both hotels and banquet facilities rely on their salespeople to reserve meeting space for groups effectively. Ensuring that sufficient revenue is derived from this space helps determine whether function space is maximized. Several factors go into this determination, the most basic of which is the physical setup of the room.

COMMON ROOM SETS

After the hotel or banquet facility decides to pursue a group, the function space in the facility must be secured. (From this point onward, the term **facility** refers to both hotels with function space and stand-alone catering sites unless otherwise noted.) The term **blocking space** describes the act of reserving function space for a group. Blocking function space correctly is critical to the success of the facility as well as the group.

The availability report/display of function space in a facility is vital to the management and maximization of availability. In hotels these displays are often tied into the availability display of sleeping rooms as well. Most facilities have fully computerized their function space management. Some have developed their own computer programs that allow salespeople to view an availability display of any given day and function room. Others use the sales and catering programs currently on the market. The most widely used of these are Delphi and Miracle. Some facilities use the more traditional **function space diary** or slash book, which is simply a large book that displays a facility's complete inventory of function space day by day on each page. The supplier simply turns to the day in question and slashes with a pencil all the space needed for the targeted time frame.

Whatever system a facility has in place, suppliers must have very good understandings of what groups can fit and where those groups fit best. Such an understanding entails an in-depth knowledge of common function room sets and the capacity of different styles of seating. At some point, from sheer repetition, most personnel in charge of function space sales can visualize each function room in various sets. The following sections outline some of the basic and most common room sets used in today's meeting industry and highlight the important facts and figures of each.

Banquet Style or "Rounds." Used primarily for meal functions, banquet style tables, which get their name because they are round, are generally available in three diameters: 60, 66, and 72 inches (see Figure 4–1).

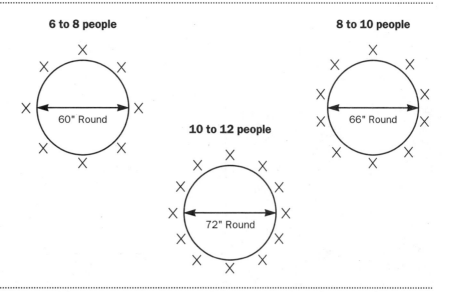

FIGURE 4–1

Banquet rounds

Each successively larger size can accommodate a few more people comfortably. Most facilities use the 72-inch round. Rounds are considered the best set for meal functions. They also work well for brainstorming or team-building sessions.

To maximize space, it is important to be able to calculate the number of rounds needed for a function. For example, a group may wish to book a dinner for 600 people. Does the facility have a large enough room to accommodate those people? Assume that the ballroom is 100 feet × 80 feet and that it is empty (see Figure 4–2).

Given dimensions, the total square footage of the ballroom can be obtained (100 × 80 = 8,000 square feet). Next determine the square feet taken by each round. Assuming the round is 6 feet (72 inches):

$$\frac{(\text{square of the diameter}) \times (\text{pi})}{4}$$

$$\frac{36 \times 3.1428}{4} = 28.28 \text{ square feet per 6-foot table}$$

Ignore the impulse to divide the total available square footage in the ballroom by 28.28, because doing so fails to consider the square footage taken by attendees with chairs, the aisle space between tables, room corners, the space needed from the walls, and the clearances dictated by fire codes. The industry rule of thumb is to multiply the square footage taken by each round table (in this case 28.28) by 4 to account for all the additional square footage needed (28.28 × 4 = 113.12 square feet per table). Now divide the square feet per table by the total available square feet:

$$\frac{8,000}{113.12} = 71 \text{ rounds}$$

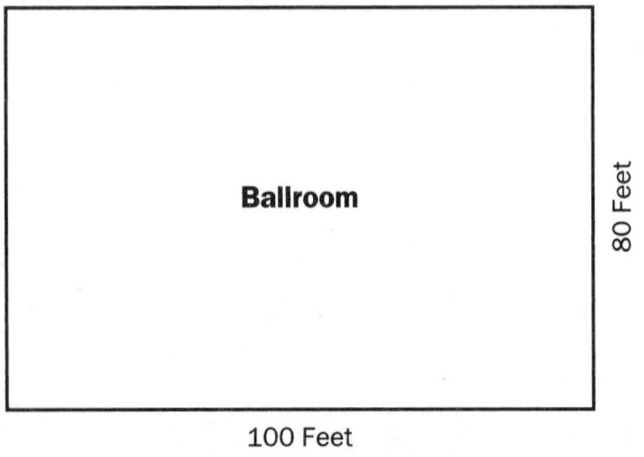

FIGURE 4–2

Ballroom diagram

If one were to sketch the rounds in the ballroom from this example, it would look like Figure 4–3.

From this point, calculate the total potential seating of the ballroom by multiplying the total number of rounds by the desired number of attendees per table.

- Eight people per round would seat 568 people (8 × 71).
- Ten people per round would seat 710 people (10 × 71).
- Twelve people per round would seat 852 people (12 × 71).

Instead of using the preceding method to calculate the number of rounds a room can accommodate, suppliers may use what are called function square footage **benchmarks** to determine how much space they actually need. A benchmark provides a rough idea of the square footage needed for a given function. A simple benchmark multiplies the number of attendees by a per-person square footage allocation. The benchmark for 72-inch rounds is approximately 12 to 13 square feet per person.

If we applied the benchmark calculation to our previous example, we would have the following:

$$600 \text{ people} \times 13 \text{ square feet per person} = 7,800 \text{ square feet}$$

Both methods of calculation yield the same result. We now know that our dinner for 600 will fit comfortably in the ballroom.

Crescent Rounds. A variation on the full round is the crescent round (see Figure 4–4). This setup is used primarily during nonmeal functions so there is a clear line of sight to the presentation source.

Because fewer people are seated at each table in this setup, the benchmark calculation for crescent rounds is double that of full rounds: 26 square feet per person.

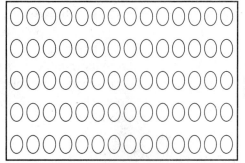

Ballroom

80 Feet

100 Feet

FIGURE 4–3

Ballroom with rounds

Presentation Source

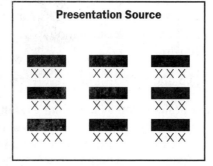

FIGURE 4–4

Crescent rounds

2 to 3 People per 6-Foot Table	or	3 to 4 People per 8-Foot Table
(2 People per 6-Foot Table Is Least Restrictive)		(3 People per 8-Foot Table Is Least Restrictive)

Presentation Source

X X X   X X X   X X X

X X X   X X X   X X X

X X X   X X X   X X X

× = Chair

Presentation Source

X X X X   X X X X   X X X X

X X X X   X X X X   X X X X

X X X X   X X X X   X X X X

× = Chair

FIGURE 4–5

Schoolroom seating

Schoolroom or "Classroom" Style. The schoolroom or "classroom" style of seating uses 6- or 8-foot-long tables (see Figure 4–5). Classroom tables are generally 18 or 30 inches wide. Classroom seating works well for presentations in which participants must work with the information they are presented because it provides a convenient surface for note taking and/or studying handouts.

The size of classroom tables is determined by one or more of the following: facility inventory, required attendee work space area, and attendee comfort level.

As was previously stated, there are certain factors that may dictate which size of tables to use. A facility's inventory may be limited to one size or the other. If attendees of the function require space to spread their materials, or if they simply feel more comfortable with more space between attendees, they may ask for less restrictive classroom seating.

The benchmark calculation for classroom seating is 14 to 16 square feet per person for setups using 18-inch schoolroom tables and 16 to 18 square feet per person for 30-inch tables.

Conference or "Boardroom" Style. In conference or "boardroom" style seating, people sit around a solid, rectangular table (see Figure 4–6). This style is very flexible because it is often set up with schoolroom-style 6- or 8-foot tables to accommodate any size group, but it tends to work better for small groups. Many facilities now incorporate one or more specialized function rooms in the conference-style arrangement.

One drawback of this seating style is that large conference-style tables can keep attendees too far apart for effective interaction. Another drawback to this seating style is that **front of room** is not clearly defined. The front of a room is the location of a speaker or another presentation source. With conference-style seating, attendees at one of the two ends would have to turn their chairs to easily see a screen or watch a speaker.

The benchmark for conference-style seating is 21 to 23 square feet per person.

Theater or "Auditorium" Style. Theater or "auditorium" seating style gets its name from its resemblance to the seating in a movie theater or lecture hall (see Figure 4–7). This is the easiest setup for most facilities, and it is the best use of space in that the most people can be seated in the

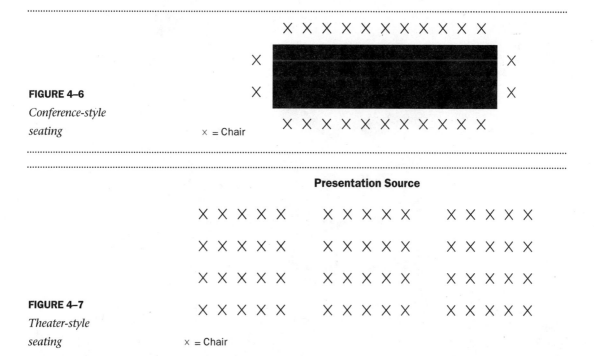

FIGURE 4–6
Conference-style seating

× = Chair

Presentation Source

FIGURE 4–7
Theater-style seating

× = Chair

least space. This seating style works best for attendees who must only listen to the presentation, because there is no work area.

The benchmark for theater style seating is 8 to 9 square feet per person.

U-Shape or "Opened End." Good for intimate or intense meetings that require interaction, the natural location of the presentation source at the front of the U-shape or "opened end" seating style (see Figure 4–8) makes it popular among meeting planners. Large U-shaped setups have the same drawback of large conference style sets: Attendees can be spread too far apart for effective interaction.

The benchmark for U-shape seating is 30 to 32 square feet per person.

Herringbone or "Chevron." A variation on schoolroom and theater style, herringbone seating (see Figure 4–9) can be helpful in making better

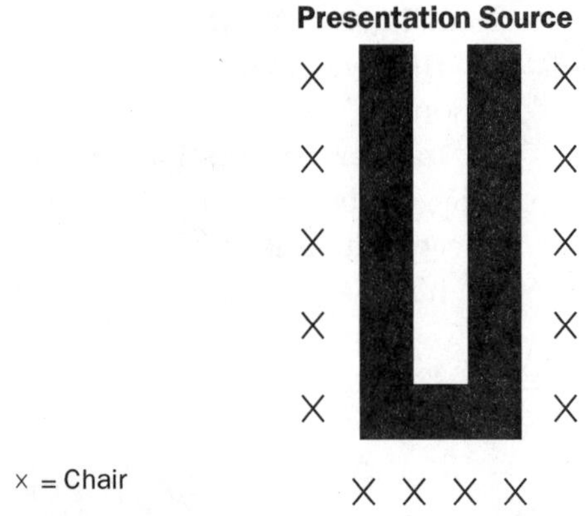

Presentation Source

FIGURE 4–8

U-shape seating

× = Chair

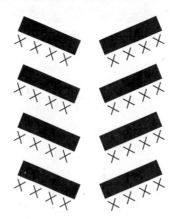

FIGURE 4–9

Herringbone seating

Herringbone Schoolroom

Herringbone Theater

× = Chair

use of space in small rooms. Odd-shaped rooms that lack straight walls may be best served with this setup.

The benchmarks for herringbone schoolroom and theater-style seating are difficult to ascertain because the angles of the setups vary. One could assume, however, that the benchmark for each is a few square feet per person less than its straight setup counterparts.

Hollow Square or "Open Conference." Not well suited for presentations but used often for board meetings, the benefits and drawbacks of hollow square or "open conference" seating (see Figure 4–10) are similar to those of conference-style seating. The space used for hollow square is no more than that for the conference-style setup. The interior is hollow, but the outside tables are of the same size and dimension as those used for equivalent conference sets. Hence, the benchmark for hollow square seating is the same as that for conference-style seating: 21 to 23 square feet per person.

Star or "Starfish." Star or "starfish" seating (see Figure 4–11) is good for diplomatic or sensitive discussions in which no one should be sitting at the "head" of any table. For this seating style, there is assumed to be no presentation source. Often, those seated at the start serve as focal points for others in the room. This is often the case for union or other types of negotiations in which those not directly involved in the meeting have vested interests in the discussion. Because this setup is shaped oddly, no benchmark for it exists.

Less Frequently Used Styles. Seating styles come in many forms and variations. Common setups can combine to create entirely new sets (see Figure 4–12). These less popular, but still used, setups have nearly infinite variety.

FIGURE 4–10

Hollow square seating

× = Chair

Presentation Source

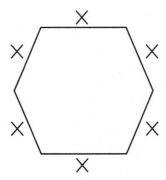

FIGURE 4–11

Star seating

As the preceding benchmarks have shown, a 40-person meeting in theater style requires a smaller room than does a 40-person meeting in schoolroom seating. Unique seating styles, and those without benchmarks, can be more difficult to determine. In some cases, facilities may have to "trial run" seating style requests to see if a function room can actually accommodate those requests. All facilities will, as part of their printed marketing collateral, have printed **room capacity charts** that outline each function room and its capacity in the most common seating configurations. Many large function rooms at a facility can be split into two or more sections. An **airwall** is a flexible partition that divides a function room. Airwalls enable facilities to allocate only as much square footage per event as is required.

When evaluating what function space to allocate to a group, the caterer should remember the extra items that will occupy usable square footage. A function room capacity chart outlines the number of people a room can accommodate with nothing else included. The hospitality industry uses the term "maxed out" to describe function room capacity in a seating style with nothing else in the room. In reality, most functions incorporate other items in the room that prohibit them from using the "maxed out" figure on its own. How does a facility account for these "other" items in a room, and what exactly are they?

In hospitality, the term **space eater** is used to describe these other items. A space eater is any item outside the primary seating style that is required in a function room. In effect, such items "eat" the available square footage. Most events require one or more space eaters to achieve their objectives. Meetings, for example, often incorporate audiovisual (AV) aids in presentations. Food functions may use AV equipment and/or additional tables, chairs, and props to achieve their objectives. It is important for suppliers to first identify space eaters, then to understand their impact on available function space.

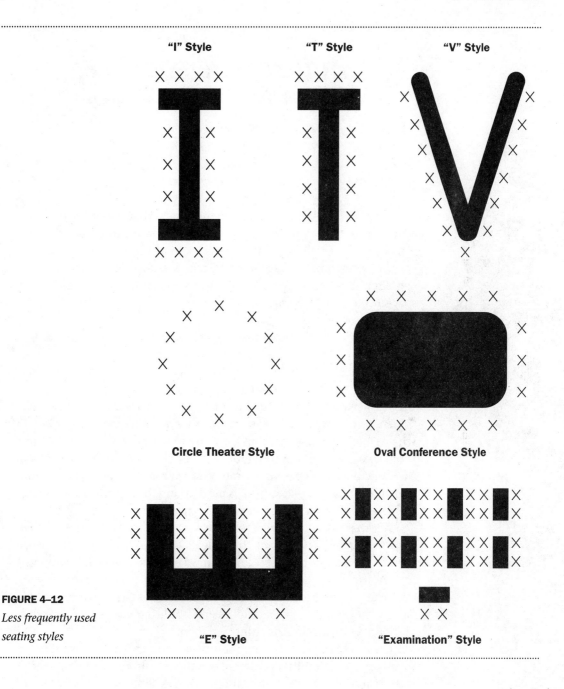

FIGURE 4–12
Less frequently used seating styles

The following sections highlight some of the most common space eaters in food or event functions: AV equipment and function equipment.

Industry Perspective
"Creative Usage of Function Space"

Penny Woodruff
Meeting Planner
Jamie Doyle
Director of Sales

Meeting facilities and hotels are unique in that they have only one opportunity to maximize revenue. Meeting space and function rooms not sold on a given day can never be sold again. From a facility perspective, maximizing space so that every possible dollar is made is crucial. From a planner's perspective, securing a venue that meets every space need exactly is rare. In some instances, creativity is needed to meet both objectives.

If traditional function space is at a premium, one might look at nontraditional options. Nontraditional function space can include outdoor courtyards, garden grounds, pool areas, lobby/foyer areas, sections of a restaurant, and even tented parking lots. If both the facility and the planner are flexible, an urgent space need can almost always be met.

Function space can be used in other ways to make the most of what is available. A group that is willing to "meet and eat" in the same room uses one function room for two purposes. A buffet meal is best in these circumstances, because it can be rolled into the meeting with minimal disruption. If a plated meal is needed, and the meeting room is large enough, a few round tables may be placed at the back of the room.

Another option for meal functions is a box lunch or dinner, which allows attendees to pick up their meals and eat wherever they wish. Groups who do not wish to supply meals for attendees but who want to give attendees meal options outside the facility restaurant may ask the facility to set up a cash food sales station near their meeting rooms. Sandwiches, boxed meals, and snacks could be offered to attendees without setting up another function room.

Creativity in meeting-room setups can go a long way toward maximizing space. Combination sets, like half-schoolroom and half-theater style, seat more people than schoolroom style alone. Rounds instead of schoolroom tables seat more people per square foot and still provide writing surfaces for attendees. Using airwalls in a ballroom to split a general session into breakouts is a good way to accomplish two goals.

Sleeping rooms can also be used as breakout rooms. Entire floors of sleeping rooms can be used in lieu of an exhibit hall, with each sleeping room housing one exhibitor. Parking garages and rooftops have served as makeshift exhibit spaces in emergencies.

A facility that cannot fully accommodate a planner's needs should not be averse to teaming with other facilities. A neighboring hotel with space available on a needed day will likely be happy to maximize its space to generate more revenue.

Overall, being creative to meet customers' needs shows that a facility has customers' best interests in mind. Going above and beyond for customers creates loyalty.

AUDIOVISUAL EQUIPMENT

The impact of technology can be felt in the hospitality industry in many ways. Technology in hospitality most commonly takes the form of **audiovisual (AV)** equipment, which is the equipment, tools, and materials used in presentations to engage the senses of hearing and sight. Because AV technology continues to advance, it is vital for caterers to understand its uses and its impact.

When blocking function space, suppliers should remember that many types of AV equipment take some of the usable square footage in a function room. Therefore, it is important that the caterer details a group's AV needs during booking. Some AV setups are so extensive that they require entire rooms.

Caterers must understand basic AV terminology. The following list includes the terms needed for a minimum level of familiarity. Suppliers must know these terms to have intelligent AV conversations with their clients and facility staff.

Amplifier—Used with some type of **audio source**, the **amplifier** enhances or, more often, intensifies sound before presentation.
Audio Monitor—The **audio monitor** is useful in any setup with a live music source. It is usually a small speaker in a stand-alone configuration.
Mixer—The **mixer** serves as a "listening ear," monitoring how sounds are heard throughout the audio system.
Audio Source—An **audio source** is any device that creates a sound to be fed into an audio presentation system. Audio sources can be presenters, speakers, live bands, and so on.

Boom Microphone—A **boom microphone** is attached to some type of extension. It is used to capture the **audio source** from a distance.

Cable—*Cable* is a generic term that covers all types of connecting cables used in most AV equipment. Sometimes called coaxial or "coax" cables, cables come in various lengths and gauges to perform various tasks.

Cart—Sometimes called an AV cart, the **cart** is used to transport AV devices such as a(n) **monitor**, **slide projector**, or **overhead projector**.

Dimmer Switch—A **dimmer switch** is a light control device that is often mounted on function room walls to control the intensity of **house lights**. Dimmer switches can be connected to remote switches to allow light control from the podium or a location away from the function room wall, or they can be stand-alone controls for portable lights.

Dissolve—When two or more projection units of any kind are faded in and out together to create a seamless presentation, they are said to **dissolve**.

Dubbing—**Dubbing** is the process by which recorded audio is transferred from one recording to another.

Equalizer—An **equalizer** is an audio device that is often used with an amplifier and/or a **public address (PA) system** to adjust bass, treble, and midrange frequencies. It can be used when the audio source is lacking sound quality or the acoustics of a room are less than ideal.

Feedback—**Feedback**, a high-pitched squeak or squeal, results when audio from the speaker system recirculates through a microphone.

Flipchart—A **flipchart** is a large pad of paper mounted on a tripod or another type of easel that is used to illustrate discussion points. The flipchart is useful in team building, brainstorming, and other types of meetings.

Freeze-frame—A **freeze-frame** is one frame of a video or motion picture that is stopped for display.

Front Projection—**Front projection** is light projection that uses a standard front reflective screen of any size. The light source (often a **projector** of some kind) must come from the front only.

Hot—The term **hot** describes a cable that is carrying a live feed or some AV device that is on or in use.

House Lights—**House lights** are the permanent lighting system of a function room.

House Sound—**House sound** is the permanent audio system in a function room.

Lavaliere Microphone—A **Lavaliere microphone** is a small microphone that can be attached to a speaker to allow free hand movement. It can be wireless or corded.

Liquid Crystal Display (LCD) Computer Panel—A **liquid crystal display (LCD) computer panel** is a unique computer monitor that allows light to pass through it. It is used with an overhead to display its screen contents to a large audience.

Computer Projector—Similar to the LCD computer panel, the **computer projector** uses its own light source (similar to a **video projector**) to project a computer's image onto a screen. There is no need for an overhead.

Level—**Level** is the measure of volume or intensity.

Mixer—A **mixer** is an audio device that combines multiple audio sources. It is often used to create a seamless recording level. A mixer must be used whenever sound is amplified or multiple microphones are used.

Monitor—**Monitor** is a common term for a television monitor. The monitor is used most often as a video playback viewer, but it can be used in many ways. It comes in sizes of common televisions. The term *monitor* is sometimes used as jargon for an audio monitor.

Multimedia—**Multimedia** is using two or more AV devices in a presentation. The term is most often used to describe high-end programs.

Overhead Projector—An **overhead projector** is a device by which light is sent through a directional lens and displayed in a forward direction. The overhead most often uses transparencies or LCD computer monitors as its presentation sources.

PA System—A **PA system**, a portable audio speaker setup that is generally used in large areas or auditoriums, is useful when the house sound does not suffice.

Pan—**Pan** is the rotation of a camera around the viewing area. The goal of panning is often to obtain a panoramic feel.

Pipe and Drape—**Pipe and drape** is the common term for portable dark draping that can be set up as a divider (useful in exhibits) or as a barrier (**rear screen**).

Podium Microphone—The **podium microphone** is attached to a podium or lectern.

Rear Screen—**Rear screen** light projection uses a rear-generated light source. The nonreflective screen then can be viewed from the front of the room. This style of light projection is useful in that no AV device can be viewed from the audience, but it tends to take a great deal of function space. Often, pipe and drape are used to hide everything behind the rear screen.

Remote—A **remote** is a device that activates an AV device from some distance. A remote can be wired, or wireless. It is often used in slide projector and video presentations.

Satellite Downlink—A **satellite downlink** is the connection made to an orbiting communication satellite to link audio and video information from other locations. Such a link is used in **video conferencing**.

Skirting—**Skirting** is using fabric or linen to wrap an AV cart or a table to make the cart or table look more polished.

Slide Projector—A **slide projector** is a video device that projects one slide at a time. Such projectors are sometimes called carousel projectors because most use carousel trays to hold and advance the slides.

Speaker Phone—A **speaker phone** is a "hands-free" phone that allows more than one person to communicate at once. It is used in **teleconferencing**.

Spotlight—A **spotlight** can be part of the house lights in a function room or it can be portable. It targets light on one person or object. It is useful in stage work.

Standing Microphone—A **standing microphone** is attached to a free-standing device that can be adjusted for height and angle.

Strobe—A **strobe** is a rapidly blinking, high-intensity light that is often used in multimedia presentations to add visual impact.

Surge Protector—A **surge protector** is an electrical device that acts as a buffer between sensitive equipment and electrical outlets. It can absorb voltage surges before equipment is damaged.

Table Microphone—A **table microphone** is attached to a small, flexible stand that is mounted on a tabletop for those who are seated. It is used in panel discussions.

Teleconferencing—**Teleconferencing** is bringing more than one remote location together via telephone. It is useful when at least one participant cannot attend. Speaker phones are widely used in this forum.

Throw—**Throw** is the measure of projection distance.

Videocassette Recorder (VCR)—A **videocassette recorder (VCR)** is used to record and play back video.

VHS—Standard VCR format. The VHS system uses ½ inch wide videotape.

Video Conference—Like the teleconference, the video conference incorporates audio and visual links to remote locations. The AV connection may require a satellite downlink.

Video Projection—**Video projection** is the display device used to project any VCR playback onto a screen. It is often used when a standard monitor is too small to be seen by all attendees.

Zoom—**Zoom** is the act of magnifying a subject over distance without moving or changing the camera or video source location.

Each of the preceding AV items can impact the usable square footage of a function room. The most widely accepted benchmark for determining the square footage needed for effective AV work is 10 square feet per person for theater-style seating and 16 square feet per person for school-room-style seating.

Benchmarks also exist for determining the distance at which attendees should sit from a screen. Audience members should sit no closer than twice a screen's height and no farther away than eight times its height. Consider Figure 4–13. In this example, a ballroom is 80 feet × 100 feet. Assume you are planning an AV presentation for 500 people in theater-style seating.

The first step is to verify that the ballroom can accommodate the function. To determine if the ballroom can accommodate the group (without miscellaneous function space items), multiply the expected attendance figure (500) by the theater-style seating benchmark of 8 square feet per person:

$$500 \times 8 = 4{,}000 \text{ square feet needed}$$

The ballroom has **8,000** square feet available (80 × 1,000). The ballroom can accommodate 500 people with nothing else in it. The next step is to apply the AV benchmark. To determine the minimum square footage required with AV for theater-style seating, multiply the number of attendees (500) by 10:

$$500 \times 10 = 5{,}000 \text{ square feet needed}$$

Because it now appears that the ballroom can accommodate the group, next determine the range at which attendees must sit to best view the screen (assume the screen size is 8 feet × 8 feet). To determine the closest distance at which attendees can sit, multiply the screen height by 2:

$$2 \times 8 = 16 \text{ feet minimum distance between the first row of attendees and the screen}$$

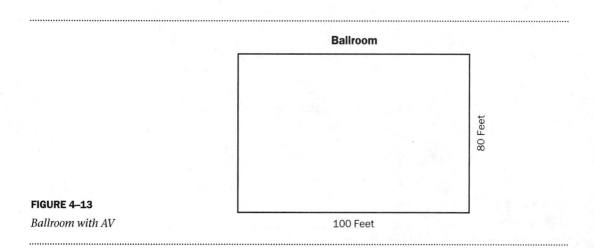

Ballroom

80 Feet

100 Feet

FIGURE 4–13

Ballroom with AV

To determine the farthest distance at which attendees should sit, multiply the screen height by 8:

$$8 \times 8 = 64 \text{ feet}$$

Figure 4–14 shows the proposed seating (not to scale).

The ballroom appeared to accommodate the 500-person group with AV. However, if 16 feet were removed from the front of the ballroom and 36 feet $(100 - 64)$ were removed from the back, the usable room length would be only 48 feet $(100 - 52)$. The new square footage figure becomes 3,840 square feet (48×80). Given that the group needs at least 5,000 square feet, how can the ballroom accommodate it?

The ballroom's dimensions change from 100×80 to 48×80 when the 8 foot $\times$ 8 foot screen is included. Screen size is the variable that must change to employ all benchmarks accurately. If the screen size were changed from 8×8 to 12×12 the diagram would look like Figure 4–15.

The new usable dimensions of the ballroom become 72 feet $(100 - 24$ in front and 4 in back) $\times$ 80 feet, which equals 5,760 square feet. That figure

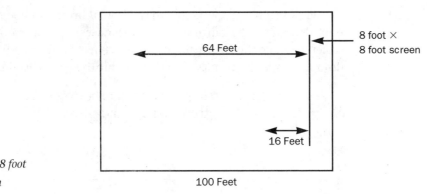

FIGURE 4–14

Ballroom with 8 foot × 8 foot screen

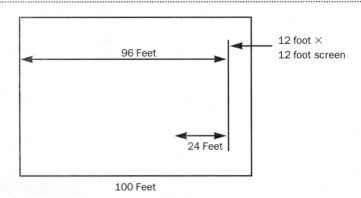

FIGURE 4–15

Ballroom with 12 foot × 12 foot screen

AUDIOVISUAL BENCHMARKS

- To ensure a clear line of sight for all seated attendees, place all screens at least 4 feet from the floor. For large groups, ceiling height may limit overall screen size. A ceiling height of 12 feet allows a screen no larger than 8 feet high. Low ceilings, therefore, may not allow for large AV presentations.
- Rear-screen video and slide projection reduce by up to one-third the available square footage for seating.
- Standard overhead projectors' maximum screen size is 10 feet × 10 feet. Larger screens tend to distort projected images. A high-intensity bulb is needed when using an LCD panel with an overhead to ensure that the computer displays clearly on the screen.
- When using video monitors in presentations, suppliers should calculate the number of attendees per monitor based on screen size. For optimal viewing, suppliers should allocate no more than 22 people per 20-inch monitor and 45 people per 27-inch monitor. When ceiling height prohibits adequate screen size for large groups, video monitors can be used toward the back of the room to supplement the front screen's reach.
- Never place attendees closer than 4 feet from the back of a slide projector, because the noise from the fan can be disturbing. In many instances, a long-throw lens can be employed. Such a lens enables the projector to be placed at the rear of a room, away from attendees. A long-throw lens cannot be focused adequately at close range (20 feet or fewer), so it is imperative that the appropriate lens be available for all uses.

surpasses the previous minimum square footage calculation of 5,000, which means the ballroom can accommodate the group. To ensure the best viewing experience for all attendees, accurately apply all benchmarks.

FUNCTION EQUIPMENT

Many items other than AV equipment can serve as space eaters when determining usable square footage. Facilities often have a number of differently sized and shaped tables to serve many roles. Most facilities have standard chairs that they use for all functions, while other facilities have chairs of different sizes for different uses. Tables and chairs, along with other items, are defined broadly as **function equipment** because they play parts in the physical makeup of the function.

BANQUET CHAIRS

Perhaps no item related to meetings and events is as important as the banquet chair. Most facilities use this chair for all seating styles. Often overlooked as a minor detail, the banquet chair may serve as an attendee's seat for 8 hours or more. It plays a major role in attendees' attention span and comfort level.

The standard banquet chair has a comfortable seat and back support. Some models have arm support, but most do not. While more comfortable, banquet chairs with arms take more square footage of function space than those that do not. Made of lightweight aluminum with rounded edges, banquet chairs are moved easily for efficient room setup. They are designed for stacking, which means they take minimal storage space.

LONG-DURATION CHAIRS

Because the standard banquet chair can be uncomfortable for long durations, some facilities provide "upgraded" models. Long-duration chairs resemble the executive desk chairs seen in many offices. Often, these chairs are leather covered. With high backs, extra-cushioned seats, and padded arm support, these chairs make attendees less conscious of their seats, and allow them to concentrate on the event.

Long-duration chairs, sometimes called "8-hour chairs," are often installed permanently in specialized function space. Rooms set in permanent conference style use long-duration chairs to invoke an "executive boardroom" feeling.

FUNCTION TABLES

Hotels and stand-alone facilities generally use various function table sizes for various events. Commonly called schoolroom tables or "schoolies," function tables are generally 30 feet high and 18 or 30 feet wide. They are usually 6 feet long, although some are 8 feet long (used 3 per 8-foot schoolroom-style seating).

Many of the seating styles reviewed earlier are "built" for each event using function tables. Figure 4–16 shows how schoolroom tables can be combined. Conference style, schoolroom style, U-shape, hollow square, and herringbone are some of the seating styles that are "built to suit" using schoolroom tables. The 18-inch schoolies are commonly used for this purpose. The 18-inch schoolie builds seating styles, while the 30-inch schoolie serves a different role. The most prominent use of function tables is in food and beverage functions, namely buffets. Buffet tables, coffee breaks, display tables, head tables, and registration tables use 6 feet × 30 inch schoolroom tables.

Buffet Tables. When blocking space for a buffet, suppliers should consider the sizes of their groups and any requisite buffet tables. The buffet table takes usable square footage that cannot be used for seating. Menu selection plays a part in the size of the buffet; extensive menus require more space, but menus may not be known when the supplier is blocking space.

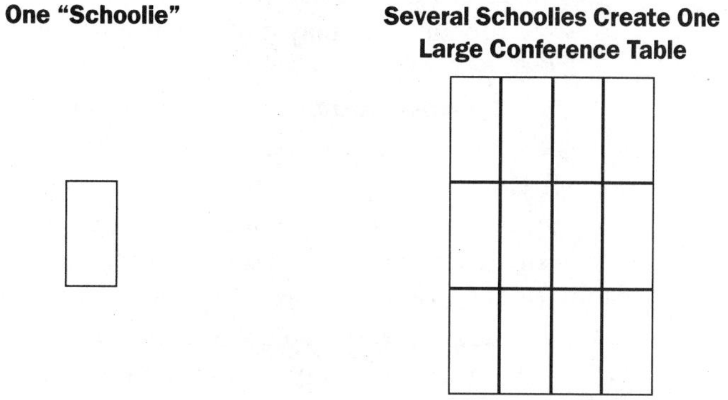

One "Schoolie"

Several Schoolies Create One Large Conference Table

FIGURE 4–16

Combined schoolroom tables

Buffet tables can be single sided or double sided, which means attendees can get their food from one or both sides of the buffet respectively. The same food items are placed side by side so that each side of the table has the same salad, entree, and so on. The benchmark that applies here is to plan for one double-sided or two single-sided buffet tables for every 100 attendees. Buffet tables can be set up inside or outside the function room depending on the space available. Setting up the buffet table outside the room gives more seating space inside, but the supplier must be cognizant of attendees' ability to access the room easily without "bottle-necking" at the entrance or interfering with other activity outside the meeting space.

Coffee Breaks. The coffee break is a food function type. It serves the role of refresher for meeting attendees. Coffee, sodas, mineral waters, and light snacks of all kinds are served at a coffee break. The 30-inch school-room table is ideal for carrying these items. Whether set up inside or outside the function room, coffee break tables can be placed out of the way of attendees. Large coffee breaks, which use several 6-foot tables, may need to be factored into usable square footage, depending on the function room.

Head Tables. A head table can be incorporated into any seating style. The head table serves as a presenter's table of location, which means the occupants of the head table play different roles in the function than do the participants seated in the general seating style. Generally in the front of a room (see Figure 4–17), the head table can seat one or more speakers, monitors, or instructors. The term *head table* derives from the term *head-master's table,* which was the table at which a teacher sat in front of his or her students.

One derivation of the head table is the **observer's table**, which is nothing more than a head table placed in the rear of the room. The observer's table is used by attendees who are not actively participating in the function but may have interest in observing the discussion or presentation.

Display Tables. Tables used in a function room to display materials and other items are called display tables (see Figure 4–18). Display tables are useful in showcasing items the presenter wants to highlight but not necessarily hold. Like other tables, display tables can impact the usable square footage. Several display tables drastically reduce the seating capacity. Six-foot schoolroom tables are most commonly used for displays.

Registration Tables. Registration tables are placed just in front or just inside the entrance to a function room (see Figure 4–19). These 6-foot

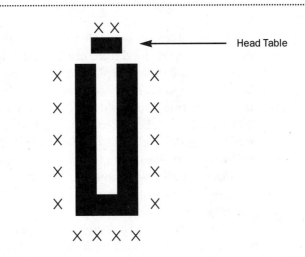

FIGURE 4–17

Head table

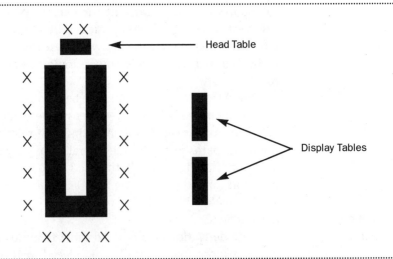

FIGURE 4–18

Display tables

tables serve as means for registering participants or distributing handouts, credentials, and other program materials.

OTHER TYPES OF FUNCTION EQUIPMENT AND THEIR USES

Cocktail Rounds. A cocktail round is a small, round table that is used most often during receptions. Unlike larger banquet rounds, cocktail rounds are generally no more than 30 inches in diameter. Sometimes called lounge-style seating, cocktail tables are intended to provide areas for mingling, networking, and eating.

When calculating the usable square footage these round tables occupy, suppliers should not attempt to place attendees at every table. Because receptions are social events, attendees tend to move around the function room. Unlike dinners and other meal functions, at which attendees must sit and be served or serve themselves and sit to eat, receptions are designed to be mobile. Reception food includes small, finger-sized food items, called **hors d'oeuvres**. Attendees can fill small plates and carry them with one hand while carrying a drink in the other. Some attendees may wish to sit and eat, while others may wish to mingle. Therefore, it is not necessary for suppliers to plan for every attendee to be seated at once, in lounge style. Most cocktail rounds accommodate up to four people comfortably. The benchmark for lounge style is, depending

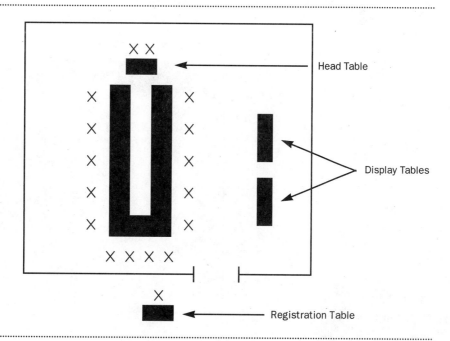

FIGURE 4–19

Registration table

on the amount of food being served, to plan on available seating for one-third to one-half the attendees at a given time. Because cocktail rounds must be spread throughout the area near the food and the bar, it is sometimes called "scattered" lounge-style seating (see Figure 4–20).

Attendees who wish to sit can do so near the food and drinks, while those who wish to mingle may stand elsewhere. The lounge tables can be standard height for seated attendees or elevated for standing attendees. American receptions tend to use seated cocktail rounds, while European receptions prefer the elevated rounds.

The ongoing discussions of seating styles and standing areas have not addressed the needs of attendees with disabilities. The Americans with Disabilities Act (ADA) mandates that public areas and facilities hosting public events ensure that the disabled have the same access as the able bodied. When planning events and calculating space usage, therefore, suppliers must be cognizant of wheelchair access. Other considerations for the disabled include sign language interpreters for the deaf, Braille program materials, access for seeing eye dogs in function rooms, and ramp access to elevated head tables, to name a few.

Serpentine Tables. Creative suppliers determined long ago that working with the straight edges of standard function tables limited layout design. The serpentine table, or "serp" as it is often called, is a curved table (see Figure 4–21). Laid end to end, the serp creates a snakelike look. Incorporating the serp with straight buffet tables creates softer lines and a unique look (see Figure 4–22).

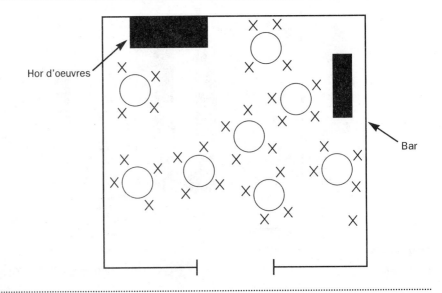

FIGURE 4–20

Lounge-style seating

FIGURE 4–21

Serpentine tables

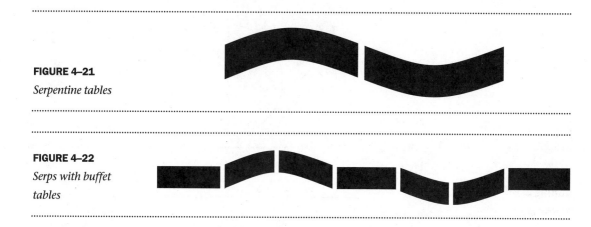

FIGURE 4–22

Serps with buffet tables

Half-Moon Rounds. The half-moon round is literally half a round table (see Figure 4–23). Half-moon rounds can be as large as the 72-inch full round or as small as the 30-inch cocktail. Not to be confused with crescent round seating, which uses full-size round tables with seating around half the table, half-moon rounds cannot seat any more than one side.

Half-moons serve two primary purposes:

1. They fit snugly against flat walls, where their fully round counter- parts would not.
2. They can be incorporated into buffet lines to reduce the harsh straight lines of standard buffet tables.

Half-moons are perfectly suited as end sections of a buffet. Specifi- cally, they work well with double-sided buffets. The double-sided buffet must have the same food items on each side to ensure that attendees on either side can access the same options. The rounded ends of a half-moon round allow double-sided buffets to share first and/or last items between sides. Most often, the first buffet item is a salad and the last is a dessert (see Figure 4–24).

Risers. Functions that require elevated elements (e.g., head tables, AV equipment) may incorporate a **riser** into the setup. A riser, also called a platform or a stage, raises function equipment to a desired height. Large functions may require risers to ensure that all attendees have clear lines of sight to the head table or a screen. Performances and other theatrical pre- sentations are commonly placed on risers.

Risers are similar to the schoolies reviewed earlier in that they are built to suit each function. Each riser section is fit with other sections to form the needed size (see Figure 4–25).

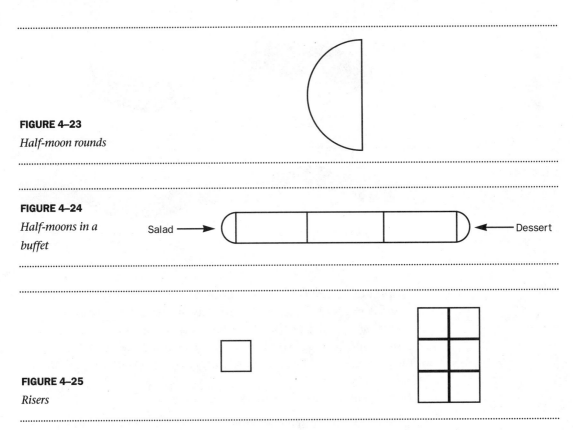

FIGURE 4–23

Half-moon rounds

FIGURE 4–24

Half-moons in a buffet

Salad →   ← Dessert

FIGURE 4–25

Risers

Individual riser sections are commonly 4 feet × 8 feet. These sections range from 6 to 32 inches high. Each riser should be built with sufficient surface areas that extend beyond the tables and chairs placed on them. The benchmark for head tables placed on risers is to ensure at least 4 feet of surface area is available behind the chairs. Participant safety must always be a primary concern of suppliers.

One derivation of the standard riser is the **tiered stage**. The tiered stage incorporates two or more stacked risers. These stages are used when individual sections are too low or when suppliers want to create a "layered" look (see Figure 4–26).

Elevated stages may require portable stairs to provide walk-up access for all attendees. Tiered stages create their own stairs. A ramp may be required if the disabled will participate.

Dance Floors. Not all functions and events are centered around meeting or eating. Social events (e.g., wedding receptions, bar mitzvah celebrations, formal balls, and parties of all kinds) are convened to have fun. A popular component of social events is dancing. Because the standard floor

Elevated for Height **Tiered for Effect**

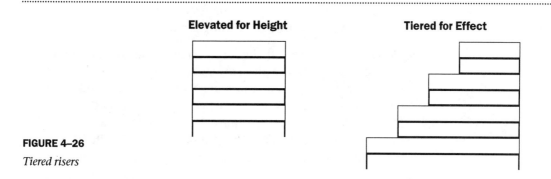

FIGURE 4–26

Tiered risers

covering in virtually all function rooms is carpeting, the supplier must plan to incorporate a **dance floor** with the other function elements.

The dance floor is yet another "built to suit" function item. Generally, dance floors come in 3 feet × 3 feet segments that are made of treated wood or wood-imitation plastic and are rimmed with reinforced steel, interlocking clamps. Each segment must fit securely next to the others to ensure attendee safety. Dance floor segments on the outside edges of the dance floor should be beveled on the sides not interlocking with other segments.

Determining the appropriate size of a dance floor is crucial to determining usable square footage. A dance floor that is too large limits available seating, while a dance floor that is too small may become too crowded. Suppliers should realize that, like lounge-style seating, dance floors need not accommodate all attendees at once. Instead, suppliers should estimate a **percentage of participation** in dancing. Each percentage has a corresponding square feet per person requirement. The benchmarks that apply here are as follows:

Estimated Participation Percentage	Required Dance Floor in Square Feet
40	2
50	3
60	4

To estimate the amount of usable square footage taken by the dance floor, the planner must first estimate the participation percentage, then multiply the corresponding square footage requirement by the total number of attendees. For example, an event of 400 people with an estimated participation percentage of 60 percent would require 1,600 square feet of dance floor (4 × 400).

It is slightly difficult to determine exact participation percentages, because the intangible factors come into play, namely the group's:

- Mood or preferences. If the group prefers dancing to a more laidback atmosphere, dance participation may increase.
- Familiarity with the music or performer. A popular band or DJ playing a string of hits may have better participation than performers playing unknown songs. The age of the participants, while not necessarily affecting the desire or ability to dance, may impact participants' familiarity with the music.

Exhibits. Functions that incorporate **exhibits** do so because they wish to display for sale or demonstration items that are in competition. **Trade shows/expositions** are functions that are centered around vendors who wish to display services and/or products for targeted markets. The exhibit is the perfect vehicle for such a display.

Exhibits come in two main forms: the **tabletop exhibit** and the **exhibit booth**. The tabletop exhibit is the simpler of the two in terms of setup and materials. A 6-foot table is used to hold items. The exhibit booth, in contrast, can be much more extensive. Not limited to 6 feet in size, the exhibit booth often incorporates a base section and a backdrop.

In many trade shows, the desire to capture the attention of the attendee has cultivated fierce competition. In these instances, the designs and layouts of booths have become extensive. Many organizations have incorporated multimedia elements of sound and light to increase the impacts of their booths. Interactive booths that encourage attendees to participate in some type of activity can increase the booths' traffic.

The square footage required by trade shows can be high, depending on the number of participants. Large expositions take place in convention centers, which can be 1 million square feet or larger. With fewer participants, or limited function space, suppliers may have fewer options. Trade shows can be parts of other functions, like sales meetings. If a trade show is occurring with another event, it might be well suited to a facility's **prefunction area**. A prefunction area is the space outside a function room (see Figure 4–27).

Suppliers must be willing to continually educate themselves on the changes in function equipment and AV. For suppliers to be effective, they must be able to answer any question or address any need. Hotels and stand-alone meeting facilities continually upgrade their services and equipment to better serve their customers. In terms of functions, those customers are the suppliers. If planners are to best use their resources, they must be one step ahead of their attendees and their facilities.

Function Rooms

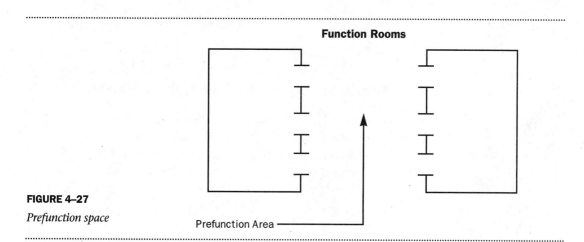

FIGURE 4–27

Prefunction space

Prefunction Area

Industry Perspective
"The Greening of the Meeting Industry"

*Kelly McNeely, Graduate nondegree Indiana
University-Purdue University, Indianapolis
Sotiris H. Avgoustis, PhD, Assistant Professor,
Department of Restaurant, Hotel, Institutional and
Tourism Management, Indiana University-
Purdue University, Indianapolis*

An increasing number of business and pleasure travelers are becoming more conscious of the natural environment and the damaging effects that result from its misuse by humankind. As a result, acceptable environmental practices will, inevitably, become key factors influencing the meeting industry and its practices. The meeting industry is already facing growing pressure from environmentally sensitive groups to reverse the effects damaging the natural environment. Those involved on the facility or hotel side must be aware of these initiatives as well. Such initiatives contribute to the "greening" of the meeting industry. To succeed, any new or existing initiative must focus on the following three goals:

1. Enhance existing collaborations and create new, inclusive partnerships between the meeting industry, local residents, and environmentalists to meet changing local needs.
2. Develop a common vision for the meeting industry and the region and provide practical, action-based ways to follow this vision to improved environmental quality through shared responsibility and diverse stakeholder participation.
3. Revitalize local communities by promoting win-win strategies that combine the dual goals of economic prosperity and natural resource preservation.

The greening of the meeting industry will alter the priorities of meeting planners. Planners will no longer look for just any available facilities to accommodate specific events; they will search for "environmentally friendly" facilities and communities. Meeting professionals who have incorporated this new approach will ask the following types of questions when searching for the right location for their next meeting or function:

- How many function rooms are equipped to conserve energy?
- What is the availability and room rate for "green" rooms? (A "green" room considers the environment. A green room may have a recycle bin, low-pressure water gauges, energy-efficient climate controls and windows, low-watt lightbulbs, and limited housekeeping services, which decrease the amount of water and chemicals used.)
- What in-house furnishings are made from recyclable materials?
- What types of conservation methods is the hotel/facility using to protect the physical environment?
- Does the hotel/facility sponsor any type of community project focused on the environment?
- Is the hotel/facility involved in any recycling programs (both internally and externally)?

Meeting Planners' Responsibilities
Jessup (1997) offers the following tips for planning greener meetings:

- Establish the types of environmental practices you wish to achieve at your meeting. For example, target a percentage of recycled material of the total amount of materials used at the meeting.
- Use recycled materials for all promotional items. Print all materials on the fronts and backs of paper. Use E-mail instead of surface mail to send notifications of upcoming meetings. Update mailing lists often to eliminate duplication.
- Educate yourself on the hotel's/facility's recycling program. Consider the types of products needed for the program and use materials that the hotel/facility can recycle for you (e.g., paper, cardboard, wooden pallets, cans and bottles). Promote recycling to delegates.
- Create exhibit booths and other items that can be reused at other functions.
- Use environmentally sound give-aways, such as recycled or plastic mugs, reusable cloth bags, or clothing items.
- Rent reusable decorations or greenery.
- Suggest that exhibitors use shredded office paper or even popcorn to pack their goods, instead of bubble wrap or polystyrene pellets.
- Encourage public transportation when appropriate.
- Reuse plastic name badges at other meetings.

- Use glass, china, and cloth instead of plastic or paper at meal events.

Meeting Delegates and Participants' Responsibilities

The "greening" of the industry cannot be fully realized without meeting participants' involvement. They, too, are responsible for helping to preserve the natural environment. Following are suggestions for meeting participants to consider when attending meetings (Jessup 1997):

- Ask to stay only in "green" rooms.
- Use public transportation when possible.
- Reuse towels and linens.
- Ask where to place recyclable items if no bin is available.
- Turn off water instead of letting it run when brushing teeth or shaving.
- Turn off all lights when leaving a room.
- Close the curtains when leaving the room to reduce energy usage.

Hotel/Facility Responsibilities

Hammer and Townsend (1993) offer the following list of steps hotels/facilities and their employees must take to protect the environment:

- Use E-mail instead of paper communication when possible.
- Decrease the need for many hard copies of documents by storing them on computer disks.
- Eliminate fax cover sheets by using a rubber stamp designed for fax use.
- Order supplies in bulk and chart the shelf lives of items; purchase only the quantities needed.
- Request that meeting attendees avoid sending excessive amounts of information in boxes, bags, and wrappings.
- Ship typewriter and computer ribbons and printer cartridges to the specified recyclers.
- Purchase nontoxic inks, biodegradable correction fluid, equipment that does not need batteries, and unbleached, chlorine-free paper to reduce hazardous waste.

Summary

As the meeting industry gets greener, hotels and other meeting facilities will be required to devise new innovative programs and practices to meet the growing expectations of environmentally aware organizations. Without doubt, the trend will continue far into the future. Meeting professionals of all disciplines need to stay current with new developments and continue to be leaders in this field.

EXERCISE

CASE STUDY The twenty-first G-7 summit was hosted from June 15 to 17 in Halifax, Nova Scotia, Canada. The Canadians welcomed leaders from Japan, the United States, France, Germany, Italy, and the United Kingdom, as well as representatives from the Russian Federation and the European Union. The Citizen Environmental Committee, consisting of representatives from over twenty environmentally conscious organizations, wanted this to be the most environmentally friendly summit ever held and for it to be a model for future events. The committee specified percentage goals through the Waste Zero Program to reduce waste on site and at local hotels. Other equally important programs were established to meet different summit goals. For example, the Green Purchasing and Procurement Program was designed to promote to summit organizers, host facilities, suppliers, and subcontractors environmentally responsible products that were endorsed by the "Environmental Choice" Eco-Loco Program of Canada. With leadership and cooperation from both civic and governmental groups, meeting attendees achieved the environmental goals set forth by the committee.

ACTIVITY

Visit the following Web site to learn more about "Greening the Halifax G-7 Summit": www.ns.doe.ca/g7/legacy4.html.

QUESTIONS

1. List the various programs that set environmental guidelines for this meeting. Explain how each contributed to the meeting's success.
2. Using the G-7 Summit as an example, choose a national conference or convention and discuss in detail how planners can set environmentally responsible goals, promote and use environmental programs during the event, and evaluate their findings to see if they were successful.

REFERENCES

Engledrum, D., & Moffitt, K. (May 1997). *Environmentally sensitive hotels* (online). Available at www.meetingsweb.com/html/green_meetings.html.

Hammer, M.S., & Townsend, J.M. (October 1993). *Ecopurchasing in hotels and motels*. The Florida Energy Extension Service, Florida Cooperative Extension Service, Institute of Food and Agricultural Sciences, University of Florida (online). Available at hammock.ifas.ufl.edu/txt/fairs/44390.

Jessup, L.S. (1997). *Going green. Meetings in the west* (online). Available at www.meetingsweb.com/html/green_meetings.html.

Lane Environmental Limited. (August 1995). *Final report, Halifax G-7 Summit, Environmental review and assessment summary. Greening the Halifax G-7 Summit* (online). Available at www.ns.doe.ca/g7/legacy4.html.

CHAPTER REVIEW

KEY CONCEPTS

Benchmark	Riser	Airwall
Front of room	Dance floor	Function space diary
Space eater	Exhibits	Blocking space
Function equipment	Percentage of	Event planning
Stay set	participation	logistics
Americans with Disabilities Act (ADA)		

REVIEW QUESTIONS

1. What size ballroom would an event planner need to seat 500 people in rounds of 10? What size screen would the planner need, and how would the screen affect the needed square footage?

2. Assuming a 40 percent participation, how many square feet are needed to accommodate a dance floor for 325 people? If those same people were to have a reception using lounge-style seating in the same room, what would the square footage figure be?

3. Explain the impact the Americans with Disabilities Act (ADA) has on event function planning.

4. Define the term *AV*. What are some of the latest AV innovations, and how do they impact events?

CHAPTER 5

Planning the
Menu

INTRODUCTION

The skills and knowledge required for catering are vast and ever changing. Indeed, the ever-evolving hospitality industry can perpetually challenge even the most knowledgeable. In catering, newly acquired skills often have unique twists. This feature attracts many to the industry. Learning something new each day can be very rewarding.

The fundamentals of catering involve the three sections of the success equation:

$$\text{Optimal Event Planning} + \text{Creative Menu Planning} \times \text{Effective Selling} = \text{Maximum Catering Results}$$

The most unique section is **menu planning**. Menu planning is formulating and implementing the food- and beverage-related aspects of an event. The discussions in this chapter assume that the meals being planned are for groups and not individuals. These group menus are preplanned, not ordered from menus individually as in restaurants.

Menu planning is unique because it has an artistic component. Culinary artists exceed menu expectations in ways the unskilled cannot. Planners who use creativity in their menus use artistic skills. Being creative is not simple, however. The culinary aspect of a menu is the most difficult to master. Before learning the aspects of menu planning, planners should learn the menu planning flow chart (see Figure 5–1). This chart highlights the steps and knowledge base a menu planner needs to plan creative and functional menus. The creative menu planning flow chart summarizes the topics covered in this chapter.

MENU COMPOSITION

> *Food is an important part of a balanced diet.*
>
> FRAN LEBOWITZ

Catering professionals seeking to plan menus must have basic knowledge of the kitchens in which they will work. Menu planners must then be able to understand the physical makeup of all possible menu selections. The **composition** of each item on a menu identifies the item's:

- Historical or geographical origins
- Preparation method

Analysis of an item's composition provides insight into the item's final appearance and taste.

FOOD ORIGINS

From the beginning of humankind, people have prepared and eaten food in an infinite number of ways. Religion, geographic location, and socio-

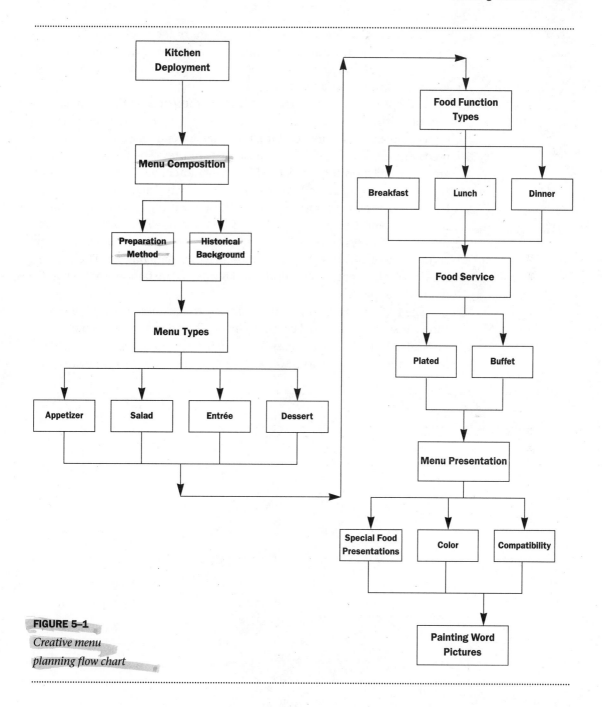

FIGURE 5–1

*Creative menu
planning flow chart*

economic factors help develop food habits. The impacts history and culture have had on culinary habits around the world could fill an entire text. Today, food tastes change as rapidly as ever.

It is necessary here to focus on the origins of food habits and tastes as they apply to North America. Within that context, the menu planner can better grasp the impact the rest of the world has made specifically on American and Canadian tastes and habits.

Perhaps no two cultures have had greater impacts on the culinary history of North America than France and Italy. Beyond the images of fast food and pizza that come to mind, the "Classic" culinary methods of food preparation owe a great deal to those two cultures. The French had their greatest impact on the terms used in today's kitchen. As the next section shows, many common culinary terms are French. Each region of France has helped food preparation evolve. The French regions of Nice, Dijon, Beaujolais, and Provence (see Figure 5–2) are renowned for their impact on sauces, cheeses, and spices. France has also contributed greatly to the enjoyment of meals with its prowess in wine preparation. The French regions of Champagne, Burgundy, and Bordeaux are famous for their ability to make spirits.

The Italian impact on food origins is perhaps most widely known to those outside of traditional culinary circles. The origins of foods commonly associated with Italy, like pizza and spaghetti, are often disputed. Pasta, for example, is argued to have been first developed by the ancient Chi-

FIGURE 5–2

Food origins in France

nese. Archeologists are said to have found recipes for pizza among the tombs of ancient Egypt. It cannot be argued, however, that the Italians did not further develop these and many other foods. The northern Italian regions of Piedmont, Lombardy, and Emilia-Romagna (see Figure 5–3) are famous for risotto, robust meats, and pasta. Tuscany is famous for its vegetables and wine and Sicily for its seafood. Like French, Italian is scattered throughout the culinary dictionary.

Within North America, regions have adopted their own distinct styles of food preparation. Again, culture and history impact food preparation, as does geographic location. Because North America is not culturally homogenous, food composition differs greatly across the continent. Cultures and traditions mesh to create hybrid preparation styles. The traditions of the earliest settlers are as evident as those of the newest immigrants. Many of the cooking traditions evident today have roots in Europe. Later, immigrants from Africa and Asia played parts in developing North American food cultures. The native people of the continent also contributed to food culture.

Each area of North America professes to have a different food culture that is based on current and/or traditional cultural makeup. While it is argued that large metropolitan areas are so diverse that they homogenize their populations, in fact many areas have to this day retained cultural and ethnic enclaves that continue to promote culinary traditions. In many areas, the cultural "Melting Pot" has led to a mixing of traditional

FIGURE 5–3

Food origins in Italy

food cultures. Indeed, the different areas of the continent have unique styles that can only be described as **culinary hybrids**. Figure 5–4 shows a few.

The significant point for a menu planner to remember here is that regions of the continent may be more familiar with certain food items than others. Hotels, caterers, and banquet facilities in certain areas should incorporate some of their regions' **signature food** items into their menus. Signature food items are items that are unique to, and/or associated with, a specific region or culture. For example, in Louisiana, signature food items are those made in Creole and Cajun style. Seafood is a signature food item in New England, because the area is close to the ocean. Salmon is often associated with the Northwest, just as Tex-Mex cooking is associated with the Southwest. There are "Chicago style" and "New York style" pizzas.

Simply put, understanding food origins and the evolution of signature food items is an important piece of the menu planner's education.

FOOD PREPARATION

After food origins, the next step to understanding menu composition is common food preparation. In this context, **food preparation** is the cook-

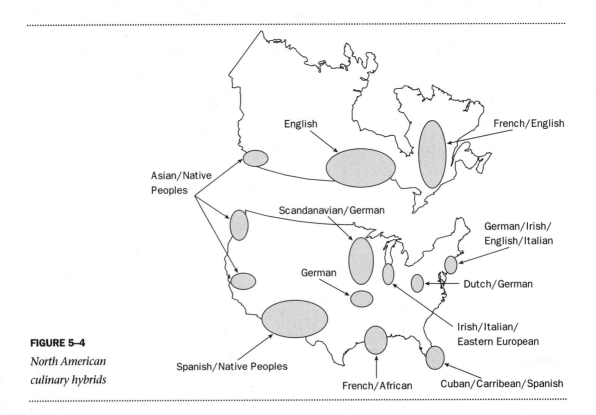

FIGURE 5–4

North American culinary hybrids

ing process a menu item undergoes before it is served. The cooking process includes physically preparing the food item and any accoutrements.

Menu planning hinges on a basic understanding of food preparation. The foundation for the remainder of this chapter is built on the assumption that menus are developed by planners who know what they are putting together. Menu planners should master the accompanying list of the most basic food preparation methods, but there are countless more ways to prepare food. New food preparation methods are developed constantly. Experienced menu planners continuously stay abreast of new preparation trends as part of their continuing education. Chefs and menu planners alike should keep Sharon Tyler Herbst's book *Food Lovers Companion* close at hand. It lists thousands of culinary definitions in detail.

BASIC FOOD PREPARATION METHODS

Preparation Method	Description
Al dente	Cooked with some firmness remaining.
Au poivre	Coated with coarse ground pepper.
Au gratin	Topped with cheese.
Au jus	Served in natural juices.
Bake	Cooked in a dry oven.
Barbecue	Cooked over coals or open heat source. Sometimes includes basting or roasting with a sauce. Also called "grilling."
Baste	Cover food with its own juices or another sauce.
Blanch	Place vegetables or fruits first into very hot water and then immediately into cold water.
Broil	Cook directly under high heat.
Cajun	Catchall phrase most often referring to cooking with ample spices.
Candied	Dipped into a warm sugar syrup that forms a crust when cool.
Caramelize	To heat sugar until it liquefies.
Chutney	Finely blended fruit with spices.
Clarify	To remove sediments from a liquid.
Coat	To cover with some type of crust.
Convection	Cooking with dry, moving heat.
Croûte	French for "crust." Foods served en croûte are often wrapped in pastry.
Dredge	Lightly coat food for frying.
Drizzled	Poured finely.
Dust	To coat food in a powder.
Emulsion	Fusion of two liquids that do not mix well.
Essence	Aromatic or flavorful oils.
Extracts	Pure flavors.
Fillet	To remove bones from meat or fish.
Flambé	French for "flaming." Foods that are flambéd are ignited with liquor before serving.

BASIC FOOD PREPARATION METHODS (*cont.*)

Preparation Method	Description
Fondue	Food item cooked or eaten in a central hot liquid. Foods can be cooked in hot oil or dipped into a fondue of warm cheese or chocolate.
French cut	Vegetables or meat cut lengthwise.
Fricassee	Cooked in butter with vegetables.
Fry	To cook in hot fat or oil.
Fumé	French for "smoked."
Garlic butter	Butter infused with garlic bits or essence.
Glacé	French for "frozen" or "glazed."
Glaze	Thin food coating.
Grill	To prepare food on a metal grate over coals or a heat source. Sometimes also called "barbecue."
Gumbo	Stewlike preparation.
Hash	Finely chopped meat or vegetables.
Home-fried	Thickly sliced, deep-fried vegetables.
Induction	Cooking using magnetic energy.
Infusion	Flavor extracted by immersing in hot liquid. Foods infused with flavors, like olive oil infused with basil, are popular.
Jerky	Dried, thin strips of meat.
Julienne	Cut into thin pieces.
Kabob	Meat, fish, and poultry cooked on a skewer over a heat source. Often accompanied by vegetables.
Kosher	Foods prepared according to Jewish laws.
Lyonnaise	French sauce made with wine and onions.
Marinade	Highly seasoned liquid in which foods are immersed before cooking.
Marsala	Italian sauce made with marsala wine and mushrooms.
Masala	Indian combinations of spices.
Medallion	Cutting meat into coinlike pieces.
Microwave	To cook food with high-frequency radio waves.
Milanese	Food coated in bread crumbs and parmesan cheese and fried in butter.
Misto	Italian for "mixed."
Mornay	Thick cheese sauce.
Mousse	French for "foam." Describes rich desserts.
Napoleon	Food with layers of pastry.
Niçoise	Foods prepared in the style of the French town of Nice. Usually includes olives and tomatoes.
Nonpareil	Decoration for candies and cakes.
Normande	Sauce with a fish or seafood base.
Open face	Sandwiches served with only one piece of bread.
Pan broil	To cook over high heat in a heavy pan with little or no oil.
Parboil	To cook briefly in hot water.
Paisienne	Sauce made with cream cheese.
Parmigiana	Food made with parmesan cheese.
Pâté	Finely ground meat preparation.
Périgourdine	Sauce made with truffles.
Pesto	Sauce made of basil, olive oil, garlic, and parmesan cheese.
Piccata	Sauce made with lemon and parsley.
Poach	To cook food in hot liquid.

BASIC FOOD PREPARATION METHODS (*cont.*)

Preparation Method	Description
Provençal	Foods prepared in the style of the French Provence region. Garlic, olive oil, onions, and tomatoes are typically included.
Purée	To blend into a thick sauce.
Ragù	Italian for "sauce."
Reduce	To boil a liquid until the volume is reduced.
Rémoulade	French sauce made with mayonnaise, mustard, and capers.
Rösti	To fry until crisp and brown.
Rotisserie	Cooking meat on a rolling spit.
Roux	Mixture of flour and butter. Used as a base for many sauces.
Salsa	Mexican for "sauce." Made of raw or cooked vegetables and spices.
Satay	Small skewers of grilled meat.
Sauté	To cook with a bit of oil.
Score	To make a series of small cuts in meat.
Sear	To cook quickly over high heat.
Smoke	To slow cook food over an enclosed heat source that emits a high level of smoke. Aromatic woods are often added to the coals to increase the smoke level.
Steam	To cook food using only the steam from boiling water. The food does not touch the water.
Stir fry	To cook food over high heat while constantly mixing.
Tandoori	Indian-style cooking.
Tartare	Raw meat mixed with spices and egg.
Teriyaki	Japanese style cooking in which meat is seasoned with soy sauce, ginger, and sugar.
Tex-Mex	Southwest cooking style. Combination of Texan and Mexican influences.
Tournedo	Cut of beef from the tenderloin.
Velouté	White sauce made from fish or poultry stock.
Vichy	Vegetables cooked with butter and sugar.
Wellington	Beef covered with paté, placed in puff pastry, and baked.
Whip	To mix ingredients until light and airy.

MENU TYPES

Throughout this text, the discussions of menus and their compositions use the preceding fundamental terms and key definitions. Knowledge of food origins, culinary hybrids, signature food items, and preparation methods is the starting point for planning a menu. Defining the type of menu requires applying that knowledge. **Menu type** is the name given to a course served during a meal. Each menu type has food items that apply to it better than others. Some meals encompass all menu types while others (e.g., fast food) include just a few. The most widely used menu types are:

- **Appetizer** The **appetizer** is typically the first item served during a meal. It can be served hot or cold. Its purpose is to prepare the eater for what is to follow. Soups fall into this category.

- **Salad**   **Salad** is usually the second course of a meal, but it can be the first if no appetizer is served. A salad can consist of any combination of greens, fruits, other vegetables, cheeses, or even flowers.

- **Entrée**   The **entrée** is considered the main course of any meal. It is the focus of the eating experience. The entrée is often served with a starch and a vegetable.

- **Dessert**   **Dessert** is typically the last course of a meal. Western tradition calls for some sweet concoction to be served. Fruits, cheeses, cakes, pies, tarts, flans, and cookies can all be served as desserts.

Menu accoutrements, like beverages, bread/butter, and condiments are not separate menu types because they are available throughout several courses.

There are other, less commonly used menu types. The courses in any meal are restricted only by budget and imagination. In the right circumstances, a menu planner may incorporate any of the following into a meal:

- **Intermezzo** The **intermezzo** is served between the salad and the entree. It is intended to cleanse the palate and prepare the eater for the next course. A sorbet (a fruit-sherbetlike treat) is usually served as the intermezzo.

- **High tea**   A British tradition, **high tea** can be considered a meal in itself. Served in the late afternoon, high tea can be used as the last course of an early dinner. A selection of small sandwiches, fruit, and/or desserts is served with tea.

- **Apéritif**   **Apéritif** is French for "a light drink." It is served at the start of a meal to excite the palate. Champagne and sherry are common apéritifs.

- **Cordials**   Served after dinner, **cordials** can include sweet liqueurs, like brandy. Coffee drinks like Irish coffee (coffee with whiskey) and Bailey's Irish Cream are popular. In rare instances, cigars are also offered.

FOOD FUNCTION TYPES

Food function types center around the focus of the meal in question and incorporate one or more menu type into their makeups. The three basic food function types mirror the three basic meals in a day: breakfast, lunch, and dinner.

Breakfast is typically a sit-down meal of traditional breakfast fare that is served in the morning. As a food function, breakfast is usually held in a separate room from a meeting or another event function. Lunch is a mid-day food function. Lunch menus are similar to those for dinner, but lunch menus offer slightly smaller portions. Dinner is the last formal food function type in a day. It can include several courses and menu items. Dinner can lead into formal business presentations or less structured events. Dances and celebrations that are scheduled after dinner are not classified as food functions because their focus is activity, not food.

FOOD SERVICE

There are two fundamental serving techniques for all food functions: plated and buffet.

PLATED FOOD SERVICE

A **plated** food function is served to attendees. Plated meals, when served to large groups, are assembled in the facility kitchen and served to all attendees at once. A server presents each meal to each seated attendee. There is an inherent time delay from the point at which the first and the last attendees are served. For large groups, it is common for 30 or more minutes to pass before all attendees are served. To shorten this delay, the menu planner may consider the **preplated** menu type. A preplated meal is simply placed on the table before attendees are seated. For example, servers need not place preplated salads before each seated person. With salads already on the table, attendees can begin eating right away, and servers can begin preparing the next course for service. Preplating is limited only by the desired service temperature. Hot soups or frozen desserts cannot be preplated because they may not be at optimal temperature when consumed.

BUFFET FOOD SERVICE

The **buffet**, the second fundamental serving technique, can be used in lieu of any plated food function. It is used when menu selection and service speed are factors. Breakfast, lunch, and dinner buffets are common. A fundamental difference between the buffet and the plated meal is choice.

A buffet typically allows an individual to choose the items they wish to eat and how much of those items. Because plated menus are predetermined, they do not allow for differences in palate and appetite. Buffets, in contrast, typically allow for more than one menu type to be served. Buffets can offer more menu choices because of the numbers of people they serve. Most banquet facilities mandate a minimum number of people for a buffet menu. A minimum is needed because buffets are designed in the kitchen to allow each person to sample each item. Therefore, the amount of food that is needed on a buffet is greater than that needed for a plated meal. Consequently, buffets may cost more than plated meals. A kitchen cannot recoup its costs for a buffet if the number of people is too low. A service charge penalty is appropriate for groups whose numbers fall short of a facility's minimum but still want buffets. A **buffet line** is an assortment of food that is laid out along a table. Because attendees move along the buffet line and choose their own food, they can get to their seats and eat quicker than they might if they waited for servers at a plated function.

Buffets are restricted somewhat in their ability to offer certain foods. All food items have preferred serving consistencies, which dictate how those items can be served. A buffet line must remain in place often for an hour or more, which means some foods will lose their desired consistencies. A **chafing dish** is a large display pan over a heat source that is used to keep food warm. This heat source, in essence, continues cooking the foods in the chafing dish. The term **hold** is used to describe how long a food item can remain on a buffet before it loses its desired consistency or temperature. Foods that do not hold well are pastas, many fried starches, and cut meats or meats cooked to specific temperatures (e.g., medium rare). Sauces are often used with food items on a buffet because they **mask** the items' consistencies. Masking is simply hiding or covering a food item with a more dominant component so that consistency is not apparent to the eye. Masking cut tenderloin in a flavorful sauce removes the need for the tenderloin to be cooked "just so"; the sauce becomes the more dominant item in the dish.

Special Buffet Exceptions. There are unique food functions that are only served in the buffet format. The continental breakfast, coffee break, reception, food station, and boxed meal are distinctive because they are never plated. They are still considered buffets because they either offer more than one choice and/or mandate that attendees serve themselves.

Continental Breakfast. The **continental breakfast** is a lighter version of the breakfast buffet that serves cold food items and hot/cold beverages in buffet style. The continental breakfast can be served in a separate room, but most often it is served in or around the central function room of a group. It is a common starting event at which attendees can congregate and get to know each other before a program begins.

Coffee Break. The **coffee break** food function is designed to break up the day for people attending meetings. The coffee break can be set up inside or outside the main function room. It allows attendees to stretch their legs and network between sessions. Coffee does not have to be served at a coffee break, but it often is during the early and mid-morning coffee breaks. Afternoon coffee breaks can include any type of beverage and snack. These breaks can be themed to match the moods and feelings of the planner and attendees.

Reception. Often a precursor to dinner, a **reception** is designed to promote mingling and communication among attendees. Hard and/or soft beverages may be served with light snacks. A formal reception may include a full bar and an assortment of hors d'oeuvres, which are commonly thought of as "heavier" finger foods, like shrimp, canapés, and fruits and cheeses. Receptions can occur at any time of day in today's market.

Food Station. The **food station**, an island set apart from a buffet line, is a unique method of presenting food. Sometimes called action stations, food stations are made of specific food items that are not found on the buffet line. Food stations can be used with standard buffet lines or as the buffets themselves. In most cases, food stations complement buffet lines.

The food station has two variations: **themed station** and **menu-type station**. Themed stations are food islands that incorporate a certain amount of theatrical flair into their presentation. Sometimes manned by a chef, themed stations focus on engaging the eater and creating more of a meal experience. A pasta station may be decorated in an Italian theme and have four different varieties of pasta. An omelet station has a chef preparing omelets made to order. A carving station is staffed by someone cutting pieces of a large meat (e.g., top round of beef or ham) and serving people individually.

Menu-type stations differ from themed stations in that they are made entirely of single menu types. A salad station, a dessert station, and an entrée station are all examples of stations that are composed of one menu type. Again, because these stations are also considered buffets, they may offer more than one choice of menu type.

Boxed Meals. **Boxed meals** are simply portable, prepackaged meals that typically include sandwiches, small bags of chips, fruit/candy desserts, and drinks. To be portable, boxed meals must have wrapped and prepackaged food items. Due to health concerns, foods that do not hold well should never be included in boxed meals. A boxed meal is used in two common situations: (1) when there is no space for a more formal meal (2) and when attendees are going offsite or there are no more planned agenda items but planners want to provide meals. The boxed meal gets its name from the firm paper carrying case many facilities use to package their meals.

MENU PRESENTATION

It is often said that the enjoyment of a meal consists of more than just the enjoyment of the food. The experience of a meal is as important as the meal. Ambiance and service level play parts in meal enjoyment. The excitement and anticipation people experience prior to the first bite are important parts of the meal experience. The moment when one first looks down at a plate set in front of them, before they ever taste anything, their mind is imagining all the possibilities of what is upcoming. That excitement is very important to the overall enjoyment of the meal experience. Anticipation and excitement are parts of **menu presentation**, which includes the ways all items are arranged and combined and the ways the items look, smell, and feel. The plate presentation affects several senses at once. The senses of sight, smell, and even sound (think of sizzling fajitas), can all come into play.

Menu planners can create superior meal experiences for their attendees using color and **compatibility** properly.

COLOR

Painters often judge the outcomes of their hard work by how well they used color. Using color correctly in art requires talent and years of practice. In culinary arts, a menu planner replaces the painter.

When looking at the color of a menu, the planner should strive to remember the concept of **balance**. Balance aims to "fit" food items together based on their colors. The concept of color in plate presentation does not apply to menu items served individually (e.g., salads, appetizers, and desserts), because there is no reason to balance those items with other food items.

Menu planners should be comfortable enough to observe the kitchens in their facilities from time to time to critique menus for color balance. When observing menus, planners should ask themselves:

- Do the colors blend?
- Are certain colors repeated over and over?
- Is one item glaringly out of place?
- What is the **eye appeal**?

The balance of colors contributes to or detracts from the eye appeal of a meal. Eye appeal, simply the way the food items on a plate look as a whole, contributes or detracts from the whole meal experience. Does the final product look appealing? Eye appeal in plate presentation is important, because the goal of presentation is to please the eye.

Each food item has a unique color that either fits well with others or not, but each unique color must be identified. Green beans are clearly green, but what color is chicken marsala? The menu planner must understand what each item on a menu will look like to understand the concept of color.

Each time an entrée is selected, the accompanying starch, vegetable, and, possibly, garnish must be selected as well. A planner may select salmon filet as an entrée, for example, as well as what should accompany it. A menu planner should select accompaniments so that balanced color results. The menu planner should strive to balance a palette of colors on each plate as the plate is created. Envisioning the final product is an important part of menu planning. A main entrée that has a brown sauce, for example, should be balanced with green broccoli and red new potatoes. An Italian entrée with a red sauce, such as veal parmesan, could use an accompaniment of tricolored bow-tie pasta and possibly a julienne of yellow squash. Color and balance are not limited to starches and vegetables, however. Color can be enhanced by sauces as well. Combination food items provide two colors at once.

Planners should only compile menu items that are available through their kitchens. Each facility is constrained by skill level, experience, capacity, and food availability. Preset **banquet menus** should be determined by the kitchen and catering management. Banquet menus should serve as guides to menu planning, because they outline the ranges and limitations of kitchens. Signature food items should be included in these menus and reviewed before menu planning. **Off-menu planning** is coordinating meals that include items not on the banquet menus. Any off-menu planning should be approved by the kitchen first. While most chefs

---

COMBINATION FOOD ITEMS

Risotto with basil	Roasted red and green peppers
Scrambled eggs with cheddar	Green beans with almonds
Wild rice with onion	Buttered cauliflower and broccoli
Baby carrots with dill	

FOOD ITEMS ENHANCED BY SAUCES

Chicken breast with tarragon wine sauce	Broiled salmon in pecan crust with chardonnay sauce
Veal in a dijon mustard sauce	Beef tenderloin in green peppercorn sauce
Pork with mushrooms and Granny Smith apple chutney	Grilled bass in grapefruit and thyme sauce

enjoy "stretching" their culinary skills, they do not wish to produce less-than-ideal outcomes because their kitchens were not equipped. For example, planners should not sell unique pastas they enjoyed at restaurants over the weekend without checking with their kitchen staff first.

Many individuals, for whatever reasons, have attended many catered meal functions. These individuals have seen the same plate presentations of chicken, beef, pork, or seafood often. Therefore, they can have predetermined negative reactions to the food being served at functions, before they see the plates. Such reactions are known as "rubber chicken syndrome." Sauces and combination items can relieve some of rubber chicken syndrome. With an understanding of the attendees and the operation limitations of the facility kitchen, a menu planner can create new and unique presentations that please even the most jaded. Creativity and color balance help avoid the rubber chicken syndrome.

Like sauces and combination items, **garnish** (see Figure 5–5), a plate accoutrement whose purpose is to contribute to color balance, adds to color as well. A garnish can be edible or nonedible. Garnishes are useful when entrées, vegetables, or starches do not provide enough color to a plate on their own. The garnish that comes to mind first for many people is the sprig of parsley. The menu planner can garnish plates with something more unique, however, like a fruit salsa. A small section of appropriate cheese or a grilled tomato half with toasted breadcrumbs makes a new and exciting garnish. Fresh herb leaves and even certain edible flowers

School Lunch Room

"Hey, what's the green stuff on my tray?"

"The lunch lady said it was a garnish."

FIGURE 5–5
Garnish

make unique garnishes. Garnishes should always be used to the menu planner's advantage.

An extension of garnish is the **painted plate**, which is most often used in desserts. To create a painted plate, the pastry chef drizzles chocolate, vanilla, or some other sauce on a plate before placing the main item on the plate. The plate then gains an artistic, "painted" look.

The painted plate can be used for entrée dishes as well. A plate drizzled with a sauce that is being served over the main entrée adds to the plate presentation. Entrée plates can also be painted with dustings of dry spices around the edges of the plates.

COMPATIBILITY

In menu planning, compatibility is how well certain menu items fit together on a plate. Certain foods are compatible, while others are not. How well things "get along" is what menu planners should be aware of when putting food items together on a plate.

Compatibility is determined by three main factors: temperature, consistency, and meal flow.

Temperature. A basic law of nature dictates that hot food gets cool and cold food gets warm. Because most meals are served in areas at room temperature, both hot and cold items eventually move toward room temperature. Foods must be served at **prime temperature** to avoid foodborne illnesses and contamination. The need to serve food at prime temperature impacts which foods can be served together on the same plate. One example would be something very hot and something very cold on the same plate. Because these foods will move eventually to room temperature, they will assume different temperatures than their intended ones. A menu planner must never combine items of drastically different serving temperatures because those items will not be compatible when served, and even less so when their temperatures change.

Consistency. Food compatibility is also rooted in consistency. A **dominant food item** overpowers a **recessive food item** combined with it in terms of taste, flavor, and smell. **Neutral food items** do not affect other food items but also do not readily absorb other taste and flavor elements. Whenever possible, dominant food items should be combined with other dominants or neutrals, and recessives should be combined with other recessives or neutrals. For example, a strong fish with a heavy cream sauce (dominant) should not be accompanied by rice (recessive), because the rice will absorb the fish odor as well as much of the sauce. The starch on the plate must be able to "hold its own" with the fish. A neutral starch like potato will not absorb the fish and sauce elements but also will not transmit its flavor to the fish. The reverse also applies. In certain instances the desire may be to transmit the flavor from one food item to another. When serving chicken marsala, a soft starch like pasta (recessive) fits perfectly because the chicken is not overpowering and the pasta benefits from the sauce. The kitchen staff at any facility should be able to answer questions of recessive/dominant/neutral traits for any food item on a banquet menu.

Meal Flow. Compatibility can also be understood in the context of entire meals. For example, the compatibility of the salad to the appetizer, entrée, and dessert can work for or against the meal flow. A spicy entrée like blackened Cajun chicken fits well with a Caesar salad, which is also flavorful. A relatively bland meal like baked chicken might do better with a straight house salad and a choice of traditional dressings. Planners should remember compatibility when putting together buffets. The colors of the different items on the buffet and how they fit together (compatibility) are viewed as one food experience. A **themed buffet** is a good example of compatibility in a buffet. A themed buffet aims to combine foods of similar origin, taste, or look. An Italian buffet should include compatible items like Caesar salad, pastas, various sauces, sausage and peppers, antipasto tray, and garlic bread. The menu planner should not insert nonrelated items, like teriyaki chicken or hot dogs, because they would be obviously out of place.

SPECIAL FOOD FUNCTION PRESENTATIONS

The preceding section analyzed color and compatibility in basic, single-entrée plate presentations and buffets. The following section applies these principles to different presentations and function types, namely dual and multiple entrées and receptions. These presentation methods are not limited to specific food function types, which are breakfast, lunch, and dinner. Each function type can have a meal served via single-entrée plate, buffet, dual entrée, and multiple entrée. One can have a breakfast

COMMON MENU THEMES	
Theme	**Possible Menu Items**
Italian	Caesar salad, chicken marsala, risotto, pesto bread
Asian	Teriyaki beef, fried rice, spring rolls, fortune cookies
Mexican	Fajitas, refried beans, spicy rice, empanadas
Greek/Middle Eastern	Stuffed grape leaves, hummus, lamb, baklava
Jamaican	Jerk chicken, sweet potato cakes, fruit
Hawaiian	Poi, roast pork, pineapple upsidedown cake

reception in the morning or a dessert buffet in the evening. This section examines the presentation, planning, and, in some instances, pricing characteristics of each.

DUAL AND MULTIPLE ENTRÉES

The color and compatibility analysis of a plate does not have to be limited to one entrée choice or buffet. There are instances when plated meals can have more than one entrée. Called a **split or dual entrée**, these menus have two distinct entrées on one plate. For example, a dual-entrée plated meal can have both a petite beef filet and sautéed chicken breast. The menu planner should suggest these options when attendees cannot decide on single entrées or when they want to please as many different palates as possible. The numbers and/or client preferences prohibit the menu planner from selling a buffet, however. Color considerations are aided by the addition of another entree and all the new vegetable and starch choices that are now appropriate.

One derivative of the dual-entrée plate is the **multiple-entrée** meal. To create such a meal, the planner again looks for two or more entrées for attendees of a nonbuffet format. The difference between the multiple-entrée meal and the dual-entrée meal is that the multiple-entrée meal offers attendees a choice. Predetermined commitments from attendees as to which entrées they prefer allow the kitchen to serve different entrées without resorting to a buffet format. Often, to please as many attendees as possible, the client may offer beef, chicken, seafood, and others in some combination.

The key to successful multiple-entrée events is to ensure that before the event the organization commits to exact numbers for each entrée choice. This is called a **guaranteed number**. A banquet kitchen cannot wait until the meal is being served to have attendees choose their entrées. One can imagine what would happen if each attendee coincidentally chose the same items. This reasoning is rooted in the fundamental differences between banquet food preparation and individual restaurant kitchens. The banquet kitchen is not set up to provide meals in the ways the restaurant kitchen does. A restaurant kitchen can cook each item to order, provided that the orders are relatively few and the customers are willing to wait for their meals. The banquet kitchen, in contrast, can prepare large numbers of meals in a relatively short time and can serve them at once, assuming that orders are known ahead of time and the meals differ little.

If a banquet kitchen operated as a restaurant, the chef would have to prepare enough of each entrée for each attendee, which would lead to great waste and very high food cost. Given the right restrictions, the banquet kitchen can accommodate multiple entrées because the:

- Number of each entrée is predetermined. Exact numbers of items can be purchased and prepared as needed.
- Remainder of the meal (i.e., salad, starch, vegetable, dessert) remains the same and can be mass produced.

The menu planner might suggest that each attendee commit to an entrée choice via an invitation or some other method. Attendees should bring these invitations to the event to identify their choices from their seats. If that is not possible, the planner can prepare identifying markers (e.g., differently colored papers) to identify the entrée selections (e.g., red for beef, yellow for chicken). Attendees would place their markers near their place settings. Identifying markers also help the banquet servers know which attendees get which entrées; asking each attendee is time consuming and unprofessional.

Identifying each attendee's entrée choice before the event is important for another reason: human nature. Many groups have requested item choices ahead of time without holding respondents accountable during the functions. Some attendees choose healthier or lighter entrées weeks in advance because they feel they should or because they plan to eat better then. Often, however, when the meal is served and those attendees smell the steak or see the lobster, they change their minds, which can cause problems for the kitchen.

RECEPTIONS

The reception is a unique meal function because it combines elements of the buffet, party, and others to create a more relaxed and enjoyable meal experience. Receptions are intended to provide easy, relaxed arenas for mingling and conversation; they do not have to follow fixed formats. The reception can be molded to accomplish any goal. Some receptions offer only cake and punch, while others offer extravagant meals with hors d'oeuvres and full bars. The more elaborate receptions include many different food stations to cover a wide variety of tastes. A reception is not limited to evening; organizations can have receptions at any time.

The array of choices available during a reception is hoped to bring together a wide variety of colors to create a pleasant presentation. Because the reception can serve as a full meal, the menu planner need not worry about the compatibility of the presentation. The reception, by nature, should have something for everybody's taste.

Menu Planning the Reception. The menu planning of the reception is much different from that for the other meal options. The reception should be thought of as a buffet. A reception menu is not built around the premise that each attendee gets one plate full of food that is similar to the plates of all the other attendees. A reception is unique because each person is allowed to sample different items. Therefore, reception menus should be planned so as to allow each attendee to sample each item. The foods at a reception are usually in the form of "finger food" which is easy to eat and less cumbersome to carry. Whether one is planning a breakfast reception or a fancy evening wedding reception, the menu should be planned with these finger foods in mind.

A menu planner should take the time to map where food items will be displayed. The facility will likely sell reception food items by the dozen, per piece, or per person. Regardless of how the items are priced, the reception menu must be planned to ensure that enough of each item is purchased so that every attendee can try each. A general benchmark for most finger food reception items is to plan to have 2 to 4 pieces of each item per attendee. Granted, some attendees will pile their plates full of their favorite items, and possibly prohibit other attendees from trying those items. However, these attendees will probably avoid other items, thereby allowing others to sample.

The nature and makeup of attendees affect the number of each item as well as the nature of the reception. Due simply to differences in appetite, receptions with mostly men may need to plan higher numbers of items per person than similar functions with mostly women. The nature of the reception also affects the number of pieces needed per person. A reception that is being offered in lieu of a meal function (e.g., breakfast, lunch, or dinner) may need to offer attendees more than a reception being offered with a meal function. The reception offered alone should include more pieces of each food item per person. A reception that is followed by a meal function is intended to stimulate the appetite in anticipation of the meal to follow, so the number of pieces needed will be lower.

For many receptions, planners may want to complement finger foods with less expensive **food displays**. Food displays can consist of meats, cheeses, fruit, and so on. They can be prepared creatively by skilled kitchen staff. Food displays are so-called because they are displayed on large mirrors or other unique presentation surfaces. They look striking on reception tables and can help fill empty areas in a room or on a table. They create the perception that attendees are getting more food than they really are, which helps organizations on budgets. Food displays are often priced by weight served or per person. With per person pricing, the facility chef determines how much of each item to display. A good benchmark when looking at per pound pricing, especially with the most popular fruit and cheese displays, is to plan 1 pound of food per ten people.

Other reception complements to finger food items include two of the buffet variations covered earlier: the menu-type station and the themed station. A popular menu-type station, called a **carving station**, has a large food item, like a full turkey or steamship round of beef, that is carved by an attendant for attendees as they approach. Carving stations look striking when used with other food items. In themed stations, servers prepare food items to order. In an omelet station, for example, servers make custom omelets. Servers at an Italian pasta station can prepare different pastas by request. Nonstaffed theme stations, like fajita bars or cheeseburger stations, let attendees prepare items themselves.

The accompanying boxes list some of the more popular reception food items available in North America today. Note that many signature food items and culinary hybrids are not listed because of their vast diversity.

RECEPTION FOOD DISPLAYS

- Vegetable crudite
- Imported/domestic cheese display
- Fresh fruit display
- Salmon display
- Variety pâté display
- Bread selection with baked brie
- Antipasto display

HOT HORS D'OEUVRES

- Breaded chicken strips
- Scallops wrapped in bacon
- Stuffed mushroom caps
- Beef or chicken satays
- Petite quiche
- Crab cakes
- Spring rolls
- Coconut shrimp
- Quesadillas
- Spanikopita
- Empanadas
- Rumaki
- Beef or chicken kabobs
- Buffalo wings
- Pot stickers
- Mini Reubens
- Mini Beef Wellington
- Petite lamb chops
- Jerk chicken brochettes
- Asian baby back ribs

COLD HORS D'OEUVRES

- Salami coronets
- Herb cheese-stuffed tomatoes
- Deviled eggs
- Roma tomato with fresh mozzarella
- Stuffed snowpeas
- Mini fruit kabobs
- Cold canapés
- Chilled meat medallions (beef/lobster)
- Tea sandwiches
- Chilled seafood, including:
  - Jumbo shrimp
  - Crab claws
  - Oysters on the half shell
  - "Peel and eat" shrimp
  - Clams
- Turkey or ham pinwheels

CARVING STATIONS

- Whole roasted turkey
- Baked ham
- Steamship round of beef
- Roast tenderloin of beef (or pork)
- Prime rib
- Rack of lamb

THEMED STATIONS

- Pasta station
- Baked potato bar
- Stir fry station
- Fajita station
- Dessert station

- Frozen drink station
- Pizza station
- Nacho station
- Barbeque bar

Beverages and the Reception. The last important component of receptions is the bar. A bar can be used at any reception, regardless of the time of day. Planners can set bars up to dispense coffee and espresso in the morning or beer and liquor at night. In either case, when determining how many bars are needed, the benchmark is to plan at least one bar per fifty attendees. If the organization wants a higher level of service, the ratio can be dropped to one bar per 40 or 30 attendees. For receptions at which alcoholic drinks or other drinks for a price are being served, the planner should understand the three most common pricing options: the host bar, the cash or no host bar, and the package bar.

The Host Bar. The **host bar** simply charges the organization for all drinks consumed by the group. Usually, the menu planner decides which drinks to offer. Alcoholic drinks are classified as:

- **House brands**, which are the least expensive. Sometimes called "well brands," house brands may have generic labels or the facility's label.
- **Premium brands**, which are one level higher than house brands in terms of quality and price. Sometimes called "call brands," premium brands are popular but not the most expensive.
- **Top-shelf brands**, which are the most expensive and the highest quality brand names available for each type of drink; highest quality obtainable.

Menu planners who want to offer drinks to their attendees on a hosted basis should determine the drink type based on budget and attendee makeup. The hosted bar works well in receptions in which attendees are not heavy drinkers. Its costs could become prohibitive otherwise.

The Cash Bar. The **cash bar** charges the attendees for each drink they consume. This "no host" bar eliminates the beverage costs for the client and, in some states, reduces some legal liability. The facility, which generates the revenue from these bars, might not serve as many drinks on a cash basis as they would on a host basis because people often drink less when they pay for those drinks. As a result, many facilities charge slightly higher prices per drink for cash bars than host bars.

The Package Bar. The **package bar** plan is similar to the host bar in that the attendees do not have to pay for their drinks individually and can choose from the drinks the client offers (i.e., house, premium, and top shelf). The difference is that in a package format, the organization pays a flat rate for all attendees on a per hour basis. The cost benefit to the organization is that the attendees can drink as much as they want yet the costs remain the same. Menu planners who know that they have many heavy drinkers in attendance can appreciate the flexibility of this pricing structure. The only potential drawback is that the organization gets charged whether the attendees drink or not.

Whatever bar setup planners choose, most facilities hold organizations accountable for minimum expenditures at each bar. The most common requirement is a bartender fee. The bartender fee is imposed if the sale figure or the consumption for each bar does not exceed a certain predetermined figure.

PAINTING WORD PICTURES

This chapter has mentioned the similarities between menu planning and art. Color and all the other tools in plate presentation relate to art. The art of cuisine is a time-honored tradition that people have enjoyed for thousands of years.

The artistic components of menu planning begin before the day of the event. Menu planning must invoke positive reactions from clients at every step in the process. A catering artist uses the words on a menu to evoke positive mental images at the beginning of menu planning. This skill is called **painting word pictures**.

A well-written book lets the reader's imagination create the intended images. This is called painting a picture with words. This principle applies when planning menus. A menu that creates word pictures starts clients enjoying their meals long before they sit down to eat.

Basically, painting word pictures involves simply upgrading the words used to describe menu items. Menus can be written in a straightforward, simple way, or they can be written in a creative way that invokes thought in the reader. Descriptive words are most effective. Words like *fresh, lean,* and *light* convey the feeling of being healthy. Because the French culture has had such an impact on the art of cuisine, people often assume that any menu item using French words is more elegant or better tasting. "Broccoli au beurre" sounds better to some people than does "broccoli with butter." As menus are prepared, planners will want to use words that describe the food items and their preparation properly.

CREATING WORD PICTURES

Generic Description	Possible Word Picture
Fruit and cheese tray	International and domestic cheese display garnished with fresh fruit and served with assorted crackers
Vegetable dip	Crudite of fresh vegetables served with peppercorn ranch dip
Fruit tray	Market-fresh seasonal fruit display
After-dinner drinks	Aperitifs, cordials, and liqueurs
Continental breakfast	Assorted fresh-chilled juices, seasonal sliced fresh fruits, variety of breakfast breads and pastries, freshly brewed coffee, decaffeinated coffee, and tea service
Deli buffet lunch with soup of the day and cookies	Soup du jour; assorted sliced lean deli meats that include roast beef, smoked turkey, ham, and pastrami; a variety of sliced cheeses that include swiss, american, and provolone; relish tray with appropriate condiments; assorted rolls and sliced breads; fresh-baked chocolate chip and peanut butter cookies

It might be safe to assume that word pictures make food items seem more appealing, but extreme word pictures can be counterproductive. Overused jargon or inappropriate words can invoke negative reactions or even be misleading. A strip steak, for example, cannot be described as a filet mignon. A menu done completely in French or Italian may look great, but it is a poor tool if people cannot understand it. Using words that describe menu items appropriately but are somewhat unique is the best route. New word pictures can enhance menus without changing any items.

SAMPLE MENUS

Each food function type, when plated, has standard menu items that are appropriate and unique. Buffets also have appropriate food items depending on which food function roles they are fulfilling. Menu planners must become familiar with what clients and their attendees expect for each type. Each food function type has a virtually unlimited number and combination of menu items. Food origins and signature food items contribute to the diversity of food function menu items. Each food function type has a standard list of accepted menu items in North America.

Most facilities only slightly differentiate their plated lunch and dinner menus. The biggest differences are portion size and price. Each of these two food function types includes a salad (and/or soup), vegetable, starch, dessert, and coffee/tea/decaffeinated coffee (C/T/D). Dinner portions may also include an additional vegetable and garnish. Complimentary accoutrements to these meals often include water/iced tea, bread,

ACCEPTED MENU ITEMS FOR PLATED BREAKFAST

- **"Traditional"** Scrambled eggs, bacon and/or sausage, pancakes, breakfast potato
- **Eggs benedict** Poached eggs and Canadian bacon on an English muffin topped with Hollandaise sauce
- **"Healthy/Lite"** Like "traditional," but with substitutions to promote healthy eating (e.g., Egg Beaters® or turkey sausage)

Other items commonly used for plated breakfasts include:

- French toast
- Omelets/crepes
- Quiche
- Fruit/cheese
- Waffles
- Eggs cooked in various styles (e.g., hard/soft boiled, "sunny side" up/down, poached, scrambled)
- Breakfast steak (smaller cut of beef than that served for lunch or dinner)
- Breakfast breads (e.g., toast, bagels, pastries, muffins, croissants, English muffins)
- Oatmeal

ACCEPTED MENU ITEMS FOR PLATED LUNCH AND DINNER

Salads
- Caesar
- Tossed mixed greens
- Tossed field greens (selection of exotic greens)
- Fruit salad
- Pasta salad
- Spinach salad
- Cobb/chef's salad (salad with meats)

Soups
- Consommé (clear broth)
- Bisque (creamy seafood soup)
- French onion soup (onion soup baked with cheese on top)
- Soup du jour (soup of the day)

Desserts, while also numerous, can include:

- Assorted pies and cakes
- Tortes (European-style cakes made with little flour)
- Cheesecake
- Cobbler
- Tiramisu (sponge cake dipped in liqueur and topped with chocolate)
- Crème brûlée (custard topped with caramelized sugar)
- White or dark chocolate mousse
- Bananas Foster (bananas mixed with rum and brown sugar and served over ice cream, often lighted before serving)
- Cherries Jubilee (cherries mixed with sugar and brandy; also often lighted before serving over ice cream)

and butter. The dinner, because it is traditionally the heavier meal, may include an appetizer and/or intermezzo. The salad and dessert should be

ACCEPTED MENU ITEMS FOR BUFFETS

Breakfast Buffets

Continental Breakfast Buffet
- Assorted juices (e.g., orange, apple, tomato, grapefruit)
- Assorted breakfast breads with butter and preserves
- C/T/D

"Deluxe" Continental Buffet
Includes all items on the continental breakfast buffet plus one or more of the following:

- Whole or sliced fruit
- Assorted cereals with milk
- Assorted yogurts

Hot Breakfast Buffet
- Assorted juices
- Fresh fruit
- Scrambled eggs
- Bacon and/or sausage
- Breakfast potatoes
- Assorted breakfast breads

Lunch Buffet

"Deli-Style" Buffet
(A popular choice because it is quick and allows meeting participants to continue working through lunch)

- Choice of salads
- Soup du jour
- Relish tray (assorted sliced vegetables, like tomatoes, lettuce, onions, and pickles)
- Sliced deli meats (including turkey, roast beef, ham, corned beef, and salami)
- Sliced cheeses (including Swiss, provolone, American, and cheddar)
- Variety of breads (including rye, white, wheat, pumpernickel, kaiser rolls, and bagels)
- Appropriate condiments (including yellow and/or brown mustard, mayonnaise, and horseradish)
- Dessert
- C/T/D

Coffee Breaks
The coffee break is a special buffet exception. Some facilities create themed coffee breaks similar to the themed stations offered during receptions. While not intended as meals, coffee breaks can include many different food items. It is understood that C/T/D is also served.

- Any item listed in the continental breakfast menu box
- Assorted cookies
- Brownies

ACCEPTED MENU ITEMS FOR BUFFETS (*cont.*)

- Popcorn
- Dry snacks (including popcorn, chips, pretzels, nuts, and dips)
- Candy bars
- "Trail mix"
- Vegetable crudite
- Soft drinks
- Mineral waters
- "Make your own" sundae bar, which includes:
  - Variety of ice creams
  - Assorted toppings (including hot fudge, strawberry, caramel, chopped nuts, whipped cream, cherries, chopped cookies, and candy bits)

selected to adhere to the compatibility requirement of plate presentation.

The variations on buffets are also numerous. The widely used buffets in the accompanying box should become familiar to the menu planner.

OTHER MENU-PLANNING TIPS

- Keep the attendees' level of culinary sophistication in mind when determining the compatibility of meal items. "Meat and potato" types, who are not very adventurous, would probably enjoy their meals more if you supply familiar choices with mild preparations.
- Always try to provide at least two entrée choices of different **food categories** in every buffet. The most widely accepted food categories are beef, pork, chicken, fish, and vegetarian. For example, at an Italian buffet, the categories may be chicken picatta and veal parmesan. Those entrées enhance the color guideline while remaining compatible. An Asian-themed dinner buffet could make use of teriyaki chicken and possibly a sweet and sour pork. The rest of the buffet could include compatible items such as stir fry rice, spring rolls, and fortune cookies.
- **Menu Restrictions** Menu planners need to be cognizant of the requirements individuals and/or organizations may place on menu planning.
  - *Kosher* The Kosher meal preparation involves a combination of specific cooking techniques and the blessing of the kitchen by a rabbi. No pork can be offered. Not all facilities can provide kosher meals. The Muslim religion also forbids the eating of pork, but the other restrictions do not apply.
  - *Other Religious* The vast variety of religions in society often have disparate and unique restrictions. The average person will not know them all. If the name of an organization indicates a

religion that is unfamiliar, the menu planner should ask the organization to identify any dietary restrictions. Be aware that certain religious restrictions can apply to meal content, preparation method, time of service, alcohol, and natural versus man-made components.

- *Vegetarian* Vegetarian meals entail no meat products. Menu planners should ask their attendees exactly how strictly they want to adhere to vegetarian guidelines. Strict vegetarians, sometimes called "vegans," want no dairy products, eggs, or fish, and they may not want the facility kitchen to cook their meals with utensils used to prepare nonvegetarian meals. A few vegetarian plates are requested for most meal functions, regardless of type. Make sure the kitchen knows ahead of time how many vegetarian plates to prepare. Try to offer alternatives to the standard fruit plate, perhaps a vegetable pasta or related item.

- *Dietary* Dietary restrictions can range from a low-fat or reduced-sodium diet to certain items that cause allergic reactions. If the entire menu is to be prepared according to a certain dietary restriction, the facility chef must be involved. The chef can suggest appropriate meals a facility can prepare. In today's health-conscious society, low-cholesterol and other "heart healthy" food choices are becoming more and more popular. If they do not currently offer them, facilities should consider adding healthy, low-fat, and low-sodium menu items to their standard banquet menus. As was the case with vegetarian restrictions, menu planners are likely to get a few requests for dietary restricted meals at all functions, so they should deal with them accordingly.

- Consider the buffet. Because of the vast variety of dietary and religious restrictions people have today, the buffet is a great opportunity to give as many people a chance to enjoy the meal as possible. Menu planners will find that the buffet is most useful when large portions of the group they are working with have more than one restriction. It can be common at any meal function to have at least one or two individuals request special plates due to their restrictions. Menu planners will sound much more knowledgeable to their attendees if they understand these restrictions and can offer appropriate alternatives. (Note: The chef at any facility can provide exact details as to what the specific facility will and will not do in these instances.)

- When planning a dual or multiple entrée, be aware that the charge for the combination will be higher than that for either item alone. While they may not be as cost effective as a buffet, dual/multiple entrées offer the higher level of service of a plated meal. Dual/multiple entrées also offer another buffet benefit, which is more than one menu selection.

- Visualize the final product as part of the planning process. The near infinite variety of food preparation and presentation styles can lead to inappropriate yet unintentional selections for food functions. For example, French onion soup is a favorite of many. Would it make sense to plan a buffet with this soup? Because French onion soup is prepared and baked individually, it would not make sense for a buffet. It is better served as part of a plated meal. Menu planners who visualize how the soup is served avoid this mistake.

- Try to limit multiple entrée choices to no more than three so they do not overburden the kitchen. As much as possible, try to find starch and vegetable accompaniments that go well with each item in terms of color and compatibility. When pricing these meals, the prices should not be inflated as they were with the dual-entrée plate, because no one is really getting more food than what would normally be served. Most facilities impose a fixed price for each meal, regardless of choice. The most common pricing strategy is to charge the price of the most expensive entrée. The reasoning is that the kitchen works much harder for a meal like this than it does for a regular, single-entrée meal. Also, the individuals at a facility who are responsible for calculating a client's final bill do not always have the luxury of knowing exactly who got which entrée. It is much easier to charge one flat price.

- Remember that when planning receptions, certain finger food items can differ from the other food options. In evening receptions, for example, clients often ask for shrimp, crab, or some other seafood hors d'oeuvres. These food choices are typically much more popular than the other items being offered. The general benchmark of 2 to 4 pieces per person does not suffice. For shrimp, in particular, the guideline jumps to 5 to 8 per person. Even though shrimp is typically more expensive than most food choices, menu planners must understand how quickly people eat it. Also, next to many food items that can be replenished quickly if they run out, shrimp typically takes quite a while to prepare. Therefore, when a reception runs out of shrimp, it cannot be replenished.

UNDERSTANDING WINE

The wine component of menu planning can intimidate some people. The prevailing thought is that, unless expert in the field, one should never offer an opinion on wine. This thought is false, however, and can sacrifice revenue if held by a caterer. Wine can be a significant source of beverage revenue for a caterer.

Although in many parts of the world wine is an ordinary table beverage (in France, for example, wine is commonly served at breakfast), North Americans associate wine solely with dinner and other evening functions. Caterers should master the basics of wine to use wine properly for their clientele.

WINE ORIGINS AND TYPES

In France and Italy, two countries commonly identified as "premier wine producers," the bottles are labeled by region of origin. One example is the Bordeaux region of France, which specializes in Bordeaux wine. In America and Australia, two countries rapidly establishing reputations as quality wine producers, wine is labeled by type of grape. In the Napa Valley region of California, a winery can produce several varieties of wine at one location.

The most common types of wine are called **varietals**. Sparkling wines, like champagne and Asti Spumante, are not commonly thought of as wines but should be understood as such. The easiest way to distinguish between varietals is by color and taste.

Chardonnay and Sauvignon Blanc are considered white wines, while Zinfandel, Pinot Noir, Cabernet Sauvignon, and Merlot are considered red wines. Because of its blush color, White Zinfandel falls somewhere between. Chardonnay is the most popular wine in North America. It is characterized by straw-gold coloring, a buttery feel, and a very oak flavor. It is commonly consumed as its own cocktail as well as with meals. Sauvignon Blanc is a less popular white wine. Its traditional flavors are steel and grassy, but many wine makers have begun to store it in oak barrels to

UNDERSTANDING VARIETALS		
Varietal Name	**Color**	**Flavor**
Chardonnay	Straw	Oak, buttery
Sauvignon Blanc	From light to gold	Oak, floral
White Zinfandel	Blush	Very sweet, fruity
Zinfandel	Light red	Mild fruit, floral
Pinot Noir	Dark red	Earthy, smoky
Cabernet Sauvignon	Ruby	Rich, flavorful
Merlot	Ruby	Rich, overpowering

try to bring its taste more in line with Chardonnay. Most wine drinkers are familiar with White Zinfandel. It is relatively inexpensive, plentiful, and sweet. Many who do not like varietals enjoy the mild taste of this wine.

Zinfandel is a red wine that is relatively easy to drink. It has a fruit flavor and is more mild than some of the other reds. Pinot Noir is a very earthy red with a deep ruby color. Cabernet Sauvignon is a classic red wine that is enjoyed by many. Because of its popularity and harsh taste, it has given other red wines its reputation of being an "acquired taste." Traditional Cabernet Sauvignon is made to be stored for several years to tame its mouth-drying character. Few vintners can afford to age it properly, however. Merlot is rapidly becoming a very popular red wine. It can also be slightly harsh in taste if served before proper aging, but many wine makers are now creating new merlots that need little aging.

As a caterer, it is most important to learn the basics of pairing wine with food. Rules for doing so have relaxed in the past few years, but one remains: white wine with chicken and fish and red wine with meat. This rule is important, but it is more important to couple a wine the client likes with the meal being planned. If the client needs help choosing a wine, the caterer should ensure that the wine complements the meal. Neither the wine nor the food should overpower the other. A big, flavorful Cabernet might overwhelm a lightly seasoned chicken breast. Conversely, a mild Chardonnay would not stand up to a blackened, cajun tenderloin.

Unless directed by their clients, caterers should use their best judgment when pairing wines. A split- or dual-entrée plate could easily accommodate two wines. Therefore, a Chardonnay and a merlot are perfectly acceptable together. The caterer should bring suggested wines to the taste panel with a client. The taste panel is a good opportunity to determine which wine works with the menu under consideration. Ultimately, viewing wine as a meal enhancement ensures that the proper wine is served for any occasion.

TIPS ON WINE

- When feasible, have the group contact or VIP sample the wine being served before serving the rest of the guests. Presenting the cork and pouring a small sample glass with a bit of flourish adds some ceremony to the event.
- Generally serve wine from the right side of each guest. Never pick up the glass when pouring. Pouring wine properly takes practice. Many servers wrap cloth napkins around the bottles they are pouring to ensure that no wine spills on the tables or

guests. Turning the wrist slightly at the end of the pour helps reduce spillage.

- Always store wine in a climate-controlled environment. Store the bottles on their sides so that the liquid stays in contact with the cork. If not, the cork could dry and ruin the bottle.
- Generally, serve red wine warmer than white wine, which should be served warmer than sparkling wines. Red wine should be served in the mid to upper 60s and white wine in the upper 50s or lower 60s. Serve sparkling wine in the lower 50s.
- Always sell wine on a consumption basis. Unless the client requests a special order of a wine not commonly kept in inventory, which would necessitate a charge for all bottles, the wine can always be sold to another group. It is common to charge for all bottles opened, so caterers should not allow their staff to open more bottles than they need.
- As a gesture to clients with little wine knowledge, designate quality, but inexpensive, red and white wines as their **house wines**. The term "house wine" dates back to when many restaurants made and bottled their own wines. Those wines became the wine "of the house." Today, few restaurants or caterers make their own wines. Instead, they classify wines as house wines to demonstrate their tacit approval. The client can assume that the caterer has determined the quality of each house wine, so the decision-making process becomes less intimidating.
- If clients wish to bring their own wines, and the caterers approve, charge a **corkage fee**. A corkage fee, as its name implies, is paid to caterers for opening and pouring the wine clients bring. It is also paid to offset some of the lost beverage revenue. A corkage fee of anywhere between $5 and $10 per bottle is common.

Industry Perspective

"Creating or Revising Banquet Menus"

Kathy Ray, CMP
Director of Catering and Convention Services
Hyatt Regency, Indianapolis

Background: Ms. Ray began her hospitality career over 20 years ago. She spent 5 years with Marriott Corporation in various sales roles, moving up the ladder progressively. She crossed over into catering as a catering manager then director with Hyatt. She relocated to the west coast and spent four years with the Ritz-Carlton Corporation. She moved back to the midwest, to Indianapolis, where she has resided for the past nine years. She served as the Director of Catering and Convention Services for the Westin Hotel for seven years. After subsequently working as a meeting planner for BTI Americas and McGettigan Partners she returned to Hyatt as Director of Catering and Convention Services.

Question: "How does a hotel or banquet facility create or improve its banquet menus?"

1. **Look at your competitors—Collect and analyze data**
   - Compile current competitive menus from hotels, catering venues, and private caterers.
   - Create a spreadsheet with key menu items and add competitive pricing; analyze data.
2. **Collect banquet menus from similarly sized hotels within your chain in similar cities.**
   - Collect menus from the corporate food and beverage office. Special banquet promotions or menus may have been designed by a food and beverage team to include recipes and decor ideas. Do not "reinvent the wheel."
3. **Separate your menu into the following categories:**
   - Coffee service/refreshment breaks
   - Breakfast
   - Lunch
   - Dinner
   - Reception food
   - Beverage (alcoholic)
   - Themed events

4. **After completing your spreadsheet, organize a brainstorming session with your food and beverage director, executive chef, banquet sous chef, banquet manager, and several members of your team (e.g., catering manager, conference services manager, short-term meetings manager).**
   - Brainstorm ideas for each category of your menu.
   - Make certain that you consider "light" or "heart healthy" items, color, texture, variety, and creativity.

5. **Compile brainstorming session ideas by category. The chef and director of catering should fill holes left in the menu.**

6. **The chef or director of purchasing should "cost" the menu. Based on the chef's recipe, quantity and portion size, each item is given a cost based on current supplier pricing.**
   - Based on your budgeted food cost, assign a retail price to each item or menu.
   - Revisit your spreadsheet to see if you are in line with or ahead of your competitor's pricing.
   - Senior management will direct how to position your pricing within the city.

7. **Invite key customers from several different market segments (e.g., corporate, association, social) to attend a "blue ribbon panel" focus group to discuss and taste your "new" menus.** The goal is to answer the following questions:
   - Do the menus contain "light" or "heart healthy" selections that please various tastes?
   - Do the menus contain enough variety to please everyone?
   - Are the prices high enough but not too high?
   - Are the menu items pleasing to the palate?
   - Are the items colorful? Do they look good?
   - Are there creative or trendy items on the menu that your competitor has not or would not consider but your client would?

8. **Banquet menus can be working documents.**
   - With many desktop publishing programs on the market, you can print your banquet menus in-house, saving money and enjoying flexibility.

9. **Tips for banquet menus**
   - On each page of your banquet menus, print "Prices are subject to change."
   - On each page of your banquet menu, print "All prices are subject to X percent service charge/gratuity and X percent sales tax."

- In small letters, print the date you revised or printed the banquet menus in the lower corner of each page. This will help you to recognize each new printing.
- Print the banquet menu pages so you can send only the pages the client needs in a folder with your business card. For example, if your client is hosting a reception, he or she need not receive your breakfast menus.

10. **Pricing guidelines**
- Through senior management, determine your "menu price guarantee policy." Many hotels guarantee printed prices for 90 days; others guarantee pricing for 6 months. Determine what is best for your property.
- Some food and beverage items, like seafood, have volatile pricing due to item availability. The price can be listed as "market value."
- Do not be afraid to use seasonal items or fresh products that reflect your marketplace. Price those items at "market value." This strategy offers the client the best products at the fairest prices.

CHAPTER REVIEW

KEY CONCEPTS

Menu planning	Buffet service type	Split/dual entrée
Menu composition	Hold	Multiple entrée
Culinary hybrids	Mask	Food displays
Signature food	Reception	Carving station
Food preparation	Food station	Host bar
Menu type	Menu presentation	Cash bar
Food function types	Compatibility	Package bar
Plated service type	Prime temperature	Menu restrictions

REVIEW QUESTIONS

1. Describe the evolution and origins of culinary hybrids in North America. List some.
2. What are the differences between menu types and food function types?
3. What are the components of menu presentation, and why are they so important?

4. What are the differences between split/dual entrées and multiple entrées? What are the advantages/disadvantages between them and buffets?
5. Think of examples in which menu items would be described in more appealing ways using word pictures.

CHAPTER 6

Making the Contact

INTRODUCTION

Catering and *sales* are two words that have only recently really belonged together. The history of selling in catering is short for various reasons. The management philosophy at many hotels and catering operations was to let the business come in on its own. In hotels, groups were booked by the room sales team, and the catering revenue that came with it was considered a bonus. Catering facilities and outside catering operations never capitalized on the revenue potential for other reasons, most notably, a lack of sales training. Proactive catering sales had been a misnomer. Catering salespeople will learn in this chapter how to sell their unique product: service.

The skill needed to sell a service differs greatly from that needed to sell a product. Much of the value a customer receives from a service is implied, perceived, or felt. While the main drivers of product sales are price and quality, service sales require a greater level of customer understanding. In catering, this understanding begins with the creation of a business opportunity.

The catering sales triangle (see Figure 6–1) creates that business opportunity and enables the salesperson to begin to put the following catering success equation together:

$$\text{Optimal Event Planning} + \text{Creative Menu Planning} \times \text{Effective Selling} = \text{Maximum Catering Results}$$

The event and menu-planning components of the catering success equation are multiplied by the selling portion because the number of sales dictates the opportunity to apply the event and menu-planning components. In essence, the catering success equation hinges on the ability to create a sale. Knowledge of what is done to a business opportunity after it is created is crucial to understand during the opportunity's creation. Salespeople who know the end points of their journeys make better decisions along the way.

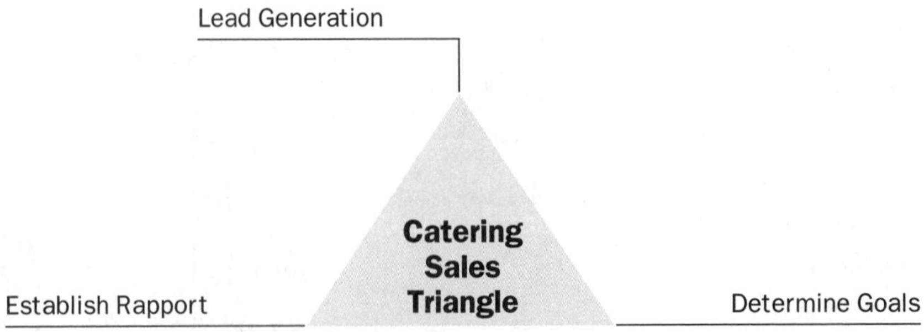

Lead Generation

FIGURE 6–1

Catering sales triangle Establish Rapport

**Catering
Sales
Triangle**

Determine Goals

Creating the sale is accomplished by implementing the points of the catering sales triangle. The catering sales triangle illustrates the notion of three sides contributing to a whole. The three main points of the sales triangle are:

1. Lead generation
2. Establish rapport
3. Determine goals

After the sale is created, it must be completed, or closed. Closing a sale is accomplished through the win triangle. Together, the win and catering sales triangles ensure that a sale is made. This chapter analyzes the two triangles and how they work together (see Figure 6–2).

In hospitality, sales situations arise that rarely can be addressed with single solutions. In fact, most sales scenarios force the salesperson to decide between three, equally important options. The catering sales triangle concept is based on the equilateral triangle (see Figure 6–3). This geometric shape has three, equal-length lines. These three sides meet at equidistant points. Taken together, these three points create the foundation for action triangles.

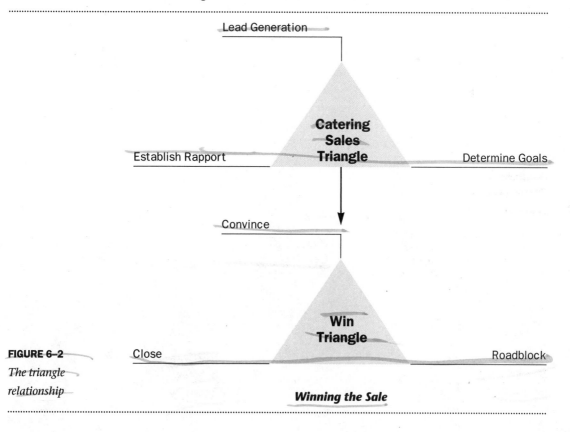

FIGURE 6–2

The triangle relationship

ACTION TRIANGLE

Each point of the sales triangle reveals additional triangles. **Action triangles** describe what salespeople must do at each point in the triangle. Action drives the process to the next step. Completing each part of the action triangle correctly compels salespeople to move along the process of creating a business opportunity. Each action triangle continues the concept of evaluating three distinct parts of one bigger whole.

After analyzing action triangles and their impact on catering sales, this chapter discusses the operational aspects of sales. Catering sales operations applies action triangles and the catering success equation to the day-to-day duties and responsibilities of a catering salesperson.

LEAD GENERATION

The most fundamental point in creating new business opportunities is the generation of interest. **Lead generation** (see Figure 6–4) is the process potential clients or salespeople undertake to generate interest. Interest creates tangible business opportunities called leads. Leads are the starting point of all catering business.

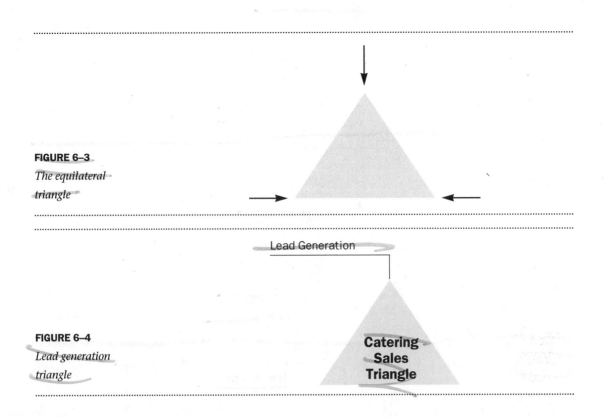

FIGURE 6–3

The equilateral triangle

FIGURE 6–4

Lead generation triangle

The action triangle within lead generation reveals the three most prevalent sources of new business: client inquiry, solicitation, and third party (see Figure 6–5).

Client Inquiry. Perhaps the most common route for catering business, inquiries originate from clients. The need for outside catering or function space at a facility generates a direct inquiry into the catering sales office (see Figure 6–6). Incoming inquiries may come in the form of a telephone call or a written **request for proposal (RFP)**. A preprinted RFP is an easy way for a client to gather proposals from many caterers at once. Inquiries generated from Internet Web sites also fall into this category. Clients who walk into facilities unannounced looking to book programs are called **walk-ins**. Walk-ins are also a client inquiry form.

Inquiries are not generated from direct actions taken by salespeople. Every catering operation has a certain level of incoming inquiry volume. Certain successful operations may not need other methods of generating new leads because their inquiry volumes are so high. It is rare for most to rely on the client inquiry exclusively.

A client who books multiple programs at once or certain programs that repeat year after year are also considered inquiry leads because there was no proactive effort taken to book the clients' subsequent business.

Solicitation. To solicit means to ask. Solicitation is the process by which salespeople proactively seek new business opportunities (see Figure 6–7). The sources for soliciting new business opportunities are numerous.

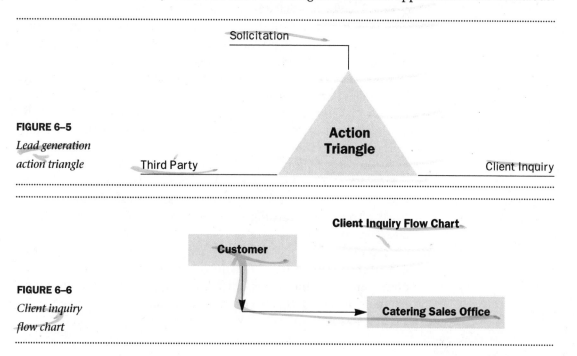

FIGURE 6–5

Lead generation action triangle

Solicitation

Action Triangle

Third Party

Client Inquiry

FIGURE 6–6

Client inquiry flow chart

Client Inquiry Flow Chart

Customer

Catering Sales Office

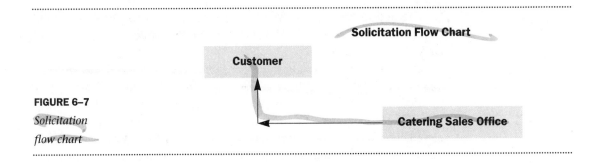

FIGURE 6–7
Solicitation flow chart

Catering operations with low client inquiry volumes often rely on these sources to generate new business.

Solicitation sources fall into four main categories: **publications**, **trace files**, **readerboards**, and **sales blitzes**. The following defines each category:

Publications. Any printed material that identifies organizations with potential catering needs is considered a publication. The following lists sample publications:

Standard & Poor's—Yearly report that publishes financial reports and data covering assets, size, profit, and so on for many companies nationwide.

Moody's Bank & Finance—Like *Standard & Poor's* in content.

Business Periodicals Index—Index of all major English-language periodicals, including *Business Week, Fortune,* and *Money.* Great resource for seeking articles on targeted businesses.

Wall Street Journal Index—Like the *Business Periodicals Index,* but strictly lists articles in the *Wall Street Journal.*

Who's Who—Reference book on top executives and major figures in the U.S. marketplace. Often lists names and phone numbers of the top-level decision makers.

Local Chamber of Commerce Directory—Listing of chamber membership.

Local Business Daily Newspapers—Usually available in large markets. Great ways to keep up on local and regional business happenings. Great resource for learning about new businesses moving into the area.

Local Telephone Book—Including telephone books of major cities nearby.

Local Office Building Roster of Tenants—If one is not available, a catering office can go to the major office buildings in the community and manually list the occupants from the directories in each lobby.

Best's Insurance Guide—A "Who's Who" of the insurance market.

The Encyclopedia of Associations—Another type of "Who's Who" listing valuable meeting information on various associations in the market-place.

National Directory of College Athletics—Lists all college coaches, athletic directors, and decision makers for the collegiate sports market.

Membership Directories of National Organizations Involved in the Hospitality Industry—Includes:

Meeting Professionals International (MPI)

Society of Government Meeting Planners (SGMP)

Professional Convention Management Association (PCMA)

American Society of Association Executives (ASAE)

Hotel Sales and Marketing Association (HSMA)

Religious Conference Management Association (RCMA)

Trace Files. Trace files are customer files that come to the attention of a salesperson on a predetermined date. This date, called a trace date, is designated by the salesperson as a time when action of some sort is needed. Trace files are collected daily by a sales assistant or appear daily on a salesperson's computer screen.

Trace files can provide tremendous information as to a client's current status, including past bookings, budget environment, where the client currently books business (if not with that catering operation), and trends in specific meeting group types and requirements. Keeping trace solicitation current avoids missed opportunities to get involved with early decisions.

The main purpose of trace files in solicitation is to stay in contact with clients. Groups who regularly book with catering operations may not need to be solicited. Groups who have not booked in a while might. Trace files are the best tool for keeping up with a client base. Trace file systems must be implemented in such a way as to ensure the catering salesperson contacts a client before the client decides on his or her next program or event. Trace file systems must be kept current, because competitive caterers also use them. Salespeople without manual or computerized trace systems can use simple notations on a calendar to solicit.

Trace files and trace dates are not used only for solicitation, however. Trace dates are useful for following up with groups for signed contracts, menu needs, and so on. They remind salespeople that something must be done. Trace file systems can also weed out organizations that have gone out of business or are no longer valid.

If, in the process of following up on trace files, salespeople find that listed contracts are not current, they should try to note the names of other contacts. Whether that name replaces the name of the original contact or the name of another potential meeting planner, it should be noted in the trace file. This process of determining new sources of business within an organization is called **account penetration**. It works well in obtaining all the business an organization offers.

Trace files cannot be the only solicitation tools salespeople use. A typical file base shrinks 1 to 5 percent per year due to factors like company moves, takeovers, and bankruptcy. A catering operation finds that over time, simply relying on existing business results in fewer and fewer opportunities.

Readerboards. The best way for banquet facilities to keep abreast of the competition is to know who is doing business with them. Most hotels and meeting centers post daily event sheets or scrolling television monitors of functions. Figure 6–8 shows a sample readerboard.

The readerboard is most valuable for stand-alone facilities that compete with hotels and other stand-alones. A catering operation can use the readerboard to identify organizations booking specific meal function types. A meal function can theoretically be put on at other venues, so the outside catering organization may be able to find new sources of business. Readerboards are therefore a great way to find out which organizations are booking at the competition. Competitive readerboards identify only new business opportunities for salespeople, because those businesses are not using the salespeople's services.

It is imperative that a catering sales team gathers readerboard information from competitive facilities in a timely manner. This duty is divided among team members. The results of this information gathering should be discussed with all sales team members, however. Salespeople should follow up on this information and find out why these organizations are not using them. The only acceptable reasons as to why the competition has business are: (1) the caterer did not want the business (i.e., the business was inappropriate for its needs) or (2) the caterer could not

FIGURE 6–8

Readerboard

accommodate the business (e.g., the menu and/or service requirements were too intricate or the group was too large).

There are more reasons clients choose competitors (e.g., quality, service levels, value). Readerboards allow salespeople to uncover those reasons, then take whatever corrective actions are needed.

Sales Blitzes. The sales blitz is a unique tool that allows for blanket sales penetration of a geographical area. The sales blitz used for catering is similar to the sales blitz used by manufacturers of food products. In major metropolitan areas, food manufacturers often hire many individuals to stand on street corners and hand out free samples of their products. The hospitality sales blitz is limited to the sales staff on hand and there are no free samples, but the concept of creating awareness is the same.

A sales blitz should be limited to the geographical area within a caterer's **sphere of influence**. A sphere of influence is the reach of an organization's brand recognition. Sales blitzes are used primarily in the early or preopening stages of catering sales offices in hotels and stand-alone facilities. A preopening sales office is often opened before the facility is opened to generate community awareness and book business once the facility opens. A sales blitz can be a fun way for a sales office to create community awareness as a group. Existing catering operations can incorporate sales blitzes into their marketing plans as well. In addition to serving in preopening stages, blitzes can introduce new services or allow caterers to reenter areas that have been neglected.

To succeed, sales blitzes must be planned properly with proper direction. The sales team should first determine where to target and whom. Downtown facilities have an easy job, because they can saturate an office tower or a block. Regardless of location, a sales team must determine where it wants to go. A good starting point are the companies near their competition or office parks.

Once the geographical area is determined, the team must decide what it wants to accomplish during the blitz. Sales blitz objectives can include:

- Announcements of new corporate meetings programs
- Value dates or discounted menu promotions
- New catering offerings, like an "express" lunch menu that provides fast service
- Literature highlighting a new off-premise AV service that services meetings not held at a hotel or banquet facility
- Announcement of recent function room renovations or enhancements
- Contests or giveaways

Whatever the objective, implementation should be classy and creative. A catering team should avoid simply distributing brochures and menu packets. This tired practice wastes time and money. Instead, the catering team should distribute materials while introducing a new product or service. Involve kitchen staff in the sales process by including them in the blitz.

Third Party. **Third-party leads** differ from the client-inquiry and solicitation methods of generation in that another entity is included in the process. A third-party lead comes to a caterer from someone other than the client (see Figure 6–9). A third party acts on the client's behalf in the search for an appropriate meeting location or catering need.

Third parties are becoming more and more prevalent in the catering industry. Due to corporate downsizing and other factors, many organizations are looking outside of their staff for meeting and/or catering planning services. Whereas at one time most organizations had in-house departments that handled meeting/travel/catering needs, today these organizations are deciding to focus on their core strengths and to **outsource** ancillary functions. Outsourcing is the concept by which an organization

---

COMMON THIRD PARTIES

- Travel Agency—Travel agents are primarily used for individual business travel. The travel agent coordinates many aspects of a traveler's trip, including hotel, airline, and transportation. Some large agencies are adding meeting/event planning departments to handle the meeting/convention market in this era of outsourcing.
- Independent Meeting Planning Firm (or Individual)—These organizations' sole purpose is to conduct searches and aid their clients in deciding on and/or conducting meetings and conventions. In many instances, the facility has no contact with the attendees until they arrive. This type of third-party lead is becoming very common. Some of the largest third parties in today's market, namely McGettigan Partners, Conferon, Krisam and Helms Briscoe, account for a large portion of a caterer's business.
- Convention and Visitors Bureau (CVB)—The CVB is another form of third-party lead generator that is most often used as an assisting service for meeting planners from outside a particular area. The CVB determines the basic needs of the client and distributes the information to the appropriate facilities. The service a CVB provides helps eliminate wasted time for clients in that only the caterers that are appropriate for the potential function are included. Many CVBs put together calendars that list organizations booked from within the local community. These calendars, like readerboards, are good places for salespeople to find citywide and other convention-center-related business that has not booked with them.
- National Sales Office (NSO)—The NSO is a third-party lead generator available only to medium to large hotel chains. An NSO is located in major cities like New York; Washington, DC; Chicago; and Los Angeles. These NSOs are staffed with salespeople who actively seek business for their respective chains. An NSO salesperson stationed in Washington, DC, may call on national associations that have meeting needs throughout the nation and distribute the leads to his or her hotels in the appropriate locations. The NSO acts like an extension of a hotel's sales team.

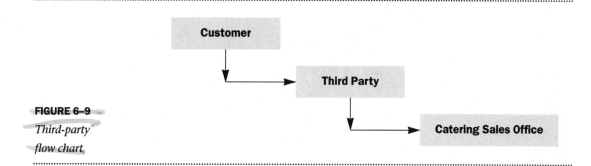

FIGURE 6–9

Third-party flow chart

focuses on its core product/service(s) and designates other organizations that specialize in ancillary functions outside these core strengths to perform on their behalf.

The outsourcing of meeting planning and/or catering services has given rise to organizations whose sole purpose is to serve others by selecting caterers and facilities. These third parties also select hotels, airlines, car-rental agencies, and other travel services.

The NSO is funded by the hotel chain, and the CVB is funded by local taxes or membership fees collected from participating hotels. Third parties outside the NSO and CVB must charge for their services in some way. Travel agencies and independent meeting planners make their money by charging flat management fees or by booking sleeping rooms at a **commissionable rate**. A commissionable rate is understood throughout the industry to include a 10 percent addition to the net room rate. This commission is paid to the travel agent or meeting planner once the guests pay for their rooms. In most cases, only agents and planners who have been issued identification numbers by the International Association of Travel Agents are eligible for a commission.

With the lead generated, it becomes time for salespeople to move along in the sales process. At this point, they must take action, which is to establish rapport (see Figure 6–10).

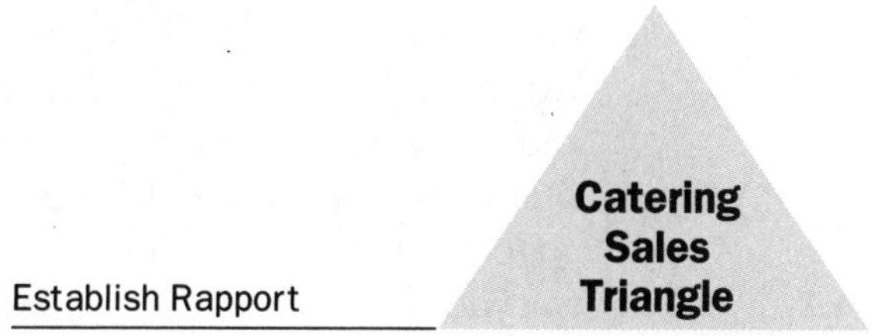

FIGURE 6–10

Establish rapport triangle

Establish Rapport

Catering Sales Triangle

Industry Perspective

"The Role of the Convention and Visitor Bureau"

John Pohl
Convention Sales Manager
Lexington Convention and Visitor Bureau

The CVB serves as an independent agent between hotels and meeting planners of all kinds. Its ultimate aim is to bring business into a city or region. Following is a list of what a CVB does and how it does it:

1. CVBs provide the meeting coordinator an avenue in which to send convention requests for proposals (RFPs) to appropriate hotels and facilities based on the room block, location or meeting space requirements, and catering need. These RFPs include detailed instructions for responses, past rate information, preferred dates, and historical information on the group room pickup. The CVB turns this RFP information into bureau leads, which are in turn sent to the hotels and facilities. These leads provide hotels with receptive organizations currently looking at their cities and/or facilities for bookings.

2. The general aim of a CVB is to conduct an overall city sell. When responding to an interested meeting planner, the CVB provides information on attractions, facilities, and other related information pertinent to the planner's meeting needs (e.g., technical tours, golf outings and field outings). The CVB represents the entire hospitality community, which may include outside caterers, restaurants, local arrangement companies, and transportation/bus companies. The CVB also provides the meeting planner information on local logistics, laws, and celebrations/events, as well as maps, assorted brochures, and quick answers that save the planner time and money.

3. Members of the CVB staff attend trade shows and exhibit-oriented events to try to promote their city and its facilities to interested planners. These exchanges occur throughout the year. Some of the larger ones include events sponsored by ASAE and MPI. Other large events are Spring Time in the Park and Destination Showcase. All these events give meeting planners opportunities to review meeting locations they may have never considered.

ESTABLISH RAPPORT

Once a lead has been generated, it must be analyzed and qualified. **Qualification** is the process a salesperson undergoes to determine the characteristics of a business opportunity. Qualification uncovers the "who, what, where, when, and why" (5 *W*s) of a piece of business. Qualification of business is considered the first step, and one of the most important, in catering sales.

What this quote says to the salesperson is "do your homework." Not in the academic sense, but do your homework in the analysis of a business opportunity. A salesperson's homework begins with qualification.

The qualification process begins and ends with questions. The salesperson must be able to ask the right questions at the right time. In fact, asking appropriate questions is a skill that applies to all aspects of hospitality sales. Asking is the only way an answer can be given. Whether administered verbally or via written correspondence, qualification must endeavor to reveal as many of the 5 *W*s as possible.

Questions that require more than one word replies are open ended. Words like *why, how,* and *what* bring people out of naturally occurring defensive states and encourage conversation. An open-ended question brings out more information than the opposite type of question, close ended. A close-ended question invariably ends with a "yes" or "no" response. Questions that begin with *is* or *if* often lead to one-word answers (yes or no).

Qualification should be considered a fact-finding mission. It is *not* an appropriate time for salespeople to make or imply commitments. The time taken to ask questions gives salespeople insight into the personalities and characters of their contacts. Qualification begins the process of establishing customer rapport. Qualification begins the thought process in the mind of the salesperson of whether to pursue or decline a business opportunity. In addition to asking qualifying questions, catering salespeople must bring their contacts into comfortable, relaxed states of mind so that as much information is gathered as is possible. Creating a sense of free and open exchange is called **establishing rapport**.

Establishing rapport between a salesperson and a client creates an environment in which both parties reveal as much information to each other as business guidelines permit. The feeling a client perceives when rapport is established allows for full qualification and analysis.

True rapport is established only when the three points of this action triangle, create comfort, ensure trust, and demand confidence, are realized (see Figure 6–11).

Rapport begins to be established with a **mental inventory**. A mental inventory is a list of specific personality traits and idiosyncrasies that

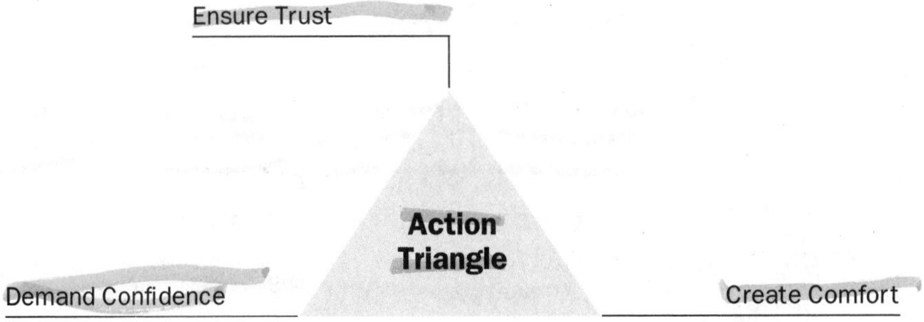

FIGURE 6–11

Establish rapport
action triangle

QUALIFYING A BUSINESS THROUGH THE 5 WS

Who
- Name and title of the client
- Name of the organization, address, telephone, fax, E-mail address
- Name of the function, if applicable
- Name(s) of the **decision maker**(s) (individual or group who makes the final decision on which caterer a business opportunity will choose). Identification of the decision makers will aid in the sales process later on.

What
- What menus are needed?
- What are the general banquet requirements? What are the function space requirements (square footage needs)? How many meetings, meals, and/or displays will be needed? How many attendees will be at each event?
- What is the organization's budget for this meeting?
- What is the purpose of the proposed function? What outcome do the planners wish to achieve?
- Is there a message that must be delivered? The message may be one of celebration, enlightenment, training, promotion, or some other general theme that the planners wish to relay to the attendees.

Where
- Is this city the only one under consideration? If so, is the client looking at other catering operations?
- Is the hotel or banquet facility a reflection of the intended message? Is the hotel or banquet facility of choice based on its location?

When
- What are the preferred dates? Is the program flexible in dates?
- Has this program been held before? What was successful in prior programs?
- How often is this program held?

Why
- Why is the particular hotel/facility under consideration?
- Why this city (if applicable)?

relate to the contact or organization in question. A salesperson who is establishing rapport with a client must first determine the client's type.

The first step in taking a mental inventory of the client is examining the catering file, if available. Each organization should have a catering file. Even if the caterer has never done business with the organization, the file should include any written correspondence and notes summarizing phone and E-mail conversations. These notes are often called a **running call report**. A running call report outlines the requests and specifics of all the business opportunities an organization has tried to bring to a catering operation.

A call report can give insight into contacts at an organization, if those contacts have been with the organization for substantial periods. If contacts continuously request specific considerations, those requests can be documented in the call report. The call report, in combination with other items, like past menus and catering contracts, indicates specific traits of the organization. These traits are called a **customer profile**.

The customer profile may be written into the call report, or it may be listed on a file cover sheet in the file. The cover sheet is intended to serve as an "at a glance" resource for a salesperson to review customer traits quickly.

The mental inventory process continues with the qualifying questions asked with each business opportunity and the range of answers that are given. The use of open-ended questions to extract information from a client adds to the salesperson's database of knowledge. This information lays the groundwork for establishing rapport.

COMMON CUSTOMER PROFILE TRAITS

- Customers are commonly conscious of banquet function budgets.
- Complimentary items are always requested. Some groups ask for free meal functions to be sponsored by the catering operation (continental breakfasts and receptions are most common). Large conventions may require that a hotel or banquet facility provide entirely complimentary accommodations for a planning committee or board that convenes months before the convention.
- Catering clients may ask to sample the food being planned for an upcoming meal function before the event to determine which items will be served. This is called a **taste panel**.
- Some clients may not respond to the salesperson in a timely manner with requisite information. The tendency to procrastinate may be a reflection of the organization, not the client.
- Organizations may require smoke-free function rooms, they may mandate strict no-alcohol policies at receptions, or they may impose certain menu restrictions on meals.

> *Endeavor to listen twice as long as you speak.*
>
> UNKNOWN

Create Comfort. The mental inventory does more than simply uncover information on customer traits. It helps the salesperson communicate well with the customer. Creating a sense of comfort with a client begins at the most basic level of human interaction, **communication**.

Communication is the process of transmitting a message from a sender to a receiver. Communication is vital to achieving goals such as selling, warning, enlightening, and entertaining. To create comfort, salespeople must get the most out of client communication. This primarily entails listening.

Listening is the only way a receiver can hear the message a sender is transmitting. Salespeople cannot fully qualify or effectively create mental inventories if they spend all their time with clients talking. Salespeople should hear the subtle hints and signals clients may give during communication.

Create comfort by listening and getting to know the client. If the client prefers to discuss the weather or other topics before discussing the program, the salesperson should do so. In contrast, salespeople should allow clients who avoid "chit chat" to quickly address topics of interest. Salespeople should avoid the trap of overusing catering jargon. Terms like *painted plate* or *food station* may be unfamiliar to inexperienced meeting planners. Unfamiliar communication often becomes uncomfortable communication. Comfortable clients provide salespeople with much more useful information. It is up to salespeople to create comfort.

Ensure Trust. Salespeople who position themselves as people who understand what is important to clients lay the foundation of trust. Trust lies at the heart of the next point in the process of establishing rapport. Ensuring that clients trust salespeople begins by creating comfort in the first stage. It continues with the salespeople's words and actions.

Salespeople can convey trust to clients by adhering to two main rules: (1) be completely honest and (2) conduct thorough followup.

Whether justified or not, the image of a "salesperson" differs greatly from person to person. Many people in modern society innately distrust salespeople, simply because they feel that salespeople must deceive to sell.

LISTENING DURING CLIENT COMMUNICATION

A client who states:	May actually mean:
"My boss will attend this meeting."	"I'm concerned with the impression of my superior."
"We want a relaxed general session."	"We picture a large, open meeting room with plenty of space."
"I cannot sign this confirmation."	"I am not the decision maker."
"We need fast meal service."	"We prefer buffet-style meals."
"We prefer a late checkout."	"We are picturing a 5:00 P.M. checkout."

In the catering industry, as in many others, clients often have preconceived notions.

In the vast majority of buyer-seller relationships, nothing is concealed and no deception ever occurs. Salespeople must dispel all the client's preconceived notions as soon as possible. The only way to do this is with complete honesty.

If salespeople cannot accurately answer client questions, they should say so immediately. Candid revelations of the sellers' weaknesses are always appreciated by clients. Caterers who cannot fully execute customer requests should explain why up front. Caterers should suggest alternatives only if those alternatives genuinely meet the customers' needs. Alternatives that do not may be perceived poorly and erode any foundation of trust.

Trust is built with honesty and commitment. Salespeople must be as committed to their clients as they are to booking business. Commitment is exemplified by thorough and complete followup on requests. When salespeople are asked to send information, research answers to questions, or return phone calls, they should do so immediately. Commitments made by catering salespeople are made on behalf of the operation, and quick, complete followup on these commitments enhances the foundation of trust.

A solid foundation of trust can elevate the salesperson-client relationship to a friend-friend relationship. A client who feels comfortable and who trusts a salesperson will return again and again. No amount of marketing or advertising can buy what trust creates in a client: genuine customer loyalty.

Demand Confidence. At this point of the establishing rapport process, the salesperson must take charge. If comfort has been created and trust ensured, the client and the salesperson move to another level. Demanding confidence in an implicit, not explicit way makes clients feel they would be remiss if they did not allow for continued action (see Figure 6–12).

A salesperson's actions speak louder than words here by reminding the client of what got the two of them to that point in the first place. The salesperson and client would not be communicating in good conscience

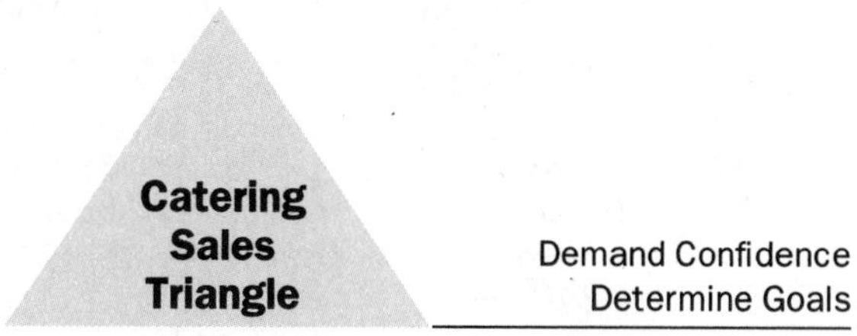

FIGURE 6–12

Demand confidence

Catering Sales Triangle

Demand Confidence
Determine Goals

were it not for the reasonable reputation of either party. The client would not allow continuing negotiations if the potential of booking was improbable. The catering salesperson would not continue establishing rapport with a client representing an inappropriate organization.

Confidence adds to the mental inventory of the salesperson by supplementing intuitive impressions with **human markers**. Human markers complete the picture of how and why clients react the ways they do.

BODY LANGUAGE

- Salespeople must be observant in face-to-face meetings with clients. In effect, the listening role moves from the ears to the eyes. Salespeople should ask themselves questions like:

  How does this person carry him- or herself?
  What is the person's expression? Is it relaxed and trusting or aggressive and confrontational?
  What does the person's mood or personality reveal? In the creating comfort stage, it can become apparent that a person is having a "bad day." An aggressive personality may want to take charge of all further discourse, while a timid person may defer to the salesperson.

- Arms crossed on the chest may indicate a defensive posture that should be noted.
- A client who leans across a desk toward a salesperson may have an aggressive personality or mood.
- Strong eye contact indicates confidence.
- A firm handshake always makes a good first impression.

DISCOURSE LEVEL

- Conversation between client and salesperson can reveal much about personality and mood (both in person and over the phone). The voice must be viewed as a tool; however a client chooses to use his or hers is another marker.

  Is the conversation often interrupted and the client distracted? That could indicate a lack of interest or time.
  Balance the vocabulary level with the client whenever possible. That may mean minimizing jargon or researching the client's organization or interests. It can be very impressive to a client when a salesperson takes the time to learn about the client's organization. Use of terminology the client can appreciate or tidbits of news that applies to the client's industry can be dramatic.

- Written communication can reveal additional insight.

  A client who favors handwritten notes over formal letters may have an informal management style, which should be noted.
  Intricate and lengthy RFPs often indicate that the client is concerned with each detail. Solid review of all aspects of a business opportunity is warranted in these cases.

Human markers help build rapport by revealing traits and insights that are not readily apparent. Some markers, like body language and discourse level, are addressed here briefly, but in-depth analysis can be found in advanced texts.

Markers can help compile a mental inventory. Thorough understanding of the client invariably leads to confidence. With confidence ensured, the process moves to the crux of hotel sales. The next action triangle addresses the "what" of a client's needs and wants: determining goals.

CHAPTER REVIEW

KEY CONCEPTS

Lead generation	Readerboards	Create comfort
Client inquiry	Sales blitz	Ensure trust
Solicitation	Third party	Demand confidence
Trace files	Establish rapport	Human markers

REVIEW QUESTIONS

1. Name solicitation sources for catering sales other than those listed in this text.
2. What goes into a salesperson's mental inventory?
3. Why does the triangle concept work so well for catering sales techniques?

CHAPTER 7

Closing the Sale

INTRODUCTION

Once the lead has been generated and rapport established, it is time to close the sale. This chapter looks at the last two steps of the action triangle sales process: **determining goals** and winning the sale. Additional tools for closing a sale in hospitality and catering are also discussed.

DETERMINING GOALS

On the surface, it may seem that many consumers simply make purchases without underlying goals as motivators. On closer examination, however, that assumption proves false.

GOAL

A **goal** in the hotel sales process is simply an objective. The objective in pursuing a hotel for services can vary greatly from one client to another. All clients have underlying goals or needs that drive their buying decisions. The motivations of individuals to select products or services must be determined by the salespeople who want to close the sales.

The goals in the accompanying case study may have triggered the consumer's buying decision, or something else may have. The point of this case is to prompt thought into the "what" or goal that all consumers share when deciding on a purchase. It is the same process for hotel consumers when they decide on caterers.

The process of determining client goals combines elements applied in the qualifying and rapport-building processes. The task of asking the open-ended questions that make clients comfortable and yield information is eased with trust.

To determine the client's goals, the salesperson may ask, "Why is quality important to you for this dinner?" The client may respond, "We

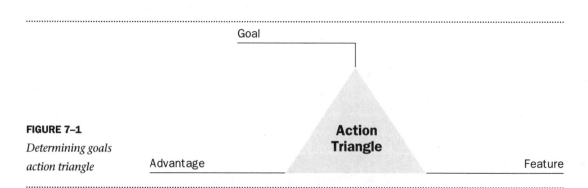

FIGURE 7–1

Determining goals action triangle

Goal

Action Triangle

Advantage

Feature

CASE STUDY

Theoretical Buying Decision

QUESTION: "What can motivate a consumer to choose one option over another?"

BACKGROUND: A consumer has an empty tank of gas. He is equidistant from two gas stations. One is on the left and one on the right. (See Figure 7–2.) Assume each is equally accessible.

What makes the consumer choose the station on the right over the one on the left? Is it a whim, or is there an underlying goal? As a consumer, what makes the individual choose between two similar options (see Figure 7–3)?

This consumer chose Station B for a reason, even if that reason is not readily apparent. The driver may not even know that reason. The motivation, or goal, of this driver may have included one or more of the following:

- Value—The price for gas at Station B may have been lower than that at Station A.
- Quality—The consumer may have wanted the performance-enhancing options of Station B's gas.
- Service—Station B may wipe windows or pump gas for the consumer.
- Reputation—Word of mouth or other forms of advertising may have triggered the consumer's decision.
- Other Factors—The convenience store in station B may have a draw, the consumer may have known the owner, the consumer may have patronized the station for years out of habit, or the station may have been brightly lighted or closer to home.

are looking to roll out a new product and the perception of the meal will reflect on us." This question uncovered two goals:

1. The salesperson understands that the new product rollout and the impression the client gives are important to the client.
2. The salesperson understands the client's attendees. With quality as a goal, the salesperson immediately knows which areas of the

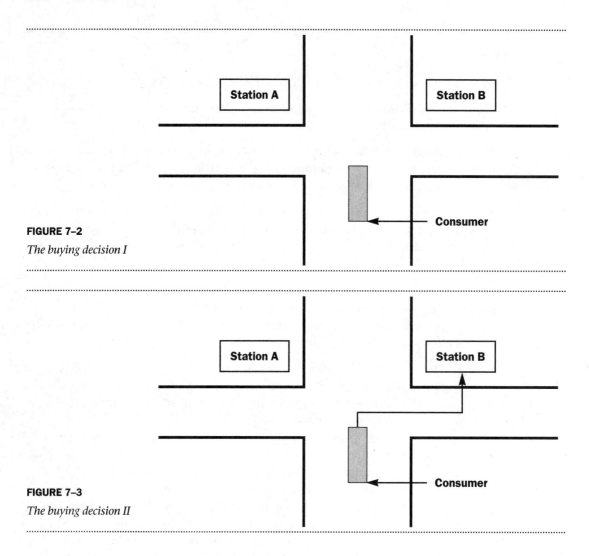

FIGURE 7–2

The buying decision I

FIGURE 7–3

The buying decision II

hotel/banquet facility to use as function space and considers menu enhancements. Budget may be less of an issue to clients concerned with image.

As goal determination continues, the salesperson should note those goals, as well as those of the organization, in the running call report and/or customer profile.

In catering sales, clients may express many goals. This chapter discusses three goals that are common across client or food function type: value, quality, and service.

A client's goals are not typically uncovered in one phone call or meeting. It may take several conversations to fully establish rapport and determine all goals. Other resources available to the salesperson in uncovering goals are research into the organization's file, discussion with sales office teammates for further insight and experience, and review of the events put on by similar organizations.

FEATURE

Uncovering goals is the first step in ensuring a sale. Knowledge of goals alone does nothing to further the sales process, however. Goals must be matched with **features** for sales to move. A feature is an aspect of the catering operation that can be shown to, felt by, or touched by the client in some way. A feature is not implied or promised. It must be demonstrable.

If a client reveals that menu creativity is a goal, for example, the caterer's matching feature would be a list of unique menu items. Salespeople who state that they can easily make different menus do not match tangible features to goals. Unique menus can be shown and appreciated by the client, which makes those menus features.

Done properly, the matching of goals to features convinces clients that caterers can meet their needs. Skilled salespeople can outsell competitors in identical catering operations, because they can make clients believe they are better suited.

Features show that caterers can meet goals with their tangible attributes. Features do not ensure that sales are made, however. Sales are made when goals and features are coupled with advantages.

ADVANTAGE

At this point in the sales process, the client has been shown that the caterer's features match his or her goals. The final step in creating a sale is to show a client how the feature-to-goal match will benefit him or her. Salespeople must show clients how it would be advantageous to buy from them.

An **advantage** is the result of matching a goal to a feature and the benefit the client gains from the combination. An advantage can be

MATCHING GOALS AND FEATURES	
Goal	**Feature**
Value	New low-season sales calendar, which offers reduced rates on menus during certain times of the year.
Quality	Industry awards, such as four star or diamond designations. Kitchen staff certifications and background.
Service	Testimonial letters from pleased clients. Employee training programs. Upgraded/new equipment.

expressed to a client in personal or intangible ways. As opposed to features, which must be seen or experienced, advantages can be implied. A picture in a client's mind of how features meet his or her goals is an advantage. The combination of goal, feature, and advantage cements the buying decision, because the sale has now become in the client's best interest.

WINNING THE SALE

The flow that was created between all three components of the catering sales triangle ensures that a sale is generated, but the process of selling does not end there. The sale must be closed, or won. Without this final step in sales, all the salesperson's work is wasted.

Winning the sale is the ultimate aim of any salesperson. To do that, the goals, features, and advantages must flow from start to finish without detour. As the arrow shows in Figure 7–4, the win triangle takes over from the sales triangle after advantages have been matched to features and goals. The points in the win triangle—convince, close, and roadblock—ensure sale closure.

CONVINCE

The convince step in the win triangle is in place for the salesperson to summarize and prepare for closure. The salesperson must review with the client the features and advantages that have been matched to the client's goals. If needed, each feature and advantage can be reinforced by restating it to the client. The best tool for ensuring reinforcement is client **affirmation**.

Gaining affirmation, or agreement, from the client that goals have been met by features and advantages is a useful sales device. A client who

RELATING GOALS, FEATURES, AND ADVANTAGES

Goal	Feature	Advantage
Value	New low-season sales calendar, which offers reduced rates on menus during certain times of the year.	Clients may now be able to afford a level of quality was not possible before without exceeding spending limits.
Quality	Industry awards, such as four star or diamond designations. Kitchen staff certifications and background.	A quality meal reflects well on the client.
Service	Testimonial letters from pleased clients. Employee training programs. Upgraded/new equipment.	A high service level ensures a lower anxiety level for a client during a function.

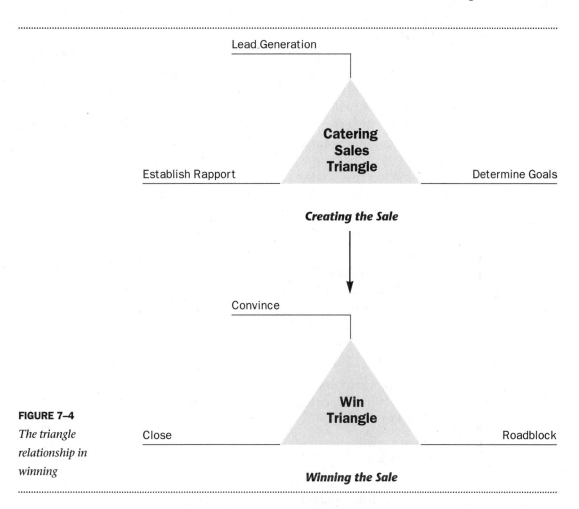

Lead Generation

Catering Sales Triangle

Establish Rapport   Determine Goals

Creating the Sale

Convince

Win Triangle

Close   Roadblock

Winning the Sale

FIGURE 7–4

The triangle relationship in winning

affirms agrees that the best choice is being discussed. Salespeople can simply ask clients to affirm that the features and advantages meet their goals using statements like, "Do you realize that our catering company has been awarded the five-star quality designation 10 years running? That fact addresses your initial goal of quality, does it not?" An affirmation indicates that the goal has been met.

This process of review and affirmation can continue, if needed, goal by goal. If the client is overwhelmingly positive, further affirmation may be unnecessary. When building rapport, the salesperson should have gotten a fairly good idea of when the client is reacting positively.

Affirmation brings the sales process to the next point in this triangle, the close. Negative reactions to all affirmation attempts take the salesperson to the last point, which is the roadblock.

CLOSE

Affirmation that all goals are met or exceeded by the features and advantages have predetermined the fate of the sale. The sale is made at this point. What often hinders salespeople from realizing final sales is the easiest step: *Ask for the business!*

Often forgotten by rookie salespeople, the simple act of asking for clients' business formally ensures sale closure. Too often salespeople take the steps of building rapport and determining goals, only to stop. The assumption that a sale has been made does not close a sale. Affirmation may signal that the client is willing to close the sale, but until the salesperson requests the business, the business is unsecure. Salespeople may ask for business using the following questions:

- May I send you a contract?
- Can we confirm this business together?
- How long do you need before I can expect a signed contract returned?
- May I start working on your final menus?
- Should I turn away other groups interested in your function space?

If the client does not provide affirmations or responds to business requests with indecision or worse, indifference, the salesperson has hit a roadblock.

ROADBLOCK

If during the convince and close phases of the win triangle the sale cannot be concluded, a **roadblock** is reached. Roadblocks can be anything, but most commonly they are uncovered or hidden client goals. It becomes obvious that something is delaying the sale when there is no affirmation during the convince phase. A roadblock can also manifest itself when the business is asked for and the client reaction is indecision.

A roadblock cannot be overcome unless the salesperson attempts to uncover it. As Figure 7–5 shows, the salesperson must return to the determining goals action triangle and try to redetermine goals.

In catering sales, there are numerous potential roadblocks. The nature of each depends greatly on the client, the client's organization, the catering operation, and the surrounding marketplace. Experienced salespeople find certain roadblocks recur due to certain factors.

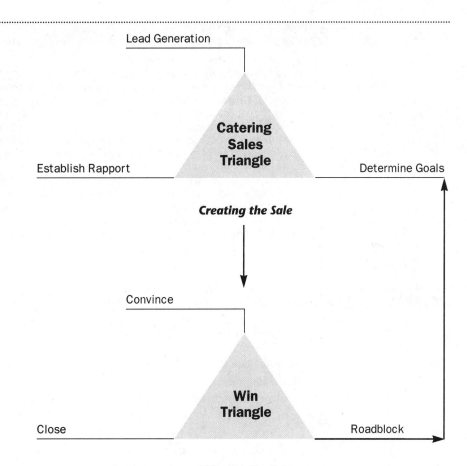

FIGURE 7–5

The roadblock

COMMON ROADBLOCKS

- **Wrong Contact**—During qualification, the salesperson did not determine the correct decision maker. A contact who is not authorized to make a decision cannot commit to a program, no matter how well needs were met.
- **Catering Menu Prices**—Roadblocks generated by high catering costs are somewhat difficult to overcome. If the impact of a business opportunity is high enough, upper management may allow for discounted menu prices. Many catering operations also have the opportunity to create special budget-sensitive menus that can be offered to clients with cost concerns. These menus are less substantial than regular menus. Often, small price reductions are viewed as signs of "good faith" by clients and major reductions are not necessary.
- **Room Rental**—Room rental is viewed by many facilities as a pure profit revenue source. Others mandate strict adherence to room rental dollars per square foot of function space. A client who objects to room rental due to client education level or market tolerance may be placated with a room rental **sliding scale**. A sliding scale ties room rental price to revenue performance. The more money spent, the lower the rental.

COMMON ROADBLOCKS (*cont.*)

- **Function Space Size or Condition**—If in the course of negotiation a client goes back again and again to the amount of function space being offered, the salesperson must review the entire program carefully. If the amount of space being offered at a hotel corresponds to the number of sleeping rooms being used (rooms-to-space ratio) and a banquet facility has properly allocated the function space (space intensity), additional function space may be offered at higher prices. If no other space is available and dates are not flexible, a hotel and/or banquet facility could get creative in allocating the space a group may be able to use for functions. Large suites, meeting room hallways, and prefunction areas may be designated as function space for a group if the business warrants it. Meeting quality or condition, if less than optimal, can often be overcome by discounting menus or offering complimentary **meeting packages**. A meeting package can include popular food or beverage items (e.g., continental breakfast, coffee breaks) or AV items (e.g., slide projectors, screens, flipcharts).

CATERING SALES COMMUNICATIONS

The sales principles in this text must be communicated for business to be booked. Sending a message from the originator (the catering salesperson) to a receiver (the client) is the basis of communication. The tools used in effective sales communication are varied. A strong foundation in the basics allows salespeople to apply those skills to whatever communication form is desired.

In catering, there are two basic types of communication: external and internal. **External communication**, which is needed to communicate with clients and others outside the facility, is reviewed in this chapter. **Internal communication**, which is used to inform and prepare departments within a facility, are addressed in the next chapter.

External communication forms are used in catering to effectively and eloquently express the three points of the catering success equation to clients. They are also used to communicate with competitors, third parties, suppliers, and vendors. The first two important vehicles of external communication examined here are catering sales letters and phone conversations. Later in this chapter, other communication forms are reviewed, namely booking status, contracts, and customer contacts.

CATERING SALES LETTERS

Letters come in various forms, each conveying a specific message. Today, letters can be used with computers to communicate via E-mail or the Internet. However, most business transactions in the catering industry are still communicated via traditional written letters. Each method of communication is called a vehicle, because it provides a means of letter writing. Whatever vehicle is used, the catering salesperson should know how to compose the best letters.

In every facet of catering sales, the messages must be conveyed effectively and eloquently while adhering to accepted business-letter-writing principles.

In written correspondence, as in verbal communication, clarity and accuracy are very important. Many books have been written on the art and style of letter writing. Correspondingly, a vast variety of letter styles and formats exist today. Although most catering salespeople do not actually type letters (administrative assistants usually assume that function), it still is a good idea to understand how to compose a well-written letter. One of the most commonly used letter styles today is the block letter format. On the left side of the following example is a sample letter using block letter format. On the right, each part of the letter is defined. This letter is not to scale. Actual letters include the correct number of spaces from the top of a blank page. The block letter format uses left justification.

EXAMPLE

10/20/99	Date (thirteenth line on page)
Mr. Joe Smith President ABC Hotels 123 East Lane Gotham City, NY 12345	Client's name (sixth line below date) Client's title Company name Address (Space)
Dear Mr. Smith:	Salutation (Dear Mr./Ms.): (Space)
Thank you for allowing me to write this sample letter. It is very kind of you.	Body of letter • No indentation of paragraphs
I will follow up with you on writing effective letters in a few days. Practice those skills, and I know you will succeed.	• Space between paragraphs
Sincerely,	(Space) Complimentary close (Sincerely), (Space)
XYZ Catering Co.	Firm name (organization's name) (3 spaces)
Ahmed Ismail Catering Manager	Signer (Ahmed Ismail) Title (Catering Manager) (Space)
AI/ast	Reference Initials (AI/ast) • Set the writer's initials in caps, the typist's initials in lowercase.

Block letter format is easy to read and flows logically from start to finish. The content of the letter may change, but its form should not. In the catering industry, caterers will write certain types of sales letters over and over.

As has been reviewed. the sales process allows the caterer to continuously learn and build their knowledge base. The learning curve is applied to the relationships with clients via the mental inventory process. The mental inventory can only be created through communication. That means every phone call, every letter, teaches the catering salesperson more about their client. Insight is gained into their personality traits as their letters are read. A catering salesperson also can learn about the client from their reactions to their own correspondence. All letters must be viewed as sales tools.

TIPS FOR COMPOSING EFFECTIVE LETTERS

- In the salutation, only use clients' first names if you have been given permission (if they use only their first names with you or they have told you to use their first names).
- Sign just your first name in the close if you wish. It is accepted in today's business world. (Some people however, do not like it, as it looks less professional to them. It is up to the individual.) A close relationship merits the first-names-only signature in the close.
- When signing off in the complimentary close, use an alternate to "Sincerely" or "Yours Truly" when applicable (e.g., Happy New Year or Happy Holidays). Do not use phrases like "Merry Christmas," because you may offend someone.
- Personalize letters for those with whom you have close relationships. Congratulate someone on a personal or professional success. If you know a person's birthday, add that greeting to the bottom of the letter using the post script (P.S.).
- Customize whenever possible. Avoid form letters that look like form letters. Remember, the experienced meeting planner may have several letters and various forms of communication from you. You do not want the planner to notice several copies of the same form letter in his or her files. Changing a form letter, even slightly, will make it look new and fresh.
- Use phrases that induce positive and proactive feelings in the reader. For example, "Please do not hesitate to call" envokes the thought that you feel they are undecided. Instead, use the phrase, "Please feel free to call."
- Avoid industry jargon and unnecessary words. Do not use words indicative to our industry that the reader may not know. Terms like *blocking space* or *rooming list* may mean little to an inexperienced meeting planner. Phrases like *As per our conversation* and *Per your request* sound formal.
- Close every letter with some type of action step. Let the addressee know you will be calling or stopping by. If you can be specific (e.g., "I will be in touch with you next Thursday as we discussed"), you can set up an appointment. Your contact will expect your call or visit. Make sure you take action. You will look very unprofessional if you do not follow up.

The five major types of catering sales letters are introduction/good-bye, confirmation, cover, proposal, and thank you. Each type can obviously be worked into an infinite number of different letter styles, but the basic shell of each and what their objectives are remain the same.

Introduction/Good-Bye Letter. When an introduction/good-bye letter, often called a transition letter, is sent, a relationship with a client is beginning or ending. These letters are used often when catering salespeople are starting at facilities, or when outside caterers are trying to land new clients. A promotion can also be a good time to use this letter; it can update clients on a person's new title and duties. These letters are important because they are part of a caterer's first or last impression.

Catering salespeople should, before they move to other organizations, always take the time to inform their clients of their departures and, ideally, who will be their replacements. Continuity is very important in catering. Personnel often move. Clients feel much better about continuing relationships when catering salespeople take the time to keep them abreast of any things that may affect them. (Catering personnel who switch to the competition, however, probably will not be allowed to inform their current clients. Obviously, management does not want existing clients to move with their former personnel.)

Confirmation Letter. A good confirmation letter reinforces, or confirms, what was mutually agreed upon. Typically, this letter is written following a phone conversation to "put it in writing," recapping what was agreed to, if applicable, and confirming the next course of action.

Cover Letter. Sometimes called a transmittal letter, the cover letter may be used to prepare the reader (client) for material being sent (e.g., brochures or menus). The cover letter might include the purpose of the enclosed material, the reasons for developing the material, or the way in which the information should be used. It can also contain any basic message the catering salesperson wishes to convey. It is intended as a quick,

SAMPLE INTRODUCTION LETTER

Dear _____:

Please let me take a moment to introduce myself. My name is _____ _____ and I am your new contact here at XYZ Resort and Towers.

While I know you have worked with us in the past, I look forward to personally continuing this mutually beneficial relationship. Rest assured, the superior level of service you have come to expect from XYZ will continue with my tenure.

Again _____, thank you for being a friend of XYZ. I will contact you soon to touch base. In the meantime, please feel free to call me directly at 123–4567 should you have any questions.

SAMPLE CONFIRMATION LETTER

Dear _____:

Thank you for taking the time to speak with me today. We here at the XYZ Hotel look forward to welcoming you and your attendees next March.

As we discussed, enclosed please find the menus to choose from for your Regional Sales Awards Celebration. Simply look them over to prepare for our further discussion.

Again _____, thank you for choosing XYZ. I will be in touch to finalize the menus as the arrival date nears. In the meantime, should you have any questions, please feel free to contact me directly at 123–4567.

---

informal means of business communication. A sample first sentence could be, "Just a quick note to accompany the enclosed contract . . ." In today's business environment, a fax cover sheet has replaced the cover letter in many cases.

Proposal Letter. The secret to generating a lead is to create interest. This is the goal in submitting a proposal to a catering client. A proper proposal includes the formal proposal and an accompanying proposal letter. The letter that accompanies the proposal is an integral part of that proposal. Because each catering operation has a different proposal format, discussion of proposal writing does not apply here. Instead, this section provides some ideas on the proposal letter.

Ideally, a proposal letter is no more than two pages long. In a proposal letter, the catering salesperson must address the goals of the client and show how the facility's features become the client's advantages. While the proposal addresses program specifics (e.g., banquet prices, room rental, cancellation policy), the proposal letter is the perfect vehicle for addressing the points of the catering sales triangle. The proposal letter should address the three points of the determine goals action triangle.

As was mentioned earlier, certain client goals are more common than others. Earlier review showed how the sample goals could become advantages to clients through links to a facility's features. Taking those goals one step farther by applying them to a proposal helps document them for clients. This permanent record of goals, features, and advantages compels the client to consider all three while reviewing the correspondence. The best way to compose proposals is to dedicate each paragraph to one goal, and its corresponding features and advantages. The three goals used throughout Chapter 6 are value, quality, and service.

VALUE AND THE PROPOSAL LETTER

Value is more important in today's economy than ever. Maximizing your spending dollar is paramount. We here at ABC Catering pride ourselves on providing all our guests a meal experience that exceeds monetary expectations. Our ability to provide you discounted catering prices and our skill at working within your budget allow us to help you put together a program without exceeding your financial limits.

QUALITY AND THE PROPOSAL LETTER

As a meeting planner, your selection of a facility inevitably reflects on you. Organizing a program at a facility that maintains a high standard of quality shows your attendees and your superiors that you value their satisfaction above all else. The XYZ Conference Center prides itself on our detail-oriented staff and our award-winning quality level. Our documented track record of satisfied clients only helps to show that your choice—us—is the correct one.

SERVICE AND THE PROPOSAL LETTER

You had mentioned that a superior level of service was important to you because you had so many things to worry about during your upcoming program. We here at the 123 Hotel understand your need to provide your guests a worry-free meeting environment. As the enclosed testimonial letters indicate, we have a track record of doing just that. Our industry-leading training program empowers all associates to do what is needed to relieve the burdens of a planner like you.

PROPOSAL WRITING EXERCISE

The following table shows three more goals that can be raised by clients. Try to compose your own proposal paragraphs using these or others you come up with. You will find that this skill comes more easily with practice.

Goal	Feature	Advantage
Attentive Service	Your facility's size may only allow for one major group in at once.	The group will not feel "lost" and as if they will have the staff's attention and focus.
Creativity	European-trained culinary staff and experienced catering personnel who have worked with a wide variety of groups.	Allows for menus and room sets that attendees will appreciate as unique, not the "same old thing."
Clear and Concise Billing	Daily review of banquet checks and easy-to-read master bill format. All charges are accompanied by documented backup.	The client will not be surprised with unanticipated or incorrect charges. Keeps budget numbers up-to-date while the client's group is in-house.

SAMPLE THANK-YOU LETTER

Dear _____:

On behalf of the staff and management of the XYZ Hotel, I wish to thank you for allowing us to host your recent Regional Sales Awards Celebration. We certainly appreciate the opportunity and hope your expectations were exceeded in every way.

Your thoughts and feelings about our performance are important to us. Please complete the enclosed evaluation form to let us know your overall impression. Input from our important clients, like you, allow us to continually improve our product as well as recognize the employees who helped us provide you with a quality meeting experience.

Again, _____, thank you for being a friend of the XYZ. I will be in touch in the coming months to help put together your next meeting. Should something arise in the meantime, please feel free to call me at 123–4567.

Thank-You Letter. A good thank-you letter shows a salesperson's appreciation for the client's business. It is also a great way to get feedback on the facility's performance. Many catering operations send client comment forms with their thank-you letters. Such forms are a great way for caterers to address problems before they worsen. They are also useful for identifying employees who went the "extra mile" for the client and for beginning the resolicitation process. If a client had a terrific program, the thank-you letter is the opportune time to rebook that client, because that client's impression of the facility is positive. In fact, the two best times to approach a client about booking are:

1. After a successful program with your organization and
2. After an unsuccessful program at the competition

A cover letter can be sent to a client finishing a program with a competitor. If the client's experience was poor, the letter may prompt the client's future consideration.

PHONE CONVERSATION TIPS

Written communication is important and requires skill. In today's busy world, catering salespeople may find that clients are pressed for time and need answers quickly. Some do not want to wait for letters or E-mail; they may prefer verbal conversation. In these cases, salespeople may use the telephone. Creating comfort and ensuring trust with clients may be accomplished solely over the telephone, so it is vital to make the best use of telephone time.

BASIC TELEPHONE TIPS

- Introduce yourself cheerfully. Starting the conversation with a relaxed and cheerful tone helps set the stage for a positive interaction.
- When answering the phone, inform the client immediately with whom he or she is speaking. ("Good morning, Sales and Catering. This is Anne. May I help you?")
- Be candid. Always work to build the foundation of trust.
- Convey confidence. A positive attitude will encourage your client to open up. "Honey can catch more flies than vinegar"
- Be courteous.
- Be direct and clear.
- Keep the discussion short.
- Avoid jargon.
- Be complimentary when appropriate.
- Appreciate other people's time. It is a good habit to ask the client if it is a good time to talk. People appreciate that you value their time as much as you value yours.
- Share information (e.g., industry trends, personnel changes, sports news), because the client may appreciate it.
- When leaving messages or voice mail, make sure to provide enough information to allow the client to act or gather information for you. No one likes to play "phone tag."

Catering salespeople, whether they work for outside catering companies or hotel/banquet facilities, can greatly impact their organizations' success by mastering the art of action selling. Proactive salespeople are successful, but those who implement the goals/features/advantages approach to sales are more successful.

With a business opportunity secured, the catering salesperson must assume additional analyses, which relate to booking. These analyses fall under the heading "catering sales communications" because they relate to the communication of the sale and are not centered around generating the sale. The tools, analyses, and other resources available to the catering salesperson are operational because they require more than sales triangle application to bring them to fruition.

BOOKING STATUS

Salespeople come to understand very quickly that members of the sales office view the business opportunities they work on as their own. Good salespeople take ownership as their business. Knowing this enables salespeople to judge other salespeople's work and to understand where they are in their own sales processes. The ability of catering salespeople to communicate to each other where they are in their processes is vital. Perhaps more important is the ability to communicate to customers the status of current and future business, because it ensures that caterers maximize revenue potential. That is why the catering industry developed a way to qualify the status of every business opportunity. Status can be thought of as the lifespan of a business opportunity. From adoption to retirement, each piece of business changes and grows. The typical business opportunity has three phrases: tentative, definite, and actual.

TENTATIVE STATUS (ADOPTION)

Tentative or adoption status is used to describe a piece of business that has been thoroughly qualified and determined and that both client and caterer are interested in pursuing. All tentative business represents potential revenue. The human equivalent term of adoption was used because the lead has grown past that of being generated. A lead yet to be generated could be equivalent to birth. The business opportunity was conceived (qualified) and born (put on the books). Tentative business has been adopted by the salesperson. The salesperson wants to pursue it at his or her facility or catering operation.

Some caterers classify tentative business with letter or number codes that correspond to the strength or "sureness" of booking.

The following business opportunities, for example, are rated as to their potential to sign contracts using a scale from A to D:

Tentative Business	(Classification)	Reason for Classification
ABC Ball Bearings	(A)	A verbal commitment was given to book and a formal contract was requested.
Joe's Flower Shop	(B)	The group is very interested in booking but has not yet given a firm commitment.
Fancy Apple Farms	(C)	The group has narrowed its choices, but the site inspection process has yet to begin.
123 Hardware	(D)	The qualification and determining goals process is ongoing or the agenda has yet to be planned.

Strong tentatives can also be called first-option business; weaker tentatives can be called second-option business. Usually, when business is classified as second option, the client is considering many sites or caterers. In some situations, a second option is as strong as the first option but is only called "second option" because the first option was put on the books before the second. A second option may be put on the books over a first option to ensure that something is booked in that time frame. Caterers can combine first and second options to provide some assurance that dates will be filled. In such cases, a second tentative could become the caterer's second option.

When first and second options are used, the first-option business has the right to refuse, which means that it must be approached first and be given the opportunity to sign a definite contract if a second-option opportunity is interested in the space. All second-option tentatives also must be informed that they are holding second-option dates. No group should be led to assume that it is free to confirm, at its leisure, any second-option dates.

DEFINITE STATUS (ADULTHOOD)

Definite business has committed to using a facility or caterer. In its lifespan, it has matured. The industry standard is to only consider business definite when a signed contract is received in hand. Some facilities classify as definite any business that has forwarded an advance deposit or given a verbal commitment, but this is not suggested. Without contractual assurance of the business, there is always a chance that something will prevent the business from arriving. Most sales quotas for catering salespeople are structured to reflect functions on the books. Any cancellations without signed contracts hurts the salespeople and their organizations. Definite catering functions for the current year and future years are very important. All catering budgets and forecasts are measured with definite functions.

ACTUAL STATUS (RETIREMENT)

Once the definite business has come and gone, it undergoes another change. At this point in the lifespan, salespeople can see exactly how many function rooms the group used and how many dollars it spent on catering. These numbers are called "actuals" because they are documented, true numbers. They are no longer the best guess of either the salesperson or the client. Actuals are equated with retirement, not death, because actuals still play an important role in future business. As in real life, where retired people continue to play an important and productive role in society, actuals contribute to the catering operation long after the group is gone. Any repeat business from a group can be analyzed with its actuals. Actuals are the foundations of future budgets, which look to them for realistic production goals. Actuals over several years can show patterns. A historical record is the best way for salespeople as well as their organizations to judge future performance.

WRITING BINDING CONTRACTS

For a business opportunity to move from tentative to definite status in most catering operations, it must sign a contract. A signed contract is, in most cases, a legally binding agreement between caterer and client. In the contract, both parties agree to stated prices and services. A signed contract should be the ultimate aim of a salesperson. Policies and procedures vary so greatly, that it would not be conducive here to dictate one way to prepare a contract. As was the case in the discussion of proposals, most organizations have their own contracts, which are thoroughly reviewed by the organizations' attorneys and senior management.

This section illustrates three widely accepted ways to best protect the interests of a facility: standard cancellation fee, attrition clause, and sliding scale. The cancellation and sliding scale apply to all caterers because they can be tailored to food and beverage commitments. The attrition clause discussed applies to convention service managers at hotels, because they are often responsible for monitoring and tracking overnight room usage. These are concepts that should not alter an organization's contract format in any way. They can easily be adapted to any contract.

STANDARD CANCELLATION FEE

As was stated earlier, every contract should protect the caterer's interests. What happens when a group booked 2 years ago decides 3 months before arrival that it cannot come? Given that the group booking cycle of some facilities is longer than 3 months, the sales office would likely be placed in a precarious position. The facility held this space in good faith for two years and may have turned other groups away because it expected the group with the signed contract to fulfill its obligations.

A cancellation clause in a contract says to the signer, "If you cancel your program by X date, you are obligated to reimburse the facility Y dollars." The key is to structure the cancellation clause so that the organization remains in a positive but conservative light. The best way to set up the cancellation clause is to mirror it to the group booking cycle.

For example, assume that a downtown hotel with a group booking cycle of 4 years signs the ABC Company for a citywide convention. The contract, which is slated to arrive in 5 years, takes all the rooms available in the group ceiling. In this case, the cancellation fee must be structured so that as the group nears its arrival date, it becomes obligated to pay more to break its contract.

Assume the group signed for 300 rooms for 5 nights at a confirmed rate of $150 per night. In total, this piece of business is worth $225,000 in room revenue ($150 × 5 nights × 300 rooms). The hotel stands to lose this revenue if the group cancels, and it cannot rebook those rooms. Based on the hotel's booking cycle, if the group cancels less than 4 years out, the hotel may miss a substantial amount of business coming to the city. In this case, the hotel should have the stiffer parts of the penalty clause in effect from 3 years out and less. The contract might read: Should the ABC Company cancel its program in whole or part within the following time frame, it agrees to reimburse the hotel based on the following schedule:

Time Frame (in Days)	Cancellation Fee (in Dollars)
1,825–1,460	0
1,459–1,095	22,500 (10 %)
1,094–730	112,500 (50 %)
720–0	225,000 (100 %)

The time frame should always be structured in days. Some facilities use months or years. For example:

Time Frame (in Years)	Cancellation Fee (in Dollars)
5–4	0
4–3	$22,500 (10 %)

Problems arise, however, when a cancellation falls on the line between the two.

If a group canceled exactly at 4 years, would there be a penalty? The structure set in days allows no room for such a question.

The facility should base the percentages of total revenue in each cancellation segment to reflect the booking cycle and what is potentially lost as the event draws closer. The preceding cancellation clause only considers the revenue lost through guest rooms. Due to the added potential loss of catering and outlet/ancillary revenue, additional cancellation revenue may be included in the clause.

ATTRITION CLAUSE

An attrition clause is similar to a cancellation clause in that it is structured to reimburse the facility in the event that the business does not come to fruition. It is not intended to recoup losses from canceled business but rather to regain losses from lower-than-expected revenue. The difference here is that an attrition clause covers the **slippage** (lower-than-expected usage of sleeping rooms) of business that does come in. Because the attrition clause focuses on sleeping rooms, it does not apply to outside caterers or those at stand-alone facilities. The convention service manager at a hotel will find this clause of most value.

If the ABC Company from the preceding example came in with 150 rooms per night rather than the 300 it contracted for, it would provide significantly lower revenue than was expected. Most hotels anticipate 10 to 15 percent slippage, not 50 percent slippage. What can be done in this case? An attrition clause imposes a scale of penalty that is relative to slippage.

Again, consider the ABC Company, who had contracted for 300 rooms for 5 nights at $150 a night. It actually comes in with 150 rooms, which means the hotel will lose $112,500 due to poor group performance. An attrition clause like the one following will recoup the hotel's losses:

"Should the ABC Company reduce its overall room commitment or utilization by more than 15 percent, (every group should be extended 5 to 15 percent slippage as a professional courtesy), "ABC Company agrees to reimburse the hotel X dollars."

In this example, X is the reimbursement amount deemed necessary based on the hotel's booking cycle and the hotel's value of the business. The attrition clause can also be set on a chronological scale that allows a percentage decrease with no penalty far from the scheduled arrival date and that increases as the date nears.

The attrition clause can be explained to the client as a tool for tracking expected numbers. If the hotel allows for the standard 15 percent slippage without penalty, the group could reduce its block far enough in advance so as not to adversely affect the hotel's booking cycle. In this example, the ABC contact could reduce the group's block by 10 percent 12 months out and by another 5 percent 6 months out. These time frames may not be realistic for a hotel with a 4-year booking cycle, but they allow for small reductions far enough in advance that the sales office has time to recover and, more important, book new business. The salesperson must make sure that these two reduction deadlines are realistic for both hotel and client.

The attrition clause must be used not in lieu of but in conjunction with a cancellation clause to ensure full coverage for the hotel. Wary clients can be assured that the hotel is giving them two opportunities to reduce their room needs without penalty.

SLIDING SCALE

The sliding scale is similar to the attrition clause in that it is designed to protect the hotel from lackluster group performance. It is not, however, centered strictly on sleeping rooms. The caterer can use it to cover food and beverage revenue as well.

Catering contracts can use variations of the sliding scale that tie food and beverage performance to room rental. If, for example, a group contracted for 5 days of meetings with breakfast, lunch, and dinner each day, but ended up only doing continental breakfast and coffee breaks, the caterer may have lost considerable revenue. The caterer can set the sliding scale to correspond to scheduled food functions or estimated food and beverage revenue. A resort can tie in proposed golf tournaments, tennis usage, and any other ancillary revenue source that stands to lose revenue due to lackluster group performance.

To illustrate the implementation of the sliding scale, consider the hotel example again. The sliding scale can be used with space-intensive groups, and the discussions on space intensity and rooms-to-space ratio apply. If a hotel's meeting space is completely booked, it cannot realistically add group rooms because, for the most part, group bookings always also use meeting rooms. Therefore, to maximize rooms and space, a hotel might institute a sliding scale that ties group room performance to meeting room rental.

Assume that the ABC has booked 300 rooms for 5 nights, which equals 1,500 total room nights. The hotel has committed all its meeting space. (If, for the sake of discussion, it is known that the hotel's group ceiling is 300 rooms a night, it would seem that this group would be a perfect fit.) The sliding scale should look like this:

> It is the policy of the XYZ Hotel to charge for meeting space. The amount of room rental charge is based on your projected meal functions and room night actualization. The following scale applies:

Slippage (Percent)	Total Room Nights Used	Meeting Room Rental (Per Day in Dollars)
15	1,275–1,500	Waived
20	1,200–1,274	2,000
40	900–1,119	8,000
60	600– 899	12,000

These numbers may seem high to prospective clients, which is the intention. This example shows clients that they will be guaranteed free meeting space (if so agreed to in their contracts) only if they fulfill their sleeping room commitments. This kind of scale often gives clients reason to reexamine their projections and guest room estimates. In response, they might ask to reduce their sleeping room requests in their contracts. If so, the convention service manager is then obligated to reevaluate the business and redetermine its attractiveness based on this new criteria. The convention service manager should not renegotiate a contract; that should be done by the room salesperson. The convention service manager can inform others when a group is not fulfilling a negotiated contract and allow those others to enforce the penalties.

The convention service manager's response to clients who choose to reduce their room commitments should be to inform them that there is no guarantee of additional rooms being available should their numbers return to initial projections. Sliding scale amounts and slippage percentages differ based on facility policy and booking cycle, but their aim remains the same: The client should be held as accountable as they would hold a facility.

Industry Perspective

"Contracts: An In-Depth Look"

Jil M. Froelich, CMP
Contract Compliance Manager

The contracting phase of the sales process, while deemed tedious by some, is vital. A truly thorough examination takes chapters, even volumes. Following are some of the common elements seen today, but remember that industry trends can have great impact. What were common practices 3 years ago are no longer common today, and so, too, may today's practices be different in 3 years.

The purpose of the contract is to secure a commitment from each party (facility and customer). Through the contract the facility commits to providing its product and services and the customer commits to using them. A contract should never be entered into lightly, because it is a legal document and not without risk or obligation. Much is discussed during the sales process, and the contract should outline all the important points. It cannot be assumed that verbal commitments will be remembered or honored or that the people involved will not change. For example, a customer may mention to the sales representative that the group does not want to have to move its materials out of their meeting room each night. Such a fact, and any associated rental costs, should be outlined in the contract.

It is the responsibility of each party to ensure that its needs are represented in the contract. The facility's contract likely includes clauses or language drafted by legal counsel. The sales representative's ability to modify this language may be limited. Some modifications may only be approved by the director of sales, general manager, or even the facility's legal counsel. Likewise, the customer may include specific language written by legal counsels. When the two conflict, it may be necessary to include both sides' legal counsels.

Contracting can be painless if both sides engage in open dialogue before the contract is issued. If each side has a clear understanding of what is important to the other, a mutually agreeable contract can be drafted more quickly. Because contracts are typically issued by the facility, the sales representative should ensure that the contract represents what has been discussed to date. Customers may lose their patience and confidence if incomplete or inaccurate contracts are issued.

Once the contract is issued, the customer should review it twice. The first review is to examine what is included, and the second review is to identify what is not included. Omissions do not mean that obligations do not exist. For example, if there is no clause addressing rooms attrition, it cannot be assumed that the group will not be charged. If the facility will not charge room attrition, then it should be stated in the contract. Also, some charges may be outlined in a policies and procedures document that the facility may provide only upon request or after contracting. These additional charges could result in significant costs to the client or the client's attendees. Examples include early check-out fees and shipping and storage charges for meeting materials. Certain facility policies, like use of outside vendors, could affect how the meeting is carried out. A savvy planner requests the policies and procedures before signing a contract to consider them during negotiation.

Once all contract changes have been agreed upon, a new contract should be issued by the facility. While addendums or handwritten and initialed changes may be commonplace in the industry, they pose an element of risk and are not preferred.

To be binding, the contract must be executed, which means signed by an authorized representative of each party. An authorized representative must have the legal authority to sign on behalf of the party he or she represents. The contract should identify the name of the organization, the name and title of each person signing the contract, and the date signed.

TYPICAL CONTRACT INCLUSIONS

Overnight Rooms
- **Quantity of Rooms per Type and per Night (Room Block).** Is the room type standard guest or a special class, such as business? Singles? Doubles? Kings? Are suites being held? What type? How many? When? In some cases (e.g., annual meetings being planned years out), the size of the room block may change based on the group's actual room pickup history. For example, a contract for an annual meeting being held 4 years from now may stipulate that the room block will be reviewed at specified dates and adjusted according to the pickup history of the 2 years prior plus an agreed-upon growth rate.
- **Rates per Type and per Occupancy.** (Note: If the contract is for a meeting more than 1 year out, then a rate may not yet be established. The contract should outline, however, a date on which the rate will be established and how it will be calculated. A formula may be based on a specified percentage of increase over a given rate base, such as the current rack rate (e.g., "A guaranteed rate will be established by XX/XX/XX, with a maximum rate of no more than 5 percent above the current rack rates. Current rack rates are . . ."

- **Rate Inclusions.** Does the rate include any meal or meeting expenses? For example, if the rate is European, then no meals are typically included. If it is based on the Full American Plan or the Complete Meeting Package method, then meals and/or meeting-related expenses may be included in the rate. Is access to health club included? Parking? Local phone calls?
- **Net Rate or Commissionable?** If commissionable, how much, to whom, and when?
- Will the group rate be honored before and/or after the program dates as long as the facility has availability? Will it be honored after the cut-off date?
- **Additional Charges Per Room or Per Night?** Are charges automatically added, such as baggage handling and housekeeping? What other types of charges could be added, such as parking? What are the current taxes?
- **Check-In and Check-Out Times, Policies, and Procedures.** Does the group have service requirements, such as a minimum ratio of desk agents to guests during peak hours of major arrivals and departures? Are special services being provided to the group in the way of baggage handling and storage, special check-in/-out procedures, and complimentary items, like beverage service during peak check-in?
- **Concessions.** The types of concessions requested are only limited by the imagination. Typical concessions include VIP upgrades, complimentary room nights, reduced rates for speakers and staff, complimentary hospitality suites, and free brochures or self-mail registration cards. For example, a group may request a particular ratio, such as one complimentary room for every forty paid room nights, calculated on a cumulative basis. A contract should be very clear on what concessions will be given and under what circumstances. A hotel may agree to a concession but may tack on a condition (e.g., only if the group realizes a specified percent of its room block).
- How will **no-shows** be handled, and what will be charged (1 night or all nights?)? A group may request that the no-show room be held without occupancy until a specific time, such as noon the following day. If the hotel can resell the no-show room and the group agrees, will the group receive credit? Will paid no-show charges and any rooms resold be included in the group's room usage to minimize attrition charges?
- If a guest checks out early, will the hotel charge an early check-out fee to the guest's folio? If so, how much?
- What is the hotel's policy regarding walking guests to other hotels? Does the group have requirements, such as the right to determine which of its participants are walked first or that the hotel must provide transportation, phone calls, or meals?
- **Reservation Method, Cut-Off Date, and Procedures.**
- **Payment Method for Overnight Rooms and Related Incidental Expenses.**
- **Method of Guarantee.**
- **Deposit Requirements.**
- **Performance (Attrition) Requirements.** How many room nights can the group drop and when, without charge? If the group exceeds its allotment or window of time, what charges will be assessed? Will the charge be based on lost rooms revenue or lost rooms profit, or will it

be tied to meeting room rental? Will the group receive credit for room nights resold by the hotel? Are there potential "double-dip" clauses? If a guest checks out 2 nights early, for example, will the guest be charged an early check-out penalty and will the group pay attrition on those nights? Do the tax laws allow the hotel to charge tax?

- **Customer's Requirements for Receiving Reports Regarding Room Block.** What information is required and how often?

Meetings/Banquets

The most important element is a detailed schedule of events (agenda) that identifies each meeting/function by name, date, and time, as well as any setup requirements and rental or other costs. This portion of the contract should address how the group has specified its function space requirements: by room size and dimensions, by specific room names, by square footage per person, or by detailed diagrams, including production/AV space requirements. Other, often-seen inclusions are:

- Service charge and tax percentages. Is the service charge taxable?
- When will menu prices be provided and guaranteed not to increase?
- When must menus be finalized?
- When are guarantees due to the facility for each function?
- What is the facility's overset policy?
- Performance (food and beverage reduction) requirements and policies. This can be addressed in a variety of ways, including:
  The group can drop its attendance by XX percent without charge. Drops over the allowed percentage could result in function space reassignment, additional room rental, lost revenue or profit charges, increased menu prices, or increased overnight room charges.
      The group is responsible for a guaranteed minimum amount of food and beverage revenue, either by function or for the total meeting. If the actual food and beverage spent is less than the guaranteed amount, the guarantee will be invoiced.
- Group's requirements for server ratios (e.g., one server for each twenty guests at a plated function).

Miscellaneous

Conflicting Bookings. A group may be sensitive to other types of groups booked at the facility over its dates. This could be due to the confidential nature of the meeting, such as a product launch, or because of the social or political nature of the event. The group may request a list of all other groups holding space just before, during, and after its meeting. It may also require rights of termination if the facility books a conflicting group. The facility may stipulate that as a public accommodation, the facility does not discriminate against a group or an individual on the basis of race, creed, gender, religion, or disability.

Hold Harmless/Indemnification. The purpose of these clauses is to protect against or minimize a party's liability due to the actions of the other party. The validity of these clauses varies from state to state. Be wary of clauses excusing or relieving liabilities as a result of gross negligence. When included in a contract, it is best if the clauses are mutual. For example, "Each party agrees to indemnify and hold harmless the other party. . . ." It is best to seek the advice of legal counsel regarding the implications of these clauses.

Renovations. A group may request a clause that protects it from planned renovations or construction during its program. While renovations typically infer physical modifications to a property, consideration should be made to other types of service interruption. For example, a plan to upgrade telephone or computer systems could have dramatic impact. The group may request a right of termination if it deems the activity will interfere with its meeting. These clauses are often written with an amount of ambiguity and therefore can be difficult to interpret. The best way to avoid problems is through communication. Disclosing scheduled modifications as well as a plan to minimize their impact to the group is critical. The facility should protect itself from rights of termination by the group for unplanned modifications, such as system failures. If a contract specifies that the group can cancel the meeting due to service interruptions and the air-conditioning system fails during the meeting, how likely is it that the group will be able to cancel the meeting once it has started? Both parties will need to work together to resolve the situation.

Act of God. The intent of these clauses is to protect both parties against failure of performance due to an act of God. An example of an act of God is a hurricane causing damage to a property. A great deal of room for interpretation exists, however. If a hurricane only damages the outside swimming pool area of the facility, does either party have the right to terminate? If a natural disaster affects 30 percent of the participants' ability to travel to the meeting does the group have a right to terminate? If the meeting is held, will the group be relieved of its performance requirements (e.g., room attrition, food and beverage minimums) for this portion of the group? If an agreement cannot be reached by the parties as these events occur, then legal intervention may be required.

Cancellation. Chapters could be written to address this issue alone. The typical cancellation clause is written to protect the facility in the event the group cancels the meeting. Planners often try to negotiate the terms of the clause, and some may introduce language to protect themselves in the event the facility cancels the group. A simple example is "The facility shall not have the right to cancel this meeting for the purpose of accepting other group(s) or business."

Many factors are involved in determining fair cancellation clauses. Some of these factors are:

- Group's history with the facility. If a strong relationship exists, then the facility may be more flexible knowing it will likely see additional business.
- What is the total value of this piece of business to the facility?
- What damages will the facility realize if the group cancels?
- What is the facility's ability to reduce its damages? How does the date of cancellation affect this ability?

Cancellation charges are often presented in a scale format:

Cancel more than 365 days from peak arrival	Pay X
Cancel 270 to 364 days from peak arrival	Pay X
Cancel 180 to 269 days from peak arrival	Pay X
Cancel 90 to 179 days from peak arrival	Pay X
Cancel 30 to 89 days from peak arrival	Pay X
Cancel 29 or fewer days from peak arrival	Pay X

Both the time frame and the value of X vary from contract to contract. A contract for a meeting booked 2 years out will have a scale very different from one booked 60 days out. The value of X (the amount to pay) may be identified as a:

- Flat dollar amount
- Percent of peak room night revenue
- Percent of total revenue (rooms, food and beverage, recreational activities, outlets, or any combination)
- Percent of profit (rooms, food and beverage, activities, outlets, or any combination)

Other Considerations

- Will the group receive credit if the hotel resells any of the overnight rooms? What if the hotel resells food and beverage functions?
- Will the facility collect taxes on the cancellation charges? A planner should ask the hotel not to collect taxes if they are not required by state law.
- When are cancellation charges due? Often, it is XX days after notification of cancellation or XX days after the original program date. If a resale clause is included and the facility collects the charges before the original meeting dates, the group may receive a credit after the original meeting dates have run and the hotel is able to assess what it resold.
- What concessions will be made if the group rebooks business?
  - Must it be a reschedule of the meeting?
  - Can it be a meeting of similar revenue?
  - Can it be a series of meetings?
  - What is the expiration date for the rebooked business (e.g., 6 months from original/canceled dates, within the current calendar year, 1 year from the date the cancellation notice was given)?
  - Will the cancellation charge have to be paid and a credit given to the rebooked meeting? Full credit? Partial credit? Or will the charge be paid only at the expiration date of the rebook offer?

In conclusion, the best contracts are those that are thorough, clear, and concise. Language that is ambiguous or that leaves room for multiple interpretations can lead to problems. The ultimate goal is to create a document that represents the interests of both sides in a way that can be understood by those who will be responsible for carrying out the document's mission.

FACILITY SITE INSPECTIONS

Generating client interest through written or verbal conversations leads to another customer communication form: the facility site inspection. The facility site inspection is used by potential customers to get a personal look at the site under consideration. It is the opportunity for clients to test the product before purchase.

Most experienced meeting planners expect to visit venues before booking. Inexperienced meeting planners should be encouraged to do the same. The site inspection is an opportunity for facility caterers to display their products. The site inspection may be the only opportunity for salespeople to display their facilities. An effective facility site inspection has three stages: preparation, implementation, and follow up.

PREPARING FOR THE SITE INSPECTION

Once a site inspection is confirmed, the salesperson should inform other personnel and departments. Whether it is a hotel or a stand-alone facility, senior management (e.g., director of catering, sales manager, executive chef, general manager) should be made aware of the business impact of a business opportunity. Management involvement can be invaluable in helping salespeople put their facilities in their best light. Alerting the key personnel in other departments (e.g., front desk, housekeeping, restaurants) of the impending site inspection helps create facilitywide awareness. Preparing the entire staff for an impending site inspection is necessary to ensure the best impression.

A unique idea is to post in various facility departments (e.g., bell stand, front desk, restaurant hostess stand) a picture of the arriving client with the pertinent information (e.g., name, group, date of site inspection) so employees can greet the client by name. This recognition technique starts the selling process even before the client and salesperson meet. It can be very impressive to a client when the doorperson greets him or her by name upon arrival.

Once awareness has been created, salespeople should review the specific goals they want to accomplish with the site inspection. These goals should correspond to their clients' agendas. Salespeople should not waste clients' time showing them outdoor pools if their only hotel needs are spaces for half-day meetings. Review of the client's proposed meeting agenda ensures that the salesperson will only show relevant aspects of the facility. Review of the organization's file should prompt these questions:

- Does the client need to be picked up at the airport?
- What does the client want to see upon arrival?
- Are the rooms/suites blocked properly?

- Which function rooms would be appropriate?
- Does the client want to see restaurants? Back of the house (non-public space)? Facility grounds? Parking garage? Kitchen?

Anticipation of all possible questions and variations will ensure that the facility is ready to accommodate all scenarios. Salespeople should personally check function rooms on the day of arrival to ensure they convey the best impression. If clients are visiting a hotel, a variety of sleeping rooms will be part of their site inspections. Checking these rooms before showing them is always a good idea. Salespeople should enter the designated rooms and open the shades to reveal their gorgeous views. They should also turn on some lights and a radio, softly. Salespeople should create an ambiance that is unconsciously inviting. Many hotels designate rooms as permanent show rooms. These show rooms are considered "last sell" rooms by the front desk, so they are not released unless the hotel is in a sold-out situation. Show rooms can be deep cleaned, smoke free, and polished by housekeeping to make the best impression. Show rooms allow the sales team to know where the rooms are located. Knowing where the client will be taken allows the salesperson to begin preparing an agenda of where and when each area of the hotel will be shown during the site inspection.

There have been recent reports in the hotel industry of a few unscrupulous hotels creating special show rooms that are more nicely appointed and decorated than are regular rooms. These hotels renovate these rooms more often and generally give clients false impressions. If clients ask salespeople to show rooms other than those they have already seen, it is because they have heard this story and want an honest look. A hotel that does not use this tactic will have no problem showing any room. Again, clients appreciate honesty in all dealings.

Usually, clients also want to see function space on site inspections. On the days of site inspections, catering salespeople should check their ballrooms and other meeting space of interest to the client to ensure they are clean and ordered. This assumes that the space in question is not occupied. An important piece of business might justify setting up of the meeting room to reflect how it would look when the client's group is meeting.

IMPLEMENTING THE SITE INSPECTION

Once the client is on the facility grounds, the next phase of the site inspection, implementation, begins. The effectiveness of a site inspection is directly related to its preparation. Salespeople should dress professionally and be well groomed, because the appearance and demeanor of salespeople reflect on their facilities. Clients judge facilities first based on the employees they meet.

The site inspection should begin with a greeting in the lobby, if possible. If the client arrived the night before to a hotel, the salesperson should set a time and exact location in the hotel for the two to meet. The sales office is a good place to meet a client. The client should be greeted like a VIP. At this point in the site inspection, introductions of senior managers (e.g., director of catering or general manager) have their greatest impact.

Before the tour of the facility, a brief sit-down discussion with the client is warranted. A review of where the two parties are at that point will sharpen both participants' focus during the inspection. The salesperson's summary of what he or she will show helps to ensure that both parties achieve what they want to achieve from the tour. A review of the determining goals triangle may be appropriate. If possible, hold this initial meeting in a restaurant at the facility over breakfast or lunch. This is another instance for which preparation can be beneficial. If a meal meeting is arranged, the salesperson should secure a superior server to handle the table. The rapport a salesperson has with familiar servers often translates into better service, which in turn reflects very well on the facility.

The site inspection should be well planned. Stops along the tour should flow, and the salesperson should backtrack as little as possible. Along the way, the salesperson should keep conversing with the client to continually establish rapport. The client's personality will reveal itself early, so the salesperson will know quickly whether easy conversation is desired or whether only strict business discourse will be accepted. Areas in which the facility is weak (e.g., renovations in progress, older meeting rooms, poor views) should be avoided, unless the proposed business is far into the future. In those cases, renovations can be sold as future new features. For example, if during a tour a client notices a renovation of the meeting space and the proposed business opportunity is not due until after the renovation is completed, the salesperson could impress upon the client that the meeting space will be new when the client's group arrives. A diagram or model of the finished product can be powerful.

Selling during a site inspection is constant, even if the salesperson does not speak. Clients observe all and make ongoing judgments of the property. Salespeople conducting site inspections of properties of exceptional quality or of properties with unique attractions have added benefits, because they can overcome roadblocks with visuals. Often, higher rates or less desirable dates can be less important to the client if they are overwhelmed by a top notch facility—not unlike new car buyers who, after completing a test drive, become enthralled with a car that might be out of their price range.

FOLLOWING UP ON THE SITE INSPECTION

As soon as the site inspection is completed, the salesperson should review the organization's file and recap the inspection results, noting specific items like:

- Any new additions or changes to the program
- Prices quoted for rooms or services
- Availability of meeting rooms or suites in which the client expressed interest should be checked
- Any challenges should be documented so that they can be addressed later

While everything is fresh, salespeople should write follow-up letters to the potential clients to thank them for taking the time to tour and, more important, to indicate the next action step (e.g., send a contract to book the business). Using the catering sales triangle as a guide, salespeople should create letters that address their clients' goals using the features showcased in the site inspections. This type of letter is very powerful, because the facility is now more than just a proposal on paper. The client can connect visuals with the letter.

The site inspection can be a very powerful sales tool if conducted properly, which is with proper preparation, implementation, and follow-up.

CUSTOMER APPOINTMENTS

Client schedules may preclude them from visiting facilities. This is especially true of clients who know the facilities under consideration. In these cases, it is often beneficial for salespeople to visit clients in their offices, in what is known as customer appointments, another catering sales communication tool. At some point, both facility and outside caterers will have to visit clients. This is uncomfortable for some salespeople in the industry, but most sales professionals today make the customer appointment a staple of their sales tools. Those who are selling products, not services, must show prospective buyers those products. Catering salespeople who master this ability to venture out increase their sales opportunities.

Appointments with familiar clients are easier to keep than those with unfamiliar ones. In either case, salespeople must remember that all clients value their time. If salespeople do not remember that, clients will not consent to seeing them again.

When stopping by for appointments, salespeople should take a little time to inventory the surroundings. How is the office set up? Do employees speak in hushed tones, or is the environment more relaxed? Is the office new, modern, and efficient looking, or is it disorganized? This inventory will give some idea as to how to interact with the client. However, it should not be assumed that clients are mirror images of their officemates.

The approach to the receptionist desk to announce is important. Salespeople should observe carefully on approach. Are there letters from competitors? Is the client's message box full or empty? Salespeople should adjust their approaches if it is obvious their clients are overwhelmed, and they should always be kind, courteous, and professional to the receptionist. They are often underappreciated, and a little kindness will go a long way. Salespeople should try to get receptionists' names so they can address them by name at each contact. Some salespeople direct thank-you letters to reception personnel so those personnel remember them and perhaps facilitate client interaction.

A face-to-face meeting in a client's office can be as productive as a site inspection. Rapport-building skills are effective in these instances. Face and body posture reveal clues to add to the mental inventory. Is the client in a hurry? Is the client pleased to have a distraction from routine chores? Salespeople must ask probing and open-ended questions to extract information. The longer the client allows a salesperson to ask questions, the more the salesperson will learn.

During the client appointment, the salesperson should keep eye contact strong and posture confident. This appointment may be the client's first contact with the catering organization. The salesperson represents the organization. If the salesperson gives a negative impression, the client will identify that impression with the organization.

The salesperson should finish the appointment by asking for some type of next action. A phone call can be made in a few days, but the salesperson should always send a thank-you note. Any type of action will make the appointment worthwhile. If some type of action is taken from each appointment, the salesperson can walk away with the satisfaction of accomplishment.

A salesperson should not schedule too many appointments in one day. Negative reactions are inevitable, and salespeople should not discourage themselves. These guidelines improve a salesperson's technique and improve the chances of success.

TASTE PANELS

Some of the catering sales tools addressed to this point have been facility oriented. One tool caterers of all disciplines have in common is the **taste panel**. The taste panel is a gathering of clients and catering and kitchen personnel to sample and choose a menu for an upcoming event. It is used most often when large or very important food functions are being planned and decision makers want to see, smell, and taste some of the menu items under consideration. A taste panel is a perfect venue in which to exhibit the menu-planning skills of plate presentation. It is also an opportunity for caterers to sell using visuals.

A taste panel is effective when catering salespeople sit with clients and kitchen representatives. Banquet or executive chefs can be very useful in taste panels, because their knowledge of preparation, food origins, and other culinary facts help impress clients and impart the expertise of their organizations. A taste panel is even more impressive when held inside the kitchen. In a clean and quiet area, a table can be arranged with all the salads, soups, entrées, and desserts under consideration. Within reason, as many of the options the client expressed interest in should be prepared to sample. For any catering salesperson, the taste panel should only be used when the size and nature of the business warrants it. A small dinner for ten may not warrant a taste panel, but that judgment must be made based on the size of the catering organization and the importance of the business.

One derivation of the taste panel is the **chef's table**. The chef's table is said to have originated hundreds of years ago in England. Lords, barons, and other wealthy landowners would have their chefs create lavish meals for other visiting elite. To outdo each other, these elite would ask their chefs to prepare meals more elegant and lavish than those of their neighbors. Today, the chef's table is not a competition, but it does provide caterers an opportunity to highlight some of their organizations' creativity and skill. Today a chef's table brings customers, VIPs, and other important people from the catering organization together for a meal presented by the executive chef and staff. The chef's table is not a venue in which to sample different food items. Instead, it showcases a special meal. Again, when put together in a kitchen, the chef's table can impress potential clients.

CHAPTER REVIEW

KEY CONCEPTS

Goal	Tentative	Sliding scale
Feature	Definite	Facility site inspection
Advantage	Actual	Customer
Convince	Standard cancellation	appointment
Close	fee	Taste panel
Roadblock	Attrition clause	

REVIEW QUESTIONS

1. Why are contracts so important in catering? How might one cancellation affect the catering operation?
2. What are the three booking statuses, and what do they represent?
3. What does a roadblock represent in the sales process? How is it overcome?
4. Why is asking for business so important?
5. What are the three steps to a successful site inspection?

ROLE-PLAYING EXERCISE

With a sales teammate or classmate, practice implementing the different stages of the catering sales triangle in a mock sales situation. Take turns in the roles of salesperson and client.

Create the method in which the lead was generated. Determine your own set of client goals, and have each person try selling. Use open-ended questions to qualify and establish rapport. Determine the goals of the other person, and attempt to close.

Each person should have a "hidden" goal that becomes a roadblock to closing the sale. When finished, each person should critique the other's stint as a salesperson. Share the results with your sales team or class.

CHAPTER 8

Managing the Event

INTRODUCTION

The intricacies of the day-to-day life of a catering professional are numerous. New challenges and opportunities arise each day, which allow those involved in catering to learn and grow. These learning opportunities abound in all disciplines of catering, both in facility and outside catering. Learning applies to all facets of the job, not just planning and selling. To varying degrees, all catering operations mandate a certain level of operational responsibility from each person. The term used broadly to describe the duties and responsibilities that catering staff can incur because of a function is operations.

Catering operations is the set of functions/roles/duties a caterer may engage in before, during, and after a function. The daily responsibilities of generating leads, managing the leads, and coordinating bookings are all operational. Communication, networking, and management are all crucial components of the caterer's operational skills.

Catering operations is a phrase that is also used to describe the interdepartmental relationships a caterer must build. A catering professional must be able to rely on other facility departments or on others outside the organization to deliver on the commitments made on everyone's behalf. As was stated in Chapter 7, these issues and responsibilities must be communicated. This type of communication is internal.

This chapter looks at major operational topics. It outlines what a catering or convention service manager may engage in to secure a sale and bring a program to fruition, called operational tools and documents.

OPERATIONAL TOOLS AND DOCUMENTS

The operational responsibilities of a caterer do not end with the sale. Because during qualification booking most of an organization's function details were uncovered, the total facility impact of a catering salesperson can be extensive. A typical facility booking impacts many different departments. Figure 8–1 shows the departments of a typical full-service hotel.

What would happen if everything committed with a client (e.g., function space, dinner prices) stopped? What would happen if no one besides the salesperson knew about a booking? Clearly, there would be serious problems.

All catering professionals must use the systems at their facilities to communicate the goals and objectives of a client to the proper operational departments. Caterers must pay as much attention to this aspect of written communication as they do to their client letters. Omitting operational details can seriously affect the outcome of any group function.

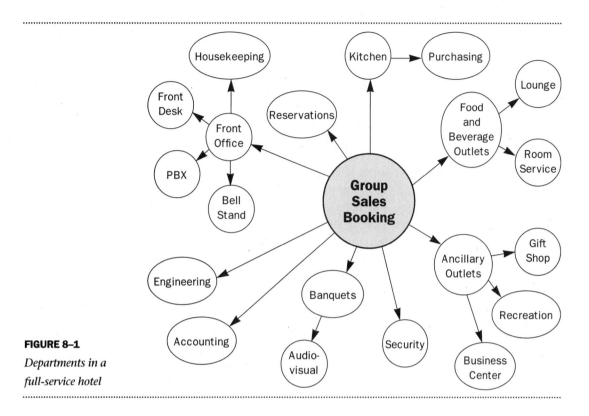

FIGURE 8–1

Departments in a full-service hotel

There is no such thing as too much information when it comes to internal communication. The more people who know what is going on, the better.

Departments rely on the message from the catering office to understand their roles in the success of a function. The documents used to transmit this message fall under the heading of "internal catering communication."

Except for meetings managers, who handle both the sales and catering aspects of small groups in hotels, catering salespeople usually create all the documents. Depending on the deployment scenario, facilities require salespeople to have different levels of responsibility in transmitting internal operations documents. It is important for all catering professionals, whether they create the documents or not, to be able to read and interpret these documents to ensure their messages are being properly transmitted.

BANQUET EVENT ORDERS

The banquet event order, sometimes called the BEO, banquet prospectus, or catering event sheet, is an important document in that it deals with all nonsleeping room needs of an organization. It is a fundamental document that communicates to the internal departments of a facility the details of any function. Outside caterers use some form of a BEO to communicate their needs to the kitchen and setup personnel. Every aspect of a function, from the name of the group to its meal choices, times of the day and prices must be detailed to ensure that what the catering salesperson and the client have agreed upon is communicated.

The BEO format differs from operation to operation. The function can also differ. In most cases, the BEO serves as a contract, thereby becoming an internal and external form of communication. In these cases, the client's signature is required on the BEO as a confirmation of details. Other operations use separate catering contracts, or letters of intent, to confirm programs.

The BEO should be completed in ample time for internal departments to prepare. Departments must allow enough time for the kitchen to purchase all the food and pose any menu questions or suggestions. The banquet floor managers must schedule appropriate staff. Early BEO completion can help avoid double-booking of function rooms and even allow all the catering/convention service managers time to move rooms for efficiency. As a general rule, BEOs should be completed at least 3 weeks before the function.

When the BEO is completed, it is ready for distribution to the appropriate operational departments. These departments can include:

- Kitchen/executive chef
- Banquet manager/captains
- A/V staff
- Accounting/credit manager
- Director of food and beverage/director of catering
- Purchasing
- Stewarding
- Engineering

A master copy of the BEO should be distributed to a central file in the catering office that is broken down by day so that any interested party can get an "at a glance" view of upcoming functions.

Every operation that uses a BEO for internal communication uses some type of daily review meeting to discuss upcoming BEOs. Some combination of representatives from departments on the distribution list and the catering/convention service managers responsible for the upcoming BEOs meet to review the BEOs and address any possible challenges. These staff often review the BEOs for the following 2 days, with Fridays covering 3 days. This means that most BEOs are reviewed twice, allowing for scrutiny of all details.

Figure 8–2 shows a sample BEO and highlights the areas all catering personnel should know.

The sample BEO on the following pages shows a fictitious Valentine's Day dance. The layout and order of the topics may differ from catering operation to operation, but the same fundamental details will be included on all.

XYZ Hotel and Towers
Banquet Event Order

BEO 1234   **SALES FILE NA555**
DATE SUBMITTED: 12/5/98   **CONV. SERV. FILE 1232**
                                               CATERING FILE 0001
                                               PAGE 1 of 2

FUNCTION DAY/DATE: Sunday, February 14, 1999
ORGANIZATION: Gotham City Valentine Couples Group
POST AS: Valentine's Day Dance

BILLING ADDRESS: 123 Lovers Lane, Gotham City, NY 01234
BOOKING CONTACT: Ms. Jane Doe
ON-SITE CONTACT(S):   Mr. John Q. Public
PHONE: (202) 555-1521
FAX: (202) 555-1522
SALES MANAGER: Mike Smith   **CONVENTION SERVICE MANAGER:** Andrew Jones
                          CATERING MANAGER: Janet Hill
ATTENDEES EXPECTED: 275   **GUARANTEED:** 290   **SET NUMBER** 305

FUNCTION TIME	FUNCTION	ROOM
3:00 P.M.–6:00 P.M.	Room Setup	Ballroom
6:30 P.M.–7:30 P.M.	Reception	Ballroom Foyer
7:30 P.M.–12 midnight	Dance	Ballroom
3:00 P.M.	Room Setup	Ballroom

No Food or Beverage Needed

6:30 P.M.	3 Host Bars*	Ballroom Foyer

House Brand Liquor @ $3.00 ++ per serving
Premium Brand Liquor @ $4.00 ++ per serving
Top-Shelf Liquor @ $5.00 ++ per serving
House White/Red Wine @ $2.50 ++ per serving
Premium and Imported Beer @ $4.50 ++ per bottle
Assorted Soft Drinks @ $2.00 ++ per serving
*Bartender fee of $35.00 + assessed per bar, should sales not exceed $300.00

BEO Continued on Next Page

BEO 1234 Continued from Previous Page **PAGE 2 of 2**

International and Domestic Cheese Display
Garnished with Fresh Fruit and Served with Assorted Crackers
@ $4.50 ++ per person

"Sweetheart" Dessert Station to Include:
Mini Raspberry Cheesecake, Chocolate-Dipped Strawberries
Assorted Valentine Candies
Heart-Shaped Cookies with Red, White, and Pink Icing
Freshly Brewed Coffee, Decaffeinated Coffee, and Tea Service
@ $10.00 ++ per person

7:30 P.M.	Valentine Dance	Ballroom
	No Food or Beverage Needed	
Note to Banquet Captain:	Please note the theme for this evening is Valentine's Day. All appropriate decorations should include red and white colors.	
Note to Banquet Kitchen:	Please ensure food items are replenished continually.	
Reception Setup:	Cocktail Lounge-Style Seating Skirted Buffet Tables 3 Banquet Bars with Bar Backs Valentine-Themed Decorations and Props	
Dance Setup:	Skirted Disc Jockey Table in Center/Front of Room Dance Floor	
Decorations/ Special Arrangements:	Additional Decorations Supplied by Client Disc Jockey Provided by Client	
AV Requirements:	Please supply power cords and outlets for disc jockey. Please adjust ballroom lighting.	
Room Rental:	Waived	
Billing Arrangements:	Advance Deposit Received Incidental Payments at Conclusion of Function	

++ Indicates 20% Service Charge and 10% Sales Tax Will Be Added
+ Indicates 10% Sales Tax Will Be Added

Approval Signature: ______________________________
If the Above Meets with Your Approval, Please Sign One Copy and Return.

FIGURE 8–2
Sample banquet event order

XYZ Hotel and Towers
Banquet Event Order

BEO 1234
DATE SUBMITTED: 12/5/98

SALES FILE NA555
CONVENTION SERVICE FILE 1232
CATERING FILE 0001

BEO Number. This number should serve as an internal control number for all BEOs. Each BEO should have a unique number. It is useful for tracking purposes.

Date Submitted. The date the BEO was created and distributed should be marked so that all the appropriate internal departments know it was submitted in a timely manner.

"File" Number. Group file numbers serve a few purposes. First, at a glance anyone can know if a BEO applied to local catering or a sleeping-room-related group. In our example, we can see that this function was group catering, because all three of the file numbers were listed. This hotel uses three-tiered deployment: sales, catering, and convention service representatives were listed. The other purpose for listing the file numbers is to give the manager in charge a little backup. If the manager were not available for some reason, another manager could pick up the file and find what he or she needed to know about the group.

FUNCTION DAY/DATE:	Sunday, February 14, 1999
ORGANIZATION:	Gotham City Valentine Couples Group
POST AS:	Valentine's Day Dance
BILLING ADDRESS:	123 Lovers Lane, Gotham City, NY 01234
BOOKING CONTACT:	Ms. Jane Doe
ON-SITE CONTACT(S):	Mr. John Q. Public
PHONE:	(202) 555-1521
FAX:	(202) 555-1522

Function Day/Date. Day of the function.

Organization. Name of the organization booking the function.

Post As. Often (as was the case in this example), the group that booked the function wants to post the name of its function differently. Posting a function is simply naming the group throughout the hotel. The reader-boards in any facility list the daily events as their sponsoring groups want them. Attendees often look for the posted name on readerboards.

Billing Address. Address of where the final bill is to go. It is listed here so that the banquet captain who prepares the bill at the conclusion of the function can include the appropriate information.

Booking Contact/On-Site Contact. Here the internal departments are informed about the person in charge of the event. Many times, the person who booked the function is not the same as the one who is on site during the function. The facility staff look much more efficient if they all know for whom to ask.

SALES MANAGER: Mike Smith	CONVENTION SERVICE MANAGER: Andrew Jones
	CATERING MANAGER: Janet Hill
ATTENDEES EXPECTED: 275	GUARANTEED: 290 SET NUMBER 305

Manager's Names. Like the section listing the file numbers, this section of the BEO has a dual purpose. First, it lists the manager(s) who booked the group. The facility can tell if the BEO applies to local or group catering functions by which type of salespeople are listed. In some cases, the salespeople who created the BEOs (catering or convention service managers) will initial their names to approve the BEOs and authorize them for distribution.

Attendees Expected. Initial number of people for which the function was booked.

Guaranteed. The "guarantee" for a function is very important in the catering industry. Full-service caterers require some type of notice from groups as to how many people they guarantee will attend. This guarantee is reinforced by the fact that most caterers bill clients for this number of attendees as minimums. Most require guaranteed numbers of attendees from clients 48 to 72 working hours before the function. This is vital for food purchasing and staff. If a group arrived with significantly more attendees than expected, the guarantee gives the caterer some time to accommodate the change.

Set Number. Serves a contingency purpose. Because there are many intangibles affecting function turnout, most caterers set functions for 5 percent over guaranteed numbers to accommodate any unexpected, last-minute attendees. Typically, a room is set for, and the kitchen prepares for, this extra 5 percent. The banquet captain in charge of the function does a head count once everyone is seated so as to inform the kitchen if that extra 5 percent or more of food is needed. Hotels should never bill for this overset, as it is sometimes called, unless the numbers of attendees dictate.

FUNCTION TIME	FUNCTION	ROOM
3:00 P.M.–6:00 P.M.	Room Setup	Ballroom
6:30 P.M.–7:30 P.M.	Reception	Ballroom Foyer
7:30 P.M.–12 midnight	Dance	Ballroom

"Summary" Information. Provides an "at a glance" look at the BEO and its contents. Each function, time, and room is posted in chronological order, usually with the "Post As" name of the group on the facility's readerboards. This informs attendees of the events the group is conducting.

The middle section of the BEO is called the "body" or "Agenda Specifics." This is where the BEO creator must clearly and articulately list everything. Again, in chronological order, each food item and service requirement is listed as it applies to the event. This is where the prices and amounts are itemized.

If an event does not need food (as in this example for the dance setup and the dance itself), it should be noted on the BEO as "No Food or Beverage Needed." The kitchen and/or banquet staff are trained to correlate functions and their possible food needs with the BEO. The BEO informs the appropriate operational departments by using this disclaimer that they asked the questions of the client and they don't want food and/or service at that particular time. This reassures those departments that there will be no last minute changes of details that were initially overlooked.

If the BEO is longer than one page (as is the example), it should be noted on both the first and second pages like this:

BEO continued on next page   **PAGE 1 of 2**

and

BEO 1234 Continued from Previous Page   **PAGE 2 of 2**

Noting that the BEO continues on the next page triggers people to look at the next page and helps them to remember to complete all BEO requirements. The notation on the second page explains to readers who may pick up the second page of the BEO that they are missing the first page. The BEO number helps those readers find the corresponding first page.

Note to Banquet Captain: Please note the theme for this evening is Valentine's Day. All appropriate decorations should include red and white color.

Note to Banquet Kitchen: Please ensure food items are continually replenished.

"Notes." In this area of the BEO, the caterer in charge takes the time to highlight certain details for specific individuals or departments to address. The example included "Notes" to the kitchen and the banquet captain that were of distinct importance to the success of the function or to the client. BEOs can include notes to any department or individuals who are part of the BEO distribution. These notes should be followed up by catering/convention service staff and again in the BEO review meeting to ensure everyone understands the point.

Event Setup. Here the BEO speaks to the banquet floor staff directly. This area should list the specific room set requirements for each event listed in the summary information section of the BEO. The example BEO listed setup requirements for the reception and the dance because they were included on the same BEO. The room setup (at 3:00 P.M.) required nothing from the facility, so the BEO did not need to dictate setup.

The BEO should be thought of as a functional document. The BEO creators should write them as if they were the ones doing the actual setups. They should be read over to ensure they can be read and interpreted by anyone.

Decorations/Special Arrangements. This section, sometimes called the "etc." section, is where a caterer makes everyone aware of any outside additions to the function. If the client was to use any outside vendors or if clients bring their own special additions, like decorations (as in the example), the BEO would list that here. It should list everything the facility is not supplying, like a DJ, production company, musicians, florist, or some other service provider of which the hotel should be aware.

A/V Requirements. This area is important because the A/V department usually does not look anywhere else on the BEO. Nothing else on the BEO applies (unless a "Note" is addressed to them). All relevant details and requirements are listed here.

Room Rental:	Waived
Billing Arrangements	Advance Deposit Received
	Incidental Payments at Conclusion of Function

Room Rental. This is the part of the BEO where the facility lists the charge for the use of the function room. Sometimes called "Setup Fee" or "Function Space Charge," the room rental can contribute a great deal to the profitability of a function. In this example, the rental was waived because the group was spending a good amount of money on the function in terms of food and beverage.

Billing. This section is arguably the most important in that it involves what the caterer is in business for, money. The BEO creator wants to inform all interested parties (namely the banquet captains who make up the bills, the accounting department that processes them, and the clients who must pay them) of their understanding of the billing process. There are typically only three options available to a client in terms of billing. (1) **Direct Billing. Direct billing** involves sending the bill to client for payment, assuming the accounting department has approved it based on the client's credit history. (2) **Advance Deposit/Prepayment.** With **advance deposit/prepayment**, the client sends money ahead of time to cover the expenses of the function. Sometimes this method is used because the client's/organization's credit history is so poor that the controller denied them direct billing. The only drawback to this payment method is that it does not cover incidental or unplanned charges. It should be used exclusively when the purchased food/beverage amounts are fixed. It can, however, be used with other payment methods if the costs are not fixed. In the example, the group sent an advance deposit, but the BEO stated that the food was to be replenished continually and bars were hosted. Therefore, there is no way to know the exact total charge in advance. The group in the example supplemented its advance deposit with the third payment method: (3) **Payment Upon Conclusion of Function.** With **payment upon conclusion of function**, the total unpaid charges are settled after the amounts are tallied. Often, it is the banquet captain's job to make sure the bill is correct and the money is collected. It should be stressed again that the billing requirements must be accurate. If the banquet captain read that the group should be direct billed and the catering salesperson mistakenly omitted the need to collect at the event's conclusion, the facility could go unpaid.

++ Indicates 20% Service Charge and 10% Sales Tax Will Be Added.
+ Indicates 10% Sales Tax Will Be Added.

"Plus/Plus" A common practice in the industry is to add a service charge and tax to the prices of food/beverage and some services. Most facilities outline this policy by adding one or two "pluses" after each quoted price. The term "plus/plus" indicates that the price needs to have both the service charge and the sales tax added. If a price were to be quoted with only one plus, only the tax was added. The actual percentages differ from property to property. The opposite of this pricing strategy is to quote prices, which is called **inclusive pricing.** Inclusive pricing simply means that the salesperson has built the service charge and tax into listed prices. Some clients prefer to have all the costs outlined and calculated up front. If a hotel uses plus/plus pricing, it should be explained on the menus and the BEOs clearly.

Approval Signature: _____
If the Above Meets with Your Approval, Please Sign One Copy and Return.

Signature Line. This last detail applies if the BEO is being used as an external confirmation document. If BEOs are sent to clients for approval, one should indicate on the signature line that by signing this document they agree with its contents. A signed BEO eliminates the possibility of clients returning and saying they "didn't expect this menu" or "these are not the prices we agreed to." If signed BEOs are required, make sure you send clients extra copies for their records.

Industry Perspective

"Group Billing and Its Impact on a Facility"

Dawn Hill
Assistant Controller
Marriott Corporation

The importance of group billing, the method by which a group pays for its rooms and/or banquet functions, is often discounted by salespeople. Hotels and other facilities are in business to make money, just like all other for-profit enterprises. Timely and complete payment of group accounts is vital to the financial health of any for-profit business.

A hotel has costs and financial obligations that it must meet, just like the organizations it books. The cash flow, the incoming and outgoing measurement of revenue, dictates how well a hotel can meet its obligations. These obligations can include: labor costs, food costs, insurance, taxes, ownership payments, capital improvement, supplies, advertising, and franchise fees. The incoming cash flow, or revenue due a hotel, is called accounts receivable. Accounts receivable play the most important role in meeting financial obligations. In any hotel, the bulk of accounts receivable is made of group and/or catering accounts. That is why the billing of these accounts is so important.

The most common payment method for groups is direct billing. This option extends credit to the group under the assumption that it will pay all hotel costs incurred in a set time frame. The direct billing application must be completed by the client thoroughly for this credit to be extended. It is the salesperson's job to ensure that all information is completed and relayed to the accounting department in a timely manner. Specific information, like hotel references and bank references, must be checked by the hotel before extending credit. An organization with a history of poor payments at other hotels, or one with too little money in the bank to cover the upcoming function, may be denied credit. The salesperson must not be timid when determining the payment method early in the qualifying process. If billing problems are addressed early enough, other arrangements can be made. The most important thing to remember when determining direct billing status is that credit is a privilege, not a right. Groups that have been direct billed at other hotels should not automatically assume that credit will be extended them.

Group salespeople should understand that booking groups that do not pay well affects the accounting department. Most hotel accounting departments are measured on how quickly groups make payments. The age of the accounts receivable (an average of the time all receivables have been outstanding) is an important measure of cash flow performance.

In summary, salespeople who book groups without sufficiently considering the groups' payment abilities may hurt, rather than help, the hotel. A salesperson can book a record number of groups, but if those groups do not pay, they are of no real use.

GROUP RESUMES

An important document that pertains exclusively to group-related catering at a hotel is the **group resume**. The group resume incorporates the sleeping room component of a group and all the group's catering needs. While primarily hotel documents, stand-alone facilities may summarize extensive or multiple-day programs with group resumes as well.

The group resume, sometimes called a group profile or group cover sheet, serves a purpose similar to the BEO in that it communicates to other facility departments specific information about a group. The biggest difference is that the group resume is distributed to all departments, not just those concerned with executing functions and events. Departments in a hotel like housekeeping and front desk are now included.

The group resume informs the facility of the size of the group, the number of overnight rooms (if applicable), the number of on-property functions, and so on. It should be completed far enough in advance of the group's arrival (like the BEO) to ensure that all affected departments have time to staff and prepare appropriately. Many facilities review the group resume in a meeting of departmental managers. The **preconvention meeting**, or precon, is similar to the BEO meeting in that all departments review the information. The biggest difference is that the precon is dedicated to one group resume and the group clients often attend to review the upcoming events with facility staff.

Group resumes are vital to projecting catering and occupancy projections as well as overall revenue numbers. These documents are helpful to departments that work with guests on the "front line" (like the front desk), because they can provide answers to many questions.

The format of the group resume differs from facility to facility, as does BEO format. It should contain as much information as possible that pertains to the upcoming group. Ideally, the resume should be no more than two pages long. Because the group resume may contain sleeping room information along with catering function details, it looks similar to portions of the group turnover document and the BEO. The resume could contain the following basic information:

XYZ Hotel Group Resume   Today's Date:
Group Name: Dates of Function:
Contact Name: Address:
Telephone: Fax:
SALES MANAGER:
CONVENTION SERVICE MANAGER:

Room Rate: ___ Single ___ Double ___ Triple ___ Quad ___ Suites
Group Billing: ___ Sign All Charges ___ Room/Tax to Master
                  ___ Individuals On Own

The preceding two lines provide a snapshot of the room rate structure and room billing.

Current Room Block: ____(date)

Day/Date	Day/Date	Day/Date	Day/Date	Day/Date	Total
___	___	___	___	___	___

Pick Up As of Today: ____(date)

Day/Date	Day/Date	Day/Date	Day/Date	Day/Date	Total
___	___	___	___	___	___

Here the resume shows the room block and room pickup of the group at the time the document was generated.

VIP	Arrival	Departure	Room Type	Billing	Amenity
M/M Jones	2/2/99	2/4/99	Suite	Sign All Charges	Yes
Ms. R. Smith	2/3/99	2/4/99	King	On Own	No
Mr. A. Willis	2/3/99	2/4/99	Twin	On Own	No

This section of the resume is important in that it lets the hotel identify the VIPs of the group. Typically, the VIPs in this listing are the on-site contacts, speakers, and assorted people deemed "important" by the group. It is a good idea to send these VIPs amenities or some other types of welcome gift upon their arrivals.

Agenda Summary. Here the resume should list briefly the catering function agenda of the group in a way similar to the "Summary Agenda" format of the BEO. The difference here is the resume should not provide any more detail than a summary of events. Actual menu selections and other function-related information is reflected in the BEO. The agenda summary might look like this:

Monday, February 15, 1999
8:00 A.M.–5:00 P.M.   Meeting
6:00 P.M.–7:00 P.M.   Reception

Tuesday, February 16, 1999
8:00 A.M.–12:00 P.M.   Meeting
12:00 P.M.–1:00 P.M.   Lunch

Some facilities also attach all BEOs to the group resume because they feel there is no such thing as too much information. Some might argue that departments like housekeeping do not need the BEOs, but others insist that the more people who know what is going on, the more attention the group can receive from the total facility.

The rest of the group resume should address each department in the facility with any relevant specifics. Most resumes lack information for all

DEPARTMENT SCENARIOS

Front Desk
- Major arrival time: 6:00 P.M. scattered departures.
- Bus arrival on second night at 3:00 P.M.
- Please key pack and preregister all VIPs.

Reservations
- Expect last-minute calls due to slow pickup.
- Please be aware of the suite reserved for M/M Jones.

Housekeeping
- Turndown service each night for all attendees.
- Please make sure all rooms are ready for the bus arrival on second night.
- Please deep-clean the suite for M/M Jones.

Banquets
- Banner to be hung during meeting.
- Materials for presentations are being stored in Security.

Room Service
- Please note amenity delivery for M/M Jones.
- Expect late-night orders on first night as group will return from activity without eating dinner.

Restaurants
- Late-night dinner possibilities on first night.
- Please set up breakfast buffet on second morning as no meal is scheduled.
- Many vegetarians in group; suggest vegetarian daily specials.

Kitchen
- See Restaurants notes.

Hotel Operator
- Wake-up calls each morning at 6:30 A.M.
- Expect high volume of messages during the meeting.

Security
- Please deliver materials being stored to Banquets before start of meeting.
- Valuable presentation equipment being used in meeting room; please check on it in the evening.

Accounting
- Please note billing requirements.

Industry Perspective

"Effective Precons"

Lori Perry
Convention Service Manager

The precon is an effective tool for a hotel or banquet facility when used properly. It is the first opportunity most of the operational staff have to meet the client. This first impression is vital to the client's comfort level and can impact the overall success of the program greatly. The team effort approach of a precon translates into client confidence; the client knows the entire facility is dedicated to the program's success. The following points are crucial to an effective precon:

- All facility personnel should arrive 15 minutes early. Nothing looks more unprofessional than facility staff arriving late. Once the meeting begins and the doors close, latecomers should not be admitted.
- All staff should be dressed well and wear their name tags. Even though introductions will be made, name tags help the client identify and remember key personnel.
- Place cards identifying participants and clients should be placed on tables.
- No pagers, beepers, or walkie-talkies should be evident. The precon is important enough that no interruptions should occur.
- All facility participants should stand and greet clients as they enter.
- Each participant should be well versed in program specifics and encouraged to ask relevant questions.
- Participants should reaffirm to the client their responsibilities and roles in the success of the group.
- The ideal room set is U shape with the client at the head of the *U*.
- An elegant or themed coffee break can add to the ambiance of the room as well as show clients the quality level of service they will receive. However, facility participants should limit themselves to drinks only. The food should be left for the clients to enjoy.

- Clients should be encouraged to review the natures of their organizations and the scopes of their upcoming functions.

The meeting should be run by the catering or convention service manager in charge of the group. Having the general manager or another high-level manager in attendance helps add weight. A well-conducted precon is crucial to the success of any large program.

departments. The nature of the group determines in large part which departments require specific notification. The accompanying examples here show what each department in a hotel might see in different scenarios.

PRECONVENTION MEETINGS

Once an organization has booked a large function at a hotel or another facility, the catering department can implement another operation tool, called the preconvention meeting (precon). It is used primarily by the catering or convention service managers assigned to the upcoming group. In the precon, the contact meets the key personnel in a facility and reviews the function agenda with those personnel. The team of leaders gathered from the facility should introduce themselves and explain what they do and how they will ensure the success of the program. The precon is most often run by the convention service manager a few days before the start of a large meeting or convention. The catering salesperson (in three-tiered deployment) should also attend given that the client probably feels most comfortable with him or her due to rapport building.

POSTCONVENTION MEETINGS

Often, large groups or convention clients request a **postconvention meeting (postcon)** at the conclusion of their functions. The postcon is used primarily to summarize all hotel details. The client should meet with the same people who attended the precon. The postcon is useful both for client and facility. It should be run by the same individual who ran the precon. Instead of reviewing a group resume, however, postcon attendees examine a postcon report that summarizes the group's activities at the facility.

The postcon report highlights the number of sleeping rooms actually used and the average rate. It lists each group function in banquets and outlines the number of attendees, called **covers**, and revenue generated. It is useful in comparing actual information to expected information. The group salesperson who booked the group, for example, would be interested in how the rooms picked up upon the group's departure. The salesperson can use this information to better evaluate this business opportunity in the future. The information summarized during a postcon can become part of a salesperson's actual information. Following is a sample **postcon report**:

....

XYZ Hotel Postconvention Report   Today's Date:
Group Name: Dates of Function:
Contact Name: Address:
Telephone: Fax:
SALES MANAGER:
CONVENTION SERVICE MANAGER:

Room Rate: ___ Single ___ Double ___ Triple ___ Quad ___ Suites

Group Billing: ___ Sign All Charges ___ Room/Tax to Master
___ Individuals on Own

Actual Rooms Used

Day/Date	Day/Date	Day/Date	Day/Date	Day/Date	Total
____	____	____	____	____	____

Actual Average Daily Rate

Day/Date	Day/Date	Day/Date	Day/Date	Day/Date	Total
$ ____	$ ____	$ ____	$ ____	$ ____	$ ____

Catering Activity Summary

Event

Day/Date	Brkfst	Breaks	Lunch	Dinner	Reception	**Totals Per Day** (Covers/Revenue)
Number of Covers						
Revenue						
Number of Covers						
Revenue						
Number of Covers						
Revenue						
Totals/Event (Covers/Revenue)						

Comments:

_____

_____

_____

_____

....

In the postcon, fresh impressions and suggestions are very meaningful. Compliments and criticisms mean more coming from clients. The postcon is also a great opportunity for the credit manager to review the master account with the client before the account is sent out. Bills for large conventions can be very involved, so any opportunity to examine them with the individuals who will be paying them will lessen future confusion and errors.

INTERNAL MEMOS

A viable form of internal written communication that covers topics not related to BEOs or group resumes is the internal memo. The internal memo plays a vital part in getting a caterer's job done effectively. Memos can be used to follow up on verbal conversations and to reinforce the issues addressed in documents like the BEO and the group resume. Items of special interest to other departments can be highlighted with memos. Memos are good to use with peers and superiors within the catering office for documentation purposes. Announcements, policy changes, and other important pieces of information can be shared with memos.

The easiest way to write a memo is to organize thoughts using the following three-step formula:

1. Communicate the purpose.
2. Relay the supporting circumstances.
3. Suggest the proposed action, if appropriate.

Organize the memo into three paragraphs, each beginning with these or similar phrases:

- "I am writing because. . . ."
- "The facts are. . . ."
- "I propose that we. . . ."

This approach works well because it is nearly impossible to complete the phrases without directly stating the memo's purpose, circumstances, and action needed. After writing the first draft using these three cues, writers may change the lead sentences to make them suit their styles.

Whenever possible, avoid substituting the memo for personal communication. The memo is a good follow-up to an initial personal contact. Many in the industry employ the "management by memo" philosophy, which entails communication almost entirely via memos. This can lead to ineffective communication, because an overwhelming number of memos from one person tend not to be reviewed with the same scrutiny as others.

Memos should not be used to voice opinions or to erect barriers between people. If someone does not have the courage to state something to another in person, the statement probably does not belong in a memo. Following is a common memo format:

XYZ HOTEL MEMORANDUM

Date:	(Today's date)
To:	(Addressee)
From:	(Individual or group name)
Re:	(Subject of the memo)
CC:	(Those to be copied on the memo)

[Body of the memo]

Memos typically do not end with signature lines. Instead, most individuals who generate memos initial next to their names on the "From" line to indicate that they approve of the memo and its contents. An effective way to ensure that important messages are communicated internally is the three-layered approach. When upcoming operational requirements of a function are intricate or out of the ordinary, caterers must guarantee that the requirements are communicated, understood, and completed. The three-layered approach employs different methods of communication, but the end goals are the same.

The first step is to contact needed personnel/departments by phone. Communicate what is needed and when clearly. No written messages or voice mail should be left for operational personnel. Large operational departments often have many different people coming and going throughout the day and night. The caterer should try again and again by phone until the right person hears the information.

The second step is to follow up the phone call with a memo or E-mail. Recap the conversation and highlight the important issues again when the receiver has those issues in writing. For extra impact, "cc" the receiver's immediate supervisor. While the issue at hand may not impact the receiver's boss, the fact that you made their boss aware of an issue will ensure that a little bit of extra attention may be given.

The third step is to personally follow up as the due date gets near. A few days before a major function, the caterer should visit the operational departments that will be called upon to perform. The face-to-face meeting will cement commitments and help ensure there are no misunderstandings.

MENU EFFICIENCY

A good catering/convention service manager incorporates all menu-planning skills effectively and consistently. A menu that has been put together with good plate presentation, acceptable food/beverage costs, and descriptive word pictures goes a long way to securing a successful function. There is, however, more a caterer can do. As a catering team, many menus may be prepared and sent to the kitchen. A catering department that creates efficient menus operates at peak performance. **Menu efficiency** is maximization of catering resources to ensure that the kitchen is not overburdened.

In today's modern catering operation, banquet kitchen staff prepare several lunches, dinners, and receptions simultaneously each day. Large facilities commonly have 15 to 20 different group meal functions at once. A catering/convention service team that incorporates menu efficiency into its meal planning by sharing or duplicating as many menu items among group functions as possible can greatly reduce stress.

That does not mean that the catering team must copy each menu word for word from each other. An efficient catering team works together to try to reduce the need for disparate and time-consuming kitchen preparation. When planning menus for a day on which the banquet kitchen already has menus, caterers should ask themselves questions like:

- Can the starches be shared?
- Can any of the meals share a vegetable or salad?
- Will that dessert work with my entrée?
- Is that soup compatible?

One can ease the load on a kitchen by checking the BEOs for any upcoming day and using the starch, vegetable, or salad, that is planned. Those BEOs can be found in the master file mentioned previously. The tenets of compatibility, color, texture, and so on must be adhered to first and foremost. Any time one can use the same vegetable or starch combination for two large, simultaneous lunches or dinners, the preparation time for the kitchen is cut dramatically. The chef can prepare one large batch of an item instead of taking the time to prepare two different ones.

Menu efficiency has another component related to food cost. As mentioned earlier, locations may have difficulty obtaining certain food items. Seasonality also impacts the availability of certain food items. Anyone who shops at a grocery store regularly knows that many food items are at their best (and cheapest) when they are in season. Caterers should not plan menus with vegetables or fruits that are out of season, because they will drive up food cost as well as make it difficult for their kitchens to deliver quality products.

Each area of the country has culinary hybrids and signature items. These food items are tied to locations by history, culture, religion, or something else. Many times, banquet kitchens become proficient and, by extension, efficient in popular local choices. Signature items can fit into clients' goal of unique or different meals. Such meals should be fairly cost effective and provide opportunities for tying in props and decorations to add to clients' satisfaction.

One method for achieving efficiency is to leave the decision making to the chef. The so-called "Chef's Choice Option" describes the school of thought that the chef would decide what accompaniments were to go with each entrée. In these cases, menu accompaniments are left to the chef to decide and can be exercised when time is a constraint or when caterers lack the knowledge to make efficient choices. Caterers who are unsure which menu accompaniments to choose can simply state "Chef's Choice of Vegetable" or "Chef's Choice of Dessert" on the BEO to ensure proper choices are made. This also allows kitchen staff to make more efficient use of the items they have on hand. Some caterers do not like this method, because they feel it takes away from their ability to sell menus with plate presentation and word pictures. Others feel that in large catering operations it is crucial to maximizing resources of which the catering salesperson may be unaware.

CUSTOMER SERVICE

Eighty percent of your business comes from 20 percent of your customers.

All people involved in catering should continually remind themselves that without satisfied clients they would be out of work. The definition of customer satisfaction in the industry needs to evolve into a notion of exceeding customer expectations. Exceeding client expectations entails incorporating all the communication and rapport-building skills.

All consumers can list a few stores and restaurants that they go back to again and again, places where they are confident they will be pleased. Most consumers can also name a few establishments to which they will never return.

The event that caused satisfaction or dissatisfaction is at the root of exceeding customers' needs. In most cases, when expectations are exceeded client loyalty is instilled in the consumer, which is worth more than any advertising could buy.

Caterers must instill in themselves and their operations the knowledge that all the work they do as salespeople in booking functions will be wasted if their operations do not provide experiences that create client loyalty.

The business that comes back again and again to a caterer makes up a vastly greater portion of total revenue than do new pieces of business. Client loyalty ensures that business returns again and again.

As was mentioned earlier, caterers sell their services against competitors with very similar products and services. The basic menu components are the same. Most sleeping rooms are very similar. Many facilities in the same location have meeting rooms of comparable sizes and dimensions. Loyalty drives clients to repeat their buying decisions.

A repeat sale is the easiest one a salesperson makes. Repeat customers typically return because they have become loyal. Salespeople with loyal customer bases have more time to solicit and seek new clients. Salespeople in all industries seek to combine increased repeat sales with more time for solicitation.

The best way for catering salespeople to instill customer loyalty, which ensures repeat sales, is to take ownership actions.

OWNERSHIP ACTIONS

Because the catering industry is service based, the value customers place on products is a direct result of the services they perceive they receive. Service perception begins with the salesperson's initial greeting and ends with the thank-you note or call. In between, clients experience various service levels from everyone they contact. Service perception of a client can begin with the facility doorperson and end with the credit manager.

Any caterer can contribute to overall service perception, even after the group is booked. Through ownership actions, caterers can communicate to their customers how important those customers are to them.

Ownership actions are the acts or services performed by caterers personally to help ensure the success of groups or functions. Caterers can take ownership of their groups by taking these actions.

Ownership actions have the dual advantage of reflecting well on both external customers (clients) and internal customers (catering operations). When caterers show both groups of customers how badly they want to exceed expectations, they win the respect of their peers and achieve customer loyalty.

"Meet and Greet." A simple but often overlooked customer-service tool is the "meet and greet," the act of greeting contacts when they arrive for their functions. If outside caterers have dinners scheduled, they should try to be at them whenever possible. Being at the front desk to welcome arriving guests is important for facility salespeople. When applicable, salespeople might go to their clients' registration desks and touch base with them during their functions. If the on-site contact is not the person who booked the program, the two may not have even spoken before the contact's arrival. Caterers should spend some time trying to establish rapport with such contacts.

An extra step that can create increased service perception in the client is to bring the general manager or another high-ranking manager to the meet and greet. Even if the contact and salesperson met at the precon, the extra effort will impress on clients how much the operation values their business.

Check Function Rooms. Catering salespeople should be very familiar with their groups' agendas. Whenever possible, they should check scheduled function rooms before start times. Caterers should visually check rooms as if they were the clients. If everything is not set up properly, there should still be time to rectify any issue.

In many facilities, banquet/floor managers as well as catering/convention servicepeople check function rooms. It is their primary responsibility. If the facility is very busy, however, floor managers may be occupied. The catering/convention service should follow up whenever possible. Caterers benefit from checking rooms: Servers, housemen, and other line personnel see that the caterers are involved and care about their groups and give caterers their respect.

BE VISIBLE AND AVAILABLE

As much as possible, caterers should try to give contacts the impression that they are available when needed. This should be caterers' main priority while groups are in-house. Without taking away from their selling duties, caterers should greet clients when they stop by their offices. Often, contacts stop by unannounced during their programs. If possible, caterers should drop their current tasks and address the clients' needs or delegate solutions. Clients should never feel that their salespeople are too busy to see them.

When clients approach catering/convention servicepeople for help, those people must take ownership. They need not personally change a meeting room set, but they should point clients in the right directions. The appropriate people must handle any problems; caterers should simply act as facilitators. Caterers should also follow up to make sure issues are resolved. These types of ownership actions are remembered, because they show that clients' needs are always in the forefront.

Management by Walking Around. The "Management by Walking Around" (MBWA) theory is that the best managers are those who are visible and accessible. This concept has generated interest recently in the hospitality trade journals. Caterers cannot be effective in their offices behind closed doors. MBWA, which simply reinforces ownership actions, applies to internal and external clients.

Customer Evaluations. Customer evaluations in the catering industry are similar to the "rate our service" cards found in many restaurants. The evaluations used for catering are a bit more involved in that they address quality, cleanliness, and satisfaction issues for each catering department. They are useful in evaluating how well a catering operation performed relative to its expectations.

INDUSTRY EXAMPLE OF MBWA

A well-respected general manger in the Midwest uses his own version of MBWA. He uses the term *walkabout* to describe the concept. Each day he walks throughout the hotel, personally checking on groups, empty function space, the outlets, sleeping rooms, and so on. He carries a small notebook on these tours and writes down anything he finds so he may address what he finds with the appropriate managers later. The impact that this has on clients and individual guests is powerful. It makes people feel important while keeping the general manager in touch. Not all general managers employ this management philosophy. Some find it difficult to make time to employ MBWA.

Catering salespeople should always send client evaluation forms with their thank-you letters. These evaluations are valuable tools for praising departments or employees who exceeded clients' expectations. It is desirable to share these positive comments with individuals mentioned by name whenever possible. Negative comments are also valuable learning tools. Challenges can be corrected before they become chronic.

If caterers feel comfortable enough in their level of rapport with clients, they may ask those clients to write letters evaluating the service and the facility (if applicable). Positive letters from clients are called **testimonial letters**. They can strongly impact prospective clients because other clients, not salespeople, praised the caterers. A collection of testimonial letters can be framed and posted in the catering reception area for people to read while they are waiting. They can also be kept in a binder, often called a "brag book," for potential clients to peruse.

ONGOING CATERING RESPONSIBILITIES

The operational aspects of catering that deal with bringing in functions and ensuring quality service for groups are crucial to master. Catering operations skills need not be strictly tied to booking and servicing groups, however. There are other operational concepts that deal with management and self-preparation that catering salespeople must be well versed in. This section covers a wide range of issues that caterers of all disciplines should employ on ongoing bases.

DEPLOYMENT

As was said throughout this book, the catering and convention service managers of any operation must be considered salespeople as much as anything. In this section, *sales team* refers to all members of the catering operation's sales team. All members of the team of salespeople who share an objective work together to achieve that objective. One can look to the great sports teams in history to find a similar shared goal, winning.

A major facet in the team approach is a caterer's marketing effort. Traditionally, **marketing** is positioning a product as ideal for a customer's needs. It is the driving force behind sales in any operation. Marketing supports selling by creating awareness of a product or service. This is especially true in the hospitality industry.

The successful marketing of catering depends on many factors. Catering/convention services staff can aid in the marketing effort. The sales team can also be viewed as a marketing team, which is why in many facilities the marketing function is headed by one person who also directs the sales and catering effort. These types of facilities (generally hotels) have directors of sales and directors of catering/convention services run their respective departments. These staff report to directors of marketing. In this way, the sales team of a hotel has a coordinated marketing effort.

Catering/convention service managers should understand their marketing role, which is essential to maximizing potential and achieving their teams' goals. The personal marketing effort of catering professionals is made up of two things. The first is getting out into the community and becoming involved in groups and activities that get their names and the names of their employers into the market. The second and more fundamental part of a personal marketing effort is to thoroughly understand and develop their roles in their sales teams' market deployment.

This section looks at two different ways of catering/convention service deployment and their respective strengths and weaknesses. Local catering deployment is another important marketing component to consider. Some catering operations deploy their local catering salespeople based on market segments. Others deploy their local catering people with no strategies; they simply let them book groups across the client-type spectrum.

Convention Service Classification. A convention service manager, by nature, is tied to another individual, the group sales or catering person depending on type of tiered deployment. Convention service people do not necessarily choose the groups with whom they work. How they become involved with a group depends on how their operation wants to classify the convention service team. The most common classifications of convention service teams are partnering and assignment. Both have strengths and weaknesses.

Partnering. **Partnering** is deploying a specific convention service manager with a specific group salesperson over and over again. Convention service managers and their sales partners handle all groups as a team. Depending on the size of the operation and the sales skill of the partner, one may have more than one partner. If one salesperson books too few groups to keep a convention service person busy, management may assign him or her two or even three group sales partners. Rarely does a facility have an equal number of sales and convention service people. Factors other than skill or effort can affect the number of groups a sales partner may book.

The sales partner may handle specific markets that are in a slump due to the nature of the economy, or one may work with a salesperson whose groups are seasonal and heavy during certain parts of the year and lighter in others.

Partnering allows for the formation of strong bonds and efficient teamwork. Partnerships are relationships. Both partners must work together to surpass a client's objectives. Both must also work to understand the other. Being able to predict each other's thoughts or actions allows each the freedom to make decisions both are comfortable with. Clients notice this comfort as well.

Working with the same partner also has the benefit of working with the same type of groups (this only applies if the sales team is deployed via market segments). Convention service managers gain in-depth understandings of how association or SMERF groups like to conduct their meetings if their sales partners book those organizations exclusively.

Assignment. Some offices prefer to use another method of deployment in convention services. A rotation of managers is assigned to each group as soon as it is turned over from the group salesperson. Often, the turnover is handed to the director of catering or convention services, and he or she assigns the next available manager.

This method of deployment is beneficial for smaller offices in which convention service managers are few. Also, assigning groups can ease the workload for those who may be swamped. This way, groups are assigned to the managers who can handle them.

Assigning groups can ease the repetition of working with the same market segment over and over again. It also eliminates the problem of partners who do not get along. The downside is that all will be assigned groups randomly. There is no way to know ahead of time the nature and size of the group to be assigned next. This can create anxiety in some people.

INTERNAL RELATIONSHIPS

If, as a convention service manager, you have overnight room responsibility, you have many more departments to interface with (e.g., reservations, front desk) than does a catering manager. Regardless of your exact responsibility, the skills needed to communicate sensibly with the group sales team and the kitchen staff are useful to examine.

GROUP SALES INTERFACE

Most appropriately for convention service managers, relating to and understanding the group salesperson is crucial to performing correctly. Many managers in catering/convention services unfortunately incorporate an "us" versus "them" mentality when communicating to and about group sales. Some in the industry designate the two sides "foodies" and "roomies" based on their separate priorities. Group salespeople want to sell rooms, and catering people want to sell food. Aside from these obvious differences, the ultimate end goals for both are the same. If the clients are happy, both sides win. Everyone's best interests are served when convention service managers can get their sales partners to work with and for them.

Chapter 7 discussed informing salespeople about situations in which groups arrive with less-than-expected overnight room reservations. Understanding what is important to group salespeople is vital in establishing rapport with them. Keeping them on top of potential problems allows salespeople to rectify situations before their bosses or others get involved. If a convention service manager comes across function room blocking errors, the salespeople should be politely asked if they meant to block the space differently.

A good relationship with a sales teammate can reward one in the end. One salesperson and convention service manager worked so well together that they were assigned to partner on all their groups. These two managers communicated so well that they could almost predict each other's thoughts. Like any good relationship, they worked on understanding each other's needs. Eventually, the relationship evolved into a real partnership. If the convention service manager was not available, the salesperson handled BEO questions. The salesperson could count on the other to field questions about cutoff dates and so on. The end result was what both desired and was always the same, satisfied clients.

Kitchen Interface. Both catering and convention service managers must be aware of the special relationship needed with a catering operation's kitchen staff. Caterers are really selling the skills of these people every day. Understanding their needs makes life easier on all involved with catering.

Chefs and their staff are typically highly trained and experienced culinary artists. Menu planners must see themselves as artists. They view their products as works of art. They should be treated with respect. Taking the time to learn about how they conduct day-to-day operations provides much insight. All catering/convention service personnel should help with **banquet plateups** when appropriate. A banquet plateup is the act of preparing large numbers of identical meals for a function. Each individual in the kitchen is assigned a part of the plate to prepare (e.g., starch, sauce, garnish), and the plate moves "along the line" to the next individual. Some plateups use moving assembly lines.

Asking questions of the chef about menu preparation, food and beverage costs, new signature items, and the like when appropriate can be very useful and keeps the caterers abreast of trends. All catering staff want their kitchen staff to look at them as allies.

CHAPTER REVIEW

KEY CONCEPTS

Catering deployment	Billing	Banquet plateup
Menu efficiency	Guest resume	Interdepartmental
Ownership actions	Banquet event order	relationships
Postconvention	Preconvention meeting	Internal documents
meeting (postcon)	(precon)	Customer service

REVIEW QUESTIONS

1. Why is managing internal relationships so important for a caterer?
2. Explain how a banquet plateup is conducted.
3. How does a catering booking impact the rest of the facility?
4. What makes internal operational documents so important?
5. Name an ownership action and its importance to sales.

VIDEOTAPE EXERCISE

Conduct a role-playing exercise with one person playing the salesperson and the other playing the client. Videotape each participant in sales scenarios such as:

- Conducting competitive analyses
- Customer phone conversations
- Site inspections
- Customer appointments
- Contract negotiations
- Pre-/postcons

When finished, review the tape with the sales team or classroom.

This is a good opportunity to tie all chapters together by taping each step in the sales process. Begin with the hotel sales triangle steps and continue through to the final guest arrival. Trade roles and critique each others' abilities. You will find that viewing yourself on tape reveals things you never expected.

Glossary

account penetration   Process of determining new sources of business within an organization.

action triangles   Triangles that outline what salespeople may encounter at each point of the catering sales triangle. The action triangle is used to describe what salespeople must do at each point in the triangle.

advance deposit/prepayment   Process in which the client sends money in advance to cover the expenses of the function. Sometimes this method is used when client's/organization's credit history is so poor direct billing was denied.

advantage   Result of matching a goal to a feature. The benefit gained from this combination is the advantage.

affirmation   Client agreement.

airwall   Flexible partition that divides a function room.

amplifier   Device used with some type of audio source that enhances or intensifies sound before presentation.

apéritif   French word for "light drink." An apéritif is served at the start of a meal to excite the palate. Champagne and sherry are common apéritifs.

appetizer   Typically the first item served in a meal, hot or cold. Its purpose is to prepare the eater for what is to follow. Soups fall into this category.

audio monitor   Device that is useful in any setup with a live music source. It is usually a small speaker in a stand-alone configuration near the mixer. It serves as a "listening ear" as to how something is being heard throughout the audio system.

audio source   Any device or entity that creates a sound to be fed into an audio presentation system. This can be a presenter, speaker, live band, and so on.

audiovisual (AV) Equipment, tools, and materials used in any type of presentation to engage the senses of sound or sight.

balance Fitting food items together on a plate based on their colors.

banquet chef Chef who ensures that all catered meal functions (i.e.: nonrestaurant functions) are completed. Not all kitchens have this level of chef. Some kitchens employ the executive sous chef in this role.

banquet menus Menus preset by the kitchen and catering management of any banquet facility.

banquet plateups Identical meals for a function.

benchmark Factor that provides a rough idea of the square footage needed for a function.

blocking space Reserving function space for a group.

booking cycle Time between the booking of a reservation and the arrival of the guests.

boom microphone Microphone that is attached to some type of extension. It is used to capture the audio source, but it cannot be used at very close range.

boxed meals Portable meals.

buffet Allows attendees to choose the types and amounts of food items. Buffets allow for more than one of each menu type to be served.

buffet line Food assortment laid along a table for attendees to serve themselves.

bundling Process by which two or more elements of a meeting's costs are combined and quoted as one.

butler style Reception service in which food is served by roaming waiters.

cable Generic term for all types of connecting cables used in most AV equipment. Sometimes called coaxial or "coax" cables, cables come in various lengths and gauges to perform various tasks.

cart Sometimes called an "AV cart," is used to transport other AV devices, such as a monitor, a slide projector, and an overhead projector.

carving station Station at which a large food is carved for each attendee individually.

cash bar Bar at which attendees pay for the drinks they consume.

catering accoutrements Suggestions for enhancing an event.

catering operations Functions/roles/duties a caterer may engage in before, during, and after a function.

chafing dish Large display pan over a heat source to keep food warm.

chef Leader of those involved in food preparation.

chef's table Brings customers, VIPs, and other important people for the catering organization together for a meal put on by the executive chef and staff.

cluster cities   Areas where catering companies have more than one operation.

coffee break   Function designed to break up the day for meeting attendees. The coffee break allows attendees to stretch their legs and network between sessions. Coffee does not have to be served, but it often is during early- and mid-morning coffee breaks. Afternoon coffee breaks can include any type of beverage and snack.

cold preparation   The kitchen staff who work with foods that need no cooking, for example, salads and fruits.

commissionable rate   Rate that includes 10 percent over the net room rate. This commission is paid to the travel agent or meeting planner once guests pay for their rooms. In most cases, only agents and planners who have been issued identification numbers by IATA are eligible for commissions.

communication   Process of transmitting a message from a sender to a receiver.

compatibility   Degree to which certain menu items fit together on a plate.

complete meeting package (CMP)   Also called the comprehensive meeting package, package used by hotels and conference centers with sleeping rooms. The CMP bundles the cost of a sleeping room with the DMP. CMP is also the accreditation awarded by the Convention Liaison Council to Certified Meeting Professionals.

composition   A food's historical or geographical origins and preparation method.

computer projector   Like the LCD panel, the projector uses its own light source to project a computer's image onto a screen. There is no need for an overhead.

conference center   Meeting and/or event facility that generally has no sleeping rooms. Some conference centers have sleeping rooms, but they do not focus on those rooms as their primary revenue source, as hotels do.

continental breakfast   Lighter version of the breakfast buffet that serves cold food items and hot/cold beverages in buffet style.

cordials   After-dinner service that can include sweet liqueurs like brandy. Coffee drinks like Irish coffee (coffee with whiskey) and Bailey's Irish Cream are popular cordials. Rarely, cigars are also offered.

corkage fee   Amount paid to caterer for opening and pouring wines that clients bring to a function.

covers   Number of attendees served in a banquet function or food/beverage outlet.

cross-training   The ability to learn the skills of more than one discipline.

culinary hybrids   Foods with mixed backgrounds resulting from the mixing of traditional food cultures.

customer profile   The call report and other items, like past menus and catering contracts, that indicate specific traits of an organization.

dance floor   "Built to suit" function item that generally comes in 3 foot × 3 foot segments. Each segment is made of treated wood or wood imitation plastic and is rimmed with reinforced steel interlocking clamps.

data mining   Extracting historical data from a database.

day meeting package (DMP)   Package that bundles the cost of the meeting space, food and beverage (often continental breakfast, coffee breaks, and lunch), and a limited amount of AV equipment.

decision maker   Individual or group who decides which caterer a business opportunity will choose.

demographics   Identifying consumers based on their buying criteria.

dessert   Typically the last course of a meal. Western tradition calls for some sort of sweet concoction to be served. Fruits, cheeses, cakes, pies, tarts, flans, and cookies can all be served as desserts.

determining goals   Uncovering and addressing a client's buying criteria so as to ensure the sale.

dimmer switch   Light control device that is often mounted on function room walls to control the intensity of house lights. Dimmer switches can be connected to remote switches to allow light control from the podium or somewhere else away from the function room wall, or they can be stand-alone controls for portable lights.

direct billing   Sending the bill to client for payment after the accounting department has approved that bill based on the client's credit history.

dissolve   Process by which two or more projection units are faded in and out together to create a seamless presentation.

dubbing   Process by which recorded audio is transferred from one recording to another.

entrée   Considered the main course of any meal. The entrée is the focus of the eating experience. The entrée is often served with a starch and a vegetable.

equalizer   Audio device often used with an amplifier and/or a PA system that allows for adjustments in bass, treble, and mid-range frequencies. It can be employed when the audio source lacks sound quality or the acoustics of the room are less than ideal.

establishing rapport   Creating a sense of free and open exchange.

event function planning   Nonfood and beverage aspects of securing function space.

event planning logistics   Arena that includes securing transportation (ground and air), program management (e.g., attendee invitations and responses, food and beverage scheduling), content (e.g., speakers, function agendas, and program materials), and activities (e.g., spouses programs, off-site locations, and recreation).

executive chef   Person responsible for the overall food production effort. He or she must control food cost while ensuring that the level of food quality is maintained. More of a manager than a hands-on chef, the executive chef coordinates the kitchen team in food production and operational menu planning.

executive sous chef   Chef who typically leads the food production. The executive chef in a large kitchen may develop into more of a manager than a "hands-on" chef. The executive sous (pronounced *sue*) chef implements the directives and ensures the team runs well.

executive steward   Person responsible for inventorying and cleaning servingware and eating utensils. The steward ensures that the restaurant has enough plates, forks, knives, and spoons. When a large catered function is scheduled, the steward plans to supply enough clean cups, glasses, and so on. Not all kitchens employ stewards.

exhibit booth   Exhibit space that incorporates a base section and backdrop for vendor displays.

exhibits   See trade shows/expositions.

external communication   Verbal or written contact with clients and others outside the facility.

eye appeal   The appetizing appearance of food items on a plate.

facility   Hotel, banquet hall, conference center, convention center, or any other venue that has space for an organization to use.

facility catering   Term used to describe the discipline of providing food/beverage and logistical support to organizations needing function space at a facility.

feature   Physical, tangible aspect of the catering operation that can be shown, felt, or touched. A feature is not implied or promised. It must be demonstrable.

feedback   High-pitched squeak or squeal that results when audio from the speaker system recirculates through a microphone.

flipchart   Large pad of paper mounted on a tripod or another type of easel that is used to illustrate points. It is useful in team-building, brainstorming, and other types of meetings.

food categories   Entrée choices including beef, chicken, pork, fish, or vegetarian.

food cost   Cost of a food item relative to its selling price. This cost is often measured as a percentage.

food displays   Display that consists of meats, cheeses, fruit, and so on. Food displays can be very creatively prepared by skilled kitchen staff.

food function types   Breakfast, lunch, and dinner.

food preparation   Process a menu item undergoes before serving.

food station   Island set up apart from a buffet line.

forecast/forecasting   To predict revenues and/or occupancy and use of rooms and space.

free sell date   Date at which space that is rapidly approaching and has not yet been sold by the group team can be sold. Short-term business opportunities are the focus of free sell windows.

freeze-frame   Single video or motion frame stopped for display.

French service   See butler style.

front of a room   Location of a speaker or other presentation source.

front projection   Style of light projection that uses a standard front reflective screen of any size. The light source (often a projector of some kind) must come from the front only.

function equipment   Tables and chairs and other items used in a facility.

function space   The meeting rooms, ballrooms, exhibit halls, and banquet spaces a facility makes available to organizations for various uses.

function space diary   Large book, sometimes called a "slash" book, that displays a facility's complete inventory of function space day by day on each page.

garnish   Plate accoutrement whose purpose is to contribute to color balance.

general-purpose vehicle   Used to transport and store fully cooked food.

goal   Objective or need that drives a buying decision.

group base   The number of group rooms currently on a hotel's books.

group booking   Multiple reservations made at a hotel for one or more nights that correspond to a specific event.

group catering   Catering revenue derived from group bookings (sleeping rooms).

group ceiling   Targeted number of group rooms needed to book on a given night.

group resume   Internal document that incorporates the sleeping room component of a group with all its catering needs.

group turnover   Method by which a catering or convention service manager becomes aware of a group and the details of its program to that point. Properly done, the turnover gives an "at-a-glance" look at where the group is, as well as valuable information on the client and contact(s).

guaranteed number   The exact numbers for each entrée that an organization commits to prior to an event.

high tea   A British tradition considered a meal in itself. A selection of small sandwiches, fruit, and/or desserts are served with tea. Served late in the afternoon, high tea can be used as the last course of an early dinner.

hold   Length of time a food item can remain on a buffet before losing its desired consistency or temperature.

holiday parties   Local catering functions that occur during the fall and early winter time frame.

hors d'oeuvres   Small finger-sized food items.

host bar   Bar at which the organization charges for each drink the group consumes.

hot   Descriptive term for the state in which a coaxial cable carries a live feed or some type of AV device that is on or in use.

hotel   Facility that rents sleeping rooms to overnight guests.

house brands   Least expensive alcoholic drinks. Sometimes called "well brands," house brands may have generic labels or facilities' labels.

house lights   Permanent lighting system of a function room.

house sound   Permanent audio system of a function room.

house wines   Wines that are stocked by a restaurant or caterer.

human markers   Aids in the rapport-building process that reveal traits and insights that are not readily apparent. Human markers, like body language and discourse level, complete the picture of "how" and "why" clients react in certain manners.

inclusive pricing   Prices with the service charge and tax built in.

intermezzo   Served between the salad and the entrée. It is intended to cleanse the palate and prepare the eater for the next course. A sorbet (fruit sherbetlike treat) is usually served.

internal communication   Verbal or written contacts among staff and departments within a facility.

kitchen capacity   Amount of food produced within safety guidelines and a set time frame.

Lavaliere microphone   Small microphone that can be attached to a speaker to allow freedom of hand movement. These microphones can be wireless or corded.

lead generation   Process undertaken by potential clients or salespeople to generate interest. The generation of interest creates tangible business opportunities called leads.

level   Measurement of volume or intensity.

liquid crystal display (LCD) computer panel   Unique computer monitor that allows light to pass through it. It is used with an overhead to display its contents on a screen to a large audience.

local catering   Revenue derived solely from the catering function (no sleeping rooms). Specifically, local catering is business in which the function or meal is the primary focus.

lost business reports (LBRs)   Listings of business opportunities that did not book at a catering operation.

"Management by Walking Around" (MBWA)   Theory that the best managers are visible and accessible.

market segment   Portion or segment of the actual or potential business pool.

market segmentation   Categorizing business into segments that share characteristics.

marketing   Positioning a product as ideal for a customer's needs. Marketing is the driving force behind sales in any operation. Marketing supports selling by creating awareness of a product or service.

mask   To hide or cover a food item with a more dominant component so that consistency is not apparent to the eye.

maximizing space   Using as much function space as efficiently as possible.

meeting packages   Packages that include popular food or beverage items (e.g., continental breakfast, coffee breaks) or AV items (e.g., slide projectors, screens, flipcharts) and the room cost for one price. Sometimes called "day meeting packages" (DMPs).

mental inventory   Set of the specific personality traits and idiosyncrasies of the client or organization.

menu efficiency   Maximization of catering resources to ensure that the kitchen is not overburdened.

menu planning   Formulating and implementing the food-and-beverage-related aspects of an event.

menu presentation   Combination of menu item arrangement, item combination, and items' looks, smells, and feels.

menu restrictions   Cultural, religious, health, or personal restrictions placed on menu options.

menu type   Name given to a course served during a meal.

menu-type station   Station made of one meal type (e.g., salad station or dessert station).

mixer   Audio device that combines audio sources. A mixer is often used to create a seamless recording level. A mixer must be used whenever sound is amplified or multiple microphones are used.

mobile kitchen   Essentially a kitchen on wheels, this vehicle is used primarily by small caterers who need not create large amounts of food in a short time.

monitor   Common term for a television monitor. They are used most often as video playback viewers, but monitors can be used in many ways. They are generally the sizes of home televisions. The term *monitor* is sometimes used as jargon for "audio monitor."

multimedia   Using two or more AV devices in a presentation. High-end and extravagant programs are most often multimedia.

multiple entrée   Choice of two or more entrées in nonbuffet format. The multiple entrée differs from the dual entrée in that the multiple entrée meal offers attendees a choice.

national holiday time frames   Periods of time in conjunction with national holidays that have a unique impact on the space intensity of functions.

networking   Meeting and talking with salespeople and potential clients.

no-shows   Employees who do not show for scheduled work shifts.

observer's table   A head table placed in the rear of a room.

occupancy level   Number of sleeping rooms occupied in a hotel.

off-menu planning   Coordinating meals that include items not on the banquet menus.

off-menu pricing   Creating then pricing menu items not currently on the preprinted banquet menus.

off-premise catering   Facility catering operations that have begun to venture into the outside catering arena. These facilities are using their large internal kitchens to provide food and beverage service to other venues.

one-tiered deployment   Scheme at a stand-alone facility that lacks a sleeping room component and does not need a convention services department. The servicing would be completed strictly by the catering personnel.

open sell date   Sales that become available to local catering when the group sales team has met the ceiling of required sleeping rooms.

opportunity cost   Measurable cost incurred when a facility has lost the opportunity to book better business.

outside catering   Providing food/beverage and the requisite logistical support and service to clients in a venue other than a hotel or a stand-alone banquet facility.

outside vendor   Resource for catering professionals to use when they cannot realistically accomplish a task.

outsource   To designate other organizations that specialize in ancillary functions outside an organization's core strengths to perform on the organization's behalf.

overhead projector   Device by which light is sent through a directional lens and displayed forward. The overhead projector most often uses transparencies or LCD computer monitors as the presentation source.

ownership actions   Acts or services personally performed by caterers to help ensure the success of a group or function.

package bar   Bar similar to the host bar at which attendees can choose their drinks (house, premium, and top shelf). For a package bar, an organization pays a flat rate for all attendees on a per hour basis.

painted plate   Plate that is drizzled with chocolate, vanilla, or some other sauce and used most often to serve desserts. The painted plate has an artistic, "painted" look.

painting word pictures   Using menu descriptions to evoke positive mental images.

pan   Rotation of a camera around the viewing area. The goal of panning is often to get a panoramic view.

partnering   Deploying a specific convention service manager with a specific group salesperson over and over again.

pastry chef   Dessert master. This chef creates all cakes, pies, cookies, tarts, breads, and so on. Often the first person in the kitchen each morning, the pastry chef works with a staff of bakers to create baked goods for breakfast as well as desserts for other meals.

payment upon conclusion of function   Settling total unpaid charges after all amounts are tallied.

percentage of participation   Used to determine dance floor size.

pipe and drape   Common term for a portable dark draping that can be set up as a divider (useful in exhibits) or as a barrier to conceal something (rear screen).

plated   Prepared meal that is served.

podium microphone   Microphone attached to a podium or lectern.

postcon report   A written summary of a group's activities at a facility.

postconvention meeting (postcon)   A forum at which relevant staff meet with contacts of a recently concluded event to review the bill and discuss what went well and what didn't.

preconvention meeting   Function at which the contact meets the key personnel in a facility and reviews with those personnel the group's meeting agenda.

preferred vendor   Supplier of goods or services that another business has certified or approved in some way.

prefunction area   Space outside a function room.

premium brands   Alcoholic drinks that are one level higher than house brands in terms of quality and price. Sometimes called "call brands," premium brands are popular but not the most expensive.

preplated   Menu type placed on the table before attendees sit.

prime selling time   Specific hours during the day in which salespeople have the best opportunity to reach current and prospective clients.

prime temperature   Safe serving point used to avoid food-borne illnesses and contamination.

profit center   Hotel area in which a product or service is sold.

projector A device that projects light or sound in a specific direction.

public address (PA) system Portable audio speaker setup that is generally used in large areas or auditoriums. PA systems are useful when house sound does not suffice.

publications Solicitation resources that identify organizations with potential catering needs.

purchasing/beverage manager Person who ensures that the right quantities of food and beverage are ordered and in stock when needed. The purchasing/beverage manager keeps all outlets supplied as well as plans for specific catered meal requirements.

qualification Process of determining the specific characteristics of a business opportunity. Qualification uncovers the "who, what, where, when, and why" (5 *W*s) attributes of a piece of business.

readerboards Posted daily event sheets or scrolling television monitors telling attendees where and when their functions are.

rear screen Style of light projection that uses a rear-generated light source. The nonreflective screen can then be viewed from the front of the room. The rear screen is useful because no AV device can be viewed from the audience, but it tends to take up a lot of function space. Often, pipe and drape are used to hide everything behind the rear screen.

reception Function designed to promote mingling and communication among attendees.

remote Device used to activate an AV device from some distance. A remote can be wired or wireless. Remotes are often used in slide projector and video presentations.

request for proposal (RFP) Document that outlines the parameters of a project.

restaurant chef Chef who directs food production for a specific outlet (food and beverage point of sale) in a hotel. Restaurants, lounges, bars, and room service are all considered outlets. Counterparts to banquet chefs, restaurant chefs need only focus on their restaurants, not catered meals. Restaurant chefs in large hotels may rotate between outlets to master different food-production skills.

riser Also called a platform or stage, raises function equipment to a desired height.

roadblock Uncovered or hidden goal.

room capacity charts Documents that outline each function room and its capacities in most common seating configurations.

room rental Cost of function space.

room rental tariff sheet Document that breaks down what management has predetermined is the value of each meeting room and all function space for specific time frames.

rooms-to-space ratio   Number of overnight rooms needed by a potential business opportunity relative to the total amount of square feet the group needs for function space.

runner   Person who brings food from its source to the preparation area for serving.

running call report   Written correspondence and list of notes summarizing phone and E-mail conversations.

salad   Usually the second course of a meal, or the first if no appetizer is served. A salad can have any combination of fruits, vegetables, cheeses, or even edible flowers.

sales blitzes   Tools that allow for blanket sales penetration of a certain geographical area.

satellite downlink   Connection to an orbiting communications satellite to link audio and video from other locations. Satellite downlinks are used in video conferencing.

service level   Amount of attention catering staff give an event.

servicing   On-property coordination of group specifics. Depending on the size of hotel, these specifics can be food-and-beverage related or sleeping-room related.

signature food   Food item unique to, and/or associated with, a specific region or culture.

skirting   The fabric or linen wrapped around an A/V cart or table to make it look more polished and professional.

slide projector   Video device used to project one slide at a time. Slide projectors are sometimes called carousel projectors because most use the carousel tray to hold and advance the slides.

sliding scale   Ties the room rental price to revenue performance; the more money spent, the lower the rental.

slippage   Lower-than-expected usage of sleeping rooms.

SMERF   Social, military, educational, religious, and fraternal marketing segments.

sous chef   Leader of a kitchen department. One sous chef may prepare sauces, while another may focus on soups. Sous chefs often rotate responsibilities to master each part of the culinary process.

space eater   Any item outside the primary seating style that is required in a function room and that uses available square footage.

space efficiency   Minimizing the labor and opportunity cost incurred by changing function rooms from one event to another.

space intensity   Amount of function space used for an event or a function versus what is considered common or typical for that facility.

space release   Method by which some hotels waive booking restrictions on local catering business, if warranted.

speaker phone   "Hands-free" phone that allows more than one person to communicate on the telephone at once. Speaker phones are used in teleconferencing.

specialized outside catering   Organizations whose sole catering ability is focused in one direction.

specialized space   Function space that cannot be used for any other function. Specialized function rooms are permanently set up to host specific food or event functions (e.g., permanent boardrooms or dining rooms cannot be changed to suit other functions).

sphere of influence   Reach of an organization's brand recognition.

split or dual entrée   Two distinct entrées on one plate.

spotlight   Can be part of the permanent lighting setup of a function room, or it can be portable. The spotlight, which allows light to be targeted on one person or object, is useful when a stage is used.

staffing   The number of servers and other operational staff needed to execute a function.

stand-alone facility   Function venue without overnight sleeping rooms.

standing microphone   Microphone attached to a freestanding device that can be adjusted for height and angle.

stay set   Function booked after another using the same setup.

strobe   Rapidly blinking, high-intensity light. A strobe is often used in multimedia presentations to add visual impact.

surge protector   Electrical device that acts as a buffer between sensitive equipment and an electrical outlet. The surge protector can absorb intermittent voltage surges before those surges damage equipment.

table microphone   Microphone that is attached to a small, flexible stand that is mounted on a tabletop for panel discussions.

tableside   Preparation that requires an attendant at each dining table to prepare the food.

tabletop exhibit   Six-foot table used as the base for item display.

taste panel   Gathering of clients and catering and kitchen personnel to sample and choose a menu for an upcoming event.

teleconferencing   Bringing more than one or more remote locations together via a telephone. Teleconference is useful when one or more participants cannot attend in person. Speaker phones are widely used in this forum.

testimonial letters   Positive letters from clients.

themed buffet   Buffet that combines foods of similar origin, taste, or look.

themed station   Station that combines foods of similar origin, taste, or look.

third-party leads   Leads that originate from someone other than the client. A third party acts on the client's behalf in the search for an appropriate meeting location or catering need.

three-tiered deployment   Scheme that requires the three branches of the hotel sales team (sales, catering, and convention service) to work together. Each branch has a specific role in the evolution of a group from booking to arrival.

throw   Measure of projection distance.

tiered stage   Two or more stacked risers.

top-shelf brands   Most expensive brand-name alcoholic drinks. Highest quality obtainable.

trace files   Customer files that come to the attention of a salesperson on a predetermined date. This date, called a trace date, is designated by the salesperson as a time when action of some sort is needed.

trade shows/expositions   Functions centered around vendors who wish to display services and/or products for a targeted market.

transient hotel guest   Individual or nongroup hotel guest.

turn time   Time it takes a facility to change a room from one event to another.

turnover   Process by which a group salesperson makes the catering and/or convention service department aware of the details of a group.

two-tiered deployment   Scheme that exists in hotels with no convention service departments. The catering department assumes the servicing and menu planning roles of all group business, as well as the booking of all local catering.

two-tiered modified deployment   Scheme that employs both the catering and convention service departments. However, the catering department does not play a role in the servicing of groups. The convention services department does all the menu planning and group servicing, while the catering department works strictly on local catering.

varietals   Common types of wines.

VHS   Standard VCR format. The VHS system uses 1/2-inch wide videotape.

video conferencing   Like teleconferencing, incorporates audio and visual links to remote locations. The connection may require a satellite downlink.

video projector   Device used to project any VCR playback onto a screen. The video projector is often used when a standard monitor is too small to be seen by all attendees.

videocassette recorder (VCR)   Device used to record and play back video.

walk-ins   Clients who walk into facilities unannounced looking to book programs.

white-glove service   See butler style.

yield management   Process of mixing low-rated group rooms with higher rated transient rooms to maximize room rates. This process tries to come as close to full occupancy each night as possible while maximizing room rate revenue.

zoom   To magnify a subject over distance without moving or changing the camera or video source location.

Index